The Forty Years that Created America

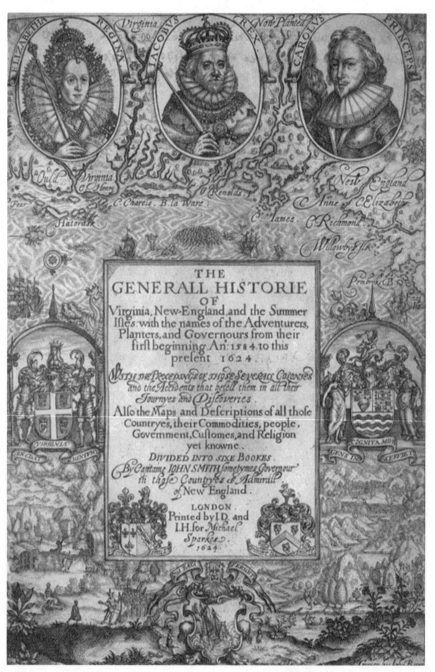

Title page of The Generalle Historie of Virginia, New England, and the Summer Isles, *by John Smith, published in 1624. Courtesy of the Library of Virginia.*

The Forty Years that Created America

The Story of the Explorers, Promoters, Investors, and Settlers Who Founded the First English Colonies

Edward M. Lamont

ROWMAN & LITTLEFIELD
Lanham • Boulder • New York • London

Published by Rowman & Littlefield
A wholly owned subsidiary of The Rowman & Littlefield Publishing Group, Inc.
4501 Forbes Boulevard, Suite 200, Lanham, Maryland 20706
www.rowman.com

16 Carlisle Street, London W1D 3BT, United Kingdom

British Library Cataloguing in Publication Information Available

Library of Congress Cataloging-in-Publication Data
Lamont, Edward M., 1926-
  The forty years that created America : the story of the explorers, promoters, investors,
and settlers who founded the first English colonies / Edward M. Lamont.
      pages cm
  Includes bibliographical references and index.
  ISBN 978-1-4422-3659-2 (cloth : alk. paper) — ISBN 978-1-4422-3660-8
(electronic) 1. United States—History—Colonial period, ca. 1600-1775. 2. Virginia—
History—Colonial period, ca. 1600-1775. 3. Massachusetts—History—Colonial period,
ca. 1600-1775. 4. Great Britain—Colonies—America. I. Title.
  E162.L35 2014
  973.3—dc23

                                                                    2014014184

Printed in the United States of America

To Buz and all the clan.

Contents

viii   *Contents*

Introduction

$\mathcal{T}$hroughout the colonial period and for the first fifty years or so of American nationhood, two English colonies that later became American states were critical in leading the development of the country—Virginia and Massachusetts. Their citizens filled the ranks of our founding fathers and early presidents. Their names inform the birth and history of our nation—George Washington, Patrick Henry, Thomas Jefferson, James Madison, and James Monroe; John Adams, Sam Adams, John Hancock, Henry Knox, John Quincy Adams—and the list goes on. Four Virginians and two Massachusetts men comprise our first six presidents. Leaders from these two colonies provided most of the intellectual ferment leading to America's successful struggle for independence. They were instrumental in the formation and development of our constitutional government.

The states of Virginia and Massachusetts sprung directly from the roots of the first two English settlements that survived in the New World—Jamestown, Virginia, and Plymouth, Massachusetts. Their settlers were the trailblazers that led the way for the flow of immigrants from the British Isles that populated the American colonies. England was America's earliest genetic, political, linguistic, and cultural parent, from whom the country first modeled its laws and practice of self-government. These two great democracies, bound by a common heritage, forged a close and special relationship in World War II, which, led by Franklin D. Roosevelt and Winston Churchill, created the alliance that defeated Germany and saved Europe from Nazi domination. Despite a few bumps in the road, that special relationship has continued. In more recent years the two countries have been staunch allies in military engagements in the Persian Gulf, Afghanistan, and Iraq. Americans have more in common with the British and their Commonwealth brothers in Canada and Australia than with the people of any other nation, and the two countries enjoy a mutual trust that is unique in world affairs. Many different streams of immigrants would come together in America to make up today's diverse culture in our country. While most Americans don't have English ancestors, the English were the first that came and stayed, and their cultural influence on American life would be foremost and long lasting.

The ventures and advocacy of early explorers, promoters, and investors were significant steps leading to planting the first two English settlements in America. Their founding was notably due to the exceptional passion for exploration and colonization of a few enterprising and visionary Englishmen—especially Sir Walter Raleigh, Bartholomew Gosnold, Richard Hakluyt, Sir Ferdinando Gorges, and Captain John Smith. The able and forceful leadership of John Smith and William Bradford during the early years of these two colonies was critical to their survival and eventual success. There is a rich history that set the stage for the founding of Jamestown and the Pilgrims' settlement at Plymouth—the record of Spanish and French colonizing endeavors and of the decades of inertia and frustrating failures by the English to establish American colonies—and finally, the tale of John Smith's persevering determination to make it happen. The forty years referred to in the book's title commence with the attempt by the English to found the colony of Roanoke in 1585 and cover the period ending with the firm establishment of Jamestown and Plymouth by 1625.

Treasure, Cod, and the Northwest Passage

On October 12, 1492, after over two months at sea, Christopher Columbus, the captain of three small caravels, stepped ashore on the sandy beach of San Salvador, probably the present-day Watkins Island in the Bahamas, and planted the royal banner of Spain. He thought he had found a direct westerly route to the Indies and the riches of the Orient. Instead he had discovered the New World and changed the course of history forever. Other Europeans had touched down in North America before him, but their activities had not led to new explorations across the western sea. The Vikings, under Leif Erikson, came to Newfoundland from Greenland around 1000 AD, and they may have built and lived in a settlement at L'Anse aux Meadows before leaving. Portuguese, Spanish, Basque, and Breton vessels had probably been fishing the waters off Newfoundland for years. They chose to be secretive about the fruitful fishing grounds that they found.

On his first voyage to the New World, Christopher Columbus explored Cuba and Hispaniola, where he left a garrison to deal with the natives. He called them *Indians*, thinking that he had reached India. The Indians gave him gold ornaments and pearls, which he brought back to Spain where he made his extraordinary report to the Spanish monarchs, Ferdinand and Isabella, who had backed his voyage of exploration. First, he declared that he had discovered a short sea passage to the Orient, which would dramatically facilitate profitable trade. Second, he disclosed the exciting prospect of vast amounts of gold in the Caribbean islands, according to the natives. The lure of gold was irresistible, spurring the conquistadores of Spain to mount a growing stream of expeditions to exploit the riches of the New World. Huge supplies of gold and silver would enable the Spanish government to pay its debts, finance its military ventures in Europe, and enrich the venturesome.

The era of Western exploration, discovery, and conquest had begun, and that of European settlements was bound to follow. In 1493 Spanish Pope Alexander VI issued two papal bulls granting virtually all the newly discovered lands to Spain, which by treaty a year later was modified to award Brazil to Portugal. Columbus himself led three more expeditions to the West Indies and the South and Central American coasts, and in 1496 his brother, Bartholomew Columbus, founded Santo Domingo, the current capital of the Dominican Republic and the first permanent European settlement in the New World.

Central and South America mainly attracted the conquistadores in their quest for riches—gold, silver, and precious stones—and their armies brutalized and enslaved the native Indians to work the mines and supply their needs. By the middle of the sixteenth century as many as sixty-five galleons left Seville each year to supply Spanish possessions in the New World, returning later to Spain laden with treasure, mainly silver from the mines of Peru and gold from Mexico. Spanish commanders and their troops also explored in North America, roaming from Florida through the Southwest to the Great Plains and West Coast seeking more riches, while their priests attempted to convert the heathen natives to Christianity.

The conquistadores, led by Hernando Cortés, seized the Aztec capital, today's Mexico City, and built new towns and ports such as San Juan, Vera Cruz, and Santa Fe to rule their conquered territories and ship their newly mined and plundered treasures back to Spain. Today the Spanish colonial sixteenth-century public buildings, missions, and churches in these towns continue to delight the eye. The Spanish also built strong forts, such as Morro Castle in Puerto Rico, to defend the Caribbean gateway to their valuable new possessions from attacks by other European powers and buccaneers eager to gain their share of the New World's wealth. Today the impressive fortifications at San Juan, Havana, and St. Augustine recall the robust military outreach of colonial Spain in the New World. Perhaps the favorite sport of the great English sea captain and privateer Sir Francis Drake was terrorizing and plundering Spanish towns and ships, but not San Juan. In 1595 the Morro Castle garrison vigorously repulsed his fleet's attack on the town and drove them off.

One wonders why England, a prosperous seafaring nation, let almost a century pass without launching its own efforts to acquire and hold parts of the newly discovered continent. The English had a tenuous claim to the new land (although no one knew its dimensions). John Cabot, a Venetian sea captain, came to England in 1495 and settled in Bristol, the country's second most important seaport. In 1497, five years after Columbus's discovery of what he thought were the Indies, English king Henry VII and the merchants from Bristol were eager to find a short sea route to the Orient in order to acquire the silks and spices—pepper, cloves, and nutmeg—that were increasingly popular in England. Backed by the Bristol merchants and sailing under a patent granted by Henry VII, Cabot's small ship *Matthew* with a crew of eighteen men left Bristol heading westward on May 20. Thirty-five days later, the *Matthew* made landfall, probably on the northern coast of Newfoundland. Going ashore, Cabot raised the cross and English flag and formally claimed the territory for the king of England, ignoring the papal bulls assigning the new lands to Spain and Portugal.

Cabot explored the Newfoundland coast for several weeks before returning to England and reporting his discoveries to King Henry. Pleased with Cabot's performance and report that he had reached the Orient, the king rewarded him with a financial annuity and granted him a patent for a second voyage. King Henry and the Bristol merchants, believing that Cabot had set foot on the continent of Asia, directed the expedition to explore the region further with the goal of establishing a trading post in the Indies to acquire the popular spices. Cabot's fleet of five ships, supplied with goods for trading, sailed from Bristol in May 1498. Soon afterward one ship in distress struggled back to port in Ireland. The other four vessels completely disappeared, probably sunk in a North Atlantic gale, and John Cabot and his crew were never seen again.

Over the next few years King Henry VII and the merchants sponsored several more voyages to explore the Newfoundland region. So did King Manuel I of Portugal, probably intending to establish grounds to dispute John Cabot's claim of the territory for England. Two ships commanded by the Corte Real brothers were lost with all hands. The English and Portuguese ships that made it back to port safely reported their discovery of great cod-fishing grounds, but once again they failed to find the eagerly sought short passage to the Orient. North Atlantic gale-force winds bringing mountainous waves and the rock-studded Newfoundland and mainland coasts, often shrouded in fog, were the treacherous obstacles facing sea captains exploring the area.

In the first decades of the sixteenth century, Portuguese vessels in growing numbers were attracted to the area by the fabulous cod fishing, especially in the Grand Banks off Nova Scotia, and, in the course of their voyages, they explored the Newfoundland and Nova Scotia coasts. In 1521 King Manuel granted a patent to João Álvares Fagundes, a Portuguese ship owner, to acquire property and govern in the region, which Fagundes had explored on an earlier voyage. Fagundes planned to set up a permanent settlement, which would preserve the fish they caught before transporting their catches back to Lisbon. When he and his fishermen arrived in the area, perhaps several years later, they built their small outpost on the shore of a protected harbor on Cape Breton Island, so named by the French fishermen from Brittany. They soon ran into unexpected difficulties. The local Indians did not welcome a new foreign settlement intending to remain permanently on their land and were hostile to the newcomers. Breton fishermen felt the Portuguese were invading their fishing grounds and retaliated by cutting their fishing lines and destroying their little houses. After a year or so, around 1525, Fagundes was forced to abandon the project, thus ending the first attempt of Europeans, since the Vikings some five hundred years earlier, to establish a permanent settlement in North America.

Spanish nobleman Juan Ponce de León, who gave Florida its name, "the land of flowers," had first come to the New World on Columbus's second voyage in 1493; he later became governor of Puerto Rico and founded the town that became San Juan. In 1513, he embarked on another exploratory voyage in the region seeking the mythical "Fountain of Youth," which was alleged by Caribbean Indians to restore physical and sexual vigor. He landed near present-day St. Augustine and claimed Florida for Spain. The Spanish were eager to colonize Florida, and in 1521 Ponce de León with 200 men attempted to start a colony on the west coast. They were repulsed by hostile natives and forced to return to Cuba, where Ponce de León, wounded by an arrow in the Indian attack, died. Five years later another Spanish expedition of five hundred colonists, including women and children, tried to start a settlement in North Carolina, probably on the Cape Fear River. Extremely severe winter weather and a shortage of provisions killed off most of the settlers. Hostile natives refused to trade for food. The survivors gave up and returned to Hispaniola. The lack of knowledge about the local Indians and the necessary preparations to cope with North American winter weather would continue to confound would-be colonizers.

One of the earliest explorers and chroniclers of his exploration of the North American coast was Giovanni da Verrazzano, a Florentine sea captain. In 1524, on a voyage commissioned by French king Francis I, Verrazzano, commanding *La Dauphine* with a crew of fifty men, left Dieppe and cruised the entire length of the coast from today's Cape Fear, North Carolina, to Newfoundland. Like others before and after, he sought in vain for a short passage to the Orient. He and his men were probably the first Europeans to enter New York Harbor, where today's great suspension bridge from Brooklyn to Staten Island bears his name. Verrazzano found the Narragansett Bay region so pleasing and the Pokanoket Indians so welcoming that he tarried there two weeks, anchoring in the future Newport Harbor. His encounters with Indians were generally friendly, except in Maine, where the natives crudely demonstrated their disdain for the strangers "by exhibiting bare buttocks and laughing immoderately at us," he wrote in a letter to the French king. On a later voyage to the Caribbean in 1528, the natives were even less friendly. When Verrazzano went ashore at Guadeloupe, he was killed and eaten by cannibals.

Breton fishermen were already fishing the Grand Banks when French king Francois I authorized an expedition commanded by master mariner Jacques Cartier from Saint-Malo to search for a passage to the Orient. In two ships, each with sixty-man crews, Cartier explored Newfoundland and the Gulf of St. Lawrence in 1534. European fishermen had been trading for some time with the Indians for furs and skins, which adorned fashionable clothing in Europe, in exchange for articles of clothing, trinkets, and metal goods, such as tools, hatchets, and copperware. In Cartier's journal of his voyage, *Premiere Relation*, he reported that he and his crew had formed friendly relations trading for pelts with the Indians they encountered. The local Huron chief, Donnaconna, even permitted his two teenage sons to go back to France with Cartier, who promised to return them to their homeland on a future voyage.

Cartier's backers and the king were pleased with his report and commissioned him to undertake another voyage of discovery in the region. In May 1535 he set out with three ships, including a smaller pinnace for close-in coastal navigation. A total crew of 112 and the two young Hurons were on board; they would serve as useful guides and interpreters in their meetings with Indians along the way. This time Cartier followed the great St. Lawrence River upstream to present-day Quebec, encountering several friendly groups of Hurons en route. Proceeding in just the pinnace, as the river became narrower west of Quebec, and later in three long boats with thirty-five men, Cartier continued following the river westward.

On October 2 Cartier's company reached Hochelaga, a large Huron town on the site of present-day Montreal, where hundreds of natives lined the shore to greet Cartier and his men. After an exchange of gifts and a warm welcoming ceremony, presided over by the local chieftain, Cartier climbed to the summit of the mountain overlooking the town, which afforded an excellent view of the region. To his dismay he observed the series of dangerous rapids, today's Lachine Rapids, on the narrow river just beyond Hochelaga. He could see that it was impossible to proceed any further by boat; the St. Lawrence River could not be the eagerly sought Northwest Passage to the Orient. On October 4 Cartier and his party in long boats joined the pinnace anchored downstream and returned to the Quebec site where the two larger ships and crews were based.

While he was upriver, these crews had built a small fort with log palisades. Cartier had decided to winter over on the St. Lawrence, perhaps to undertake further explorations in the spring. It would take weeks to retrace his steps to the open ocean, and he probably did not relish the thought of a North Atlantic crossing in the winter. The weather was brutal that winter on the St. Lawrence. Fom mid-November 1535 to mid-April the following year Cartier's ships were locked solid in the frozen-over river. All the casks of beverages were frozen, and the snow lay four feet deep on shore, reported Cartier in his account of the expedition, *Brief Recit.* Then scurvy broke out among the men in the fort, caused by a vitamin C deficiency due to the lack of fresh fruits and vegetables in their diet. By February only ten out of more than one hundred men were well enough to help the sick, "a pitiful thing to see," Cartier reported. Fortunately, many crewmembers recovered when Hurons from the local village of Stadacone introduced them to an effective curative, a tea made from spruce needles. Nevertheless, about two dozen died. When spring came Cartier abandoned the little settlement and sailed home, bringing some prize trophies to show off to his backers and the king.

Before leaving Cartier deceitfully kidnapped the local chief of the Hurons, Donnaconna, who had welcomed Cartier earlier; his two sons, who had been guides for Cartier; and several other Indians. The Hurons, who had greeted Cartier and his men with kindness as they explored the river, were naturally shocked and angry at this act of betrayal. Cartier gave them gifts, promised to bring their comrades back in about a year with more presents, and set sail for France. Cartier also took four native children, a gift from the Hurons upriver, back with him to France. None of the Hurons ever saw their native land again. In France Donnaconna became a masterful salesman in telling tall tales describing the fabulous riches in a mythical region in Canada called Saguenay. He was treated honorably in France until he died a few years later. King Francois I was intrigued by his stories and the prospects they held for enriching the royal treasury.

The mission commissioned by the king for Cartier's third expedition up the St. Lawrence was to find the fabled land of Saguenay—no more searching in vain for the passage to the Orient. Two fleets would undertake the enterprise, one led by Captain-General Jacques Cartier and the other by the French nobleman seigneur de Roberval. Cartier, in command of five ships with about two hundred passengers on board, set sail from Saint-Malo on May 23, 1541. His company of colonists contained a group of convicts, men and women, including an engaged couple. The ships also carried horses, cattle, swine, and all the provisions needed to establish a lasting settlement, which would serve as a base for the expedition as it searched for Saguenay and its riches. Roberval claimed that his ships were not yet ready to leave; he would join Cartier in Canada later.

After a rough crossing, Cartier's ships made their first landfall in northern Newfoundland, where they took on wood and water and bought bread and wine from French fishing vessels in the harbor. They sailed into the Gulf of St. Lawrence and up the great river, reaching Stadacone, the native village near today's Quebec, on August 23. While the Hurons appeared to greet the French warmly, Cartier sensed that they resented their latest intrusion and plans to stay. Furthermore, where were their comrades that Cartier had promised to return to their homes? They probably didn't buy Cartier's story that they were all living happily in France (except Donnaconna who had died) and wished to remain there. So Cartier decided to move on. He brought his ships about eight miles upstream to a spot, today's Cap-Rouge, which he had observed on his previous expedition. There the colonists went to work building a fort with palisaded walls and planting a vegetable garden. Cartier named the settlement Charlesbourg-Royal after the son of the French king. He sent two ships back to France carrying samples of bogus precious minerals his men had collected—"fool's gold" (iron pyrites) and "diamonds Canadien" (quartz crystals)—which he thought were the real thing and would impress his king.

Upon returning to the fort from a scouting excursion to the Lachine Rapids, Cartier was informed that the natives were acting ominously, no longer coming to sell food to the colonists and lurking about in the woods around the fort. Sketchy tales from crewmembers later reported that the Hurons attacked some woodcutters that winter outside the fort and killed thirty-five of them. During another brutally cold winter, scurvy broke out among the colonists. Fortunately, the spruce-based cure, learned from the Hurons on the previous voyage, saved lives once again.

However, by spring Roberval's fleet had still not showed up, and this presented a major obstacle to continuing the venture. Was it on its way, or had it been lost at sea? Cartier needed Roberval's additional provisions and manpower to go off searching for Saguenay, while leaving the fort protected from the hostile natives. He made his decision in early June 1542 to abandon Charlesbourg-Royal, and with his three remaining ships he sailed downriver to Newfoundland and home. To Cartier's great surprise, already anchored in St. John's Harbour in Newfoundland when he arrived were seigneur de Roberval's three ships.

The long-delayed Roberval had been busy raising money to finance his expedition, even resorting to piracy against English and Portuguese vessels in the English Channel. His ships were large and well provisioned, including farm animals, to build the new colony, and his total company of probably about one hundred and fifty included volunteer gentlemen and their ladies. Departing from New Rochelle, he had reached St. John's Harbour on June 7, joining twenty-seven fishing vessels already anchored there. When Cartier's ships anchored in the harbor, one can assume the ensuing conversation between the two commanders was heated. Roberval, a lieutenant general, outranked Cartier, a fact that Cartier apparently ignored. Roberval ordered Cartier to accompany him back to Charlesbourg-Royal. Cartier refused, warning Roberval of his fear that the hostile Hurons might attack and overcome the settlement. Disobeying his superior's orders, Cartier's three ships quietly slipped out of the harbor under cover of darkness the following night and headed for Saint-Malo. Cartier, the veteran master mariner and explorer, was a revered and popular figure in Saint-Malo, where he happily lived out the rest of his days.

At the end of July Roberval's ships reached Charlesbourg-Royal, which the commander promptly renamed France-Roy. He sent two of his ships back to France to report to the king and then return with supplies the following year. The colonists built a new fortified settlement on a nearby hill, completing it in time to house them when winter arrived with its icy blasts and unrelenting snowfalls. A growing shortage of food forced everyone onto short rations, and once again the deadly scurvy struck down the colonists, killing fifty of them. The Hurons kept their distance, unwilling to sell food or trade with the French. When spring came Roberval with fifty men rowed their boats upstream as far as the Lachine Rapids, where one of his boats capsized, drowning eight men. Apparently Roberval decided that his people had suffered enough. In July 1543 Roberval and his company sailed home to France.

Thus ended the early French efforts to find the fanciful land of Saguenay and to establish new colonies in Canada. The ill-prepared and poorly provisioned settlers were no match for the harsh Canadian winters. Furthermore, Cartier's kidnapping of the local Indians had severely poisoned relations with them for his own and Roberval's expeditions. Sixty-five years would pass before another intrepid French explorer and expedition leader, Samuel de Champlain, successfully founded the town of Quebec. All the Hurons and their villages had disappeared, perhaps driven west by their enemies to the great lake bearing their name.

In 1562 a new French group, probably recalling those harsh Canadian winters suffered by Cartier and his men, chose the more benign climate of the sunny South to start a new colony. Jean Ribault, a Huguenot sea captain from Dieppe, established a Huguenot outpost he named Port Royal, near to-day's Parris Island, South Carolina. Ribault sailed back to France, and within two years the colonists, poorly led, short of provisions, and discouraged, disbanded. But the French Huguenots, eager to seek refuge from Catholic France to worship freely, did not give up. In 1564 a new company of Huguenots, led by René de Laudonnière, a nobleman who had been with Ribault, built a settlement that they named Fort Caroline on the St. John's River in northern Florida. In the spring of 1565 the fragile colony was reinforced when Jean Ribault arrived with several shiploads of additional colonists and badly needed provisions. However, Spanish king Philip II had no intention of permitting this French occupation of Florida.

That same year a Spanish expedition of 1,500 prospective colonists and soldiers began fortifying a new settlement on the east coast where Ponce de León had first landed and named it St. Augustine. Following his king's orders, Pedro Menéndez de Avilés, the Spanish governor, then marched his troops about twenty-five miles north to Fort Caroline, where they torched the French settlement and brutally slaughtered the inhabitants. Another French settlement in America bit the dust.

The Spanish were serious in their campaign to bring Christianity to the heathen Indians of the New World. In 1571 a group of Jesuit priests built a mission on today's York River in Chesapeake Bay. Within a year they were massacred by the local tribe, the Powhatans. But St. Augustine endured, despite devastating attacks by English sea raider Sir Francis Drake and pirates, to become the first European settlement in North America and the northernmost outpost of the Spanish colonial empire.

Following the death of Henry VII in 1509, the English made no further attempt to establish colonies in the New World until the closing years of the sixteenth century. For decades they were reluctant to challenge Spain's territorial claims in the distant lands across the western sea. The reign of Tudor monarchs was distracted for years by internal political conspiracies and rebellious uprisings in Ireland and Scotland, the religious controversies and marital maneuvers and scandals of Henry VIII, and the realities of European power relationships. Fortified by its riches from the New World, Spain had become a prosperous and powerful nation whose support in European affairs was vital for the English to maintain. When Mary, the Catholic daughter of Henry VIII and Catherine of Aragon, became queen of England in 1553, she married King Philip II of Spain. She became known as "Bloody Mary" for condemning hundreds of Protestants to be burned at the stake.

However, her Protestant sister Elizabeth, who ascended to the throne in 1558 after Mary's death, became increasingly drawn to gaining a profitable foothold in the New World, as were the merchants of Bristol, Plymouth, and London. England was now a Protestant nation and no longer felt the need to align herself with Spain, the stronghold of Catholicism. After all, there were vast expanses of territory in America that Spain was unable to occupy and control, which, in English eyes, rendered the papal bull of 1493 meaningless. Queen Elizabeth ordered the construction of a formidable naval fleet, already started by Henry VIII, and England increasingly asserted itself as a strong European power prepared to take on the Spanish if provoked. Furthermore, there was promising news from America: captains and crews from vessels that sailed along the Atlantic coast reported their observations of fertile lands with rivers and forests to supply lumber for building ships and houses, a territory most suitable for profitable development by enterprising settlers. Moreover, the English were still eager to discover a short northwest passage to the riches of the Orient and to search for gold and silver in America, the precious metals from the New World that had so enriched her European archrival, Spain.

· 2 ·

The Elizabethan Years

In 1576 an experienced English sea captain from Yorkshire, Martin Frobisher, made the first of his three voyages to Labrador, the southeastern end of Baffin Island, and Hudson Strait in search of gold and the Northwest Passage. He failed on both counts. On his first voyage, Frobisher brought back a nugget of iron pyrite, "fool's gold," which an Italian assayer falsely declared was the real thing. On the next trip he brought back two hundred tons of the ore, and this time two German experts concluded that it could be profitably refined to produce gold. Considering the large investment by the London merchants who backed the expeditions and expected rich returns, perhaps the Germans did not dare to tell the truth. Queen Elizabeth, a major investor in the enterprise, and other backers were excited over the golden treasure that lay waiting to enrich her kingdom. Their instructions to Frobisher for his third voyage were to hold back on his search for the passage to the Orient. Concentrate on bringing home the golden ore.

Frobisher's huge fleet of fifteen ships of varying sizes set sail from Harwich on May 31, 1578, with a team of Cornish miners on board. Through violent storms, snowfalls, and battering icebergs they finally reached their destination in Frobisher Bay and began mining the ore. In view of the freezing cold weather in midsummer, Frobisher canceled the original plan to leave an outpost of one hundred men to winter over and man the mines. On September 2, with their holds filled with 1,350 tons of iron pyrite ore, the fleet headed for home. Attempts in England to smelt precious metal from the ore confirmed that their cargoes were worthless. The rocks ended up being used to repair roads, and the investors lost everything. Nevertheless, Frobisher's voyages enlivened the interest of the queen and English merchants in pursuing plans for colonization in America and added significantly to mariners' knowledge of the geography of the northern regions.

During the reign of Queen Elizabeth I, English elite, merchants, and investors first sponsored attempts to start colonies in America.
Courtesy of the Library of Virginia.

Sir Humphrey Gilbert, a veteran army officer from Devonshire, first led the way in promoting English colonization in the New World. In his essay, published in 1576, *A Discourse of a discoverie for a new passage to Cataia*, he made a strong case for finding a short northwest sea passage to the Orient and building English trading outposts along the route. The new colonies would offer another advantage: they could be manned by England's surplus population—the unemployed living in poverty and convicts from its overflowing prisons—relieving the growing strains of overcrowding in the country. (England's estimated population increased by about a third during Queen Elizabeth's forty-five-year reign ending in 1603.) Gilbert had been a backer of Frobisher's futile attempt to strike gold. Despite Frobisher's failure, the possibility of finding gold, the good fortune that had so enriched their archrival Spain, continued to be a potent lure for English explorers and their queen. Gilbert's article had a significant impact on the thinking of English merchants, mariners, and the queen.

Queen Elizabeth was grateful to Sir Humphrey Gilbert for his military service to her kingdom, and she admired him as a man. His essay closed with a dramatic flair reflecting his knightly spirit and motivation: "He is not worthy to live at all, that for fear or danger of death shunneth his country's service and his own honour; seeing death is inevitable and fame of virtue is immortal." His military success in ruthlessly subduing a rebellion in Ireland and plans for establishing colonial plantations in that country enhanced his reputation as a forceful and competent leader. Furthermore, the queen was impressed with his strategy for advancing English colonization in America. In 1578, Queen Elizabeth issued a patent to Gilbert authorizing him to establish English settlements on any land that he discovered that was not occupied by another European nation.

Unfortunately, his mission, which left Plymouth in November of that year, soon collapsed. Three of his large fleet of eleven ships broke away to engage in piracy against Spanish treasure ships. The main body of the fleet was so delayed by poor planning and foul weather late in the year that, running low on provisions, they retreated into several Irish ports. But Gilbert refused to give up and obtained the backing for another expedition from his family, including his half-brother Walter Raleigh, friends, and Southampton merchants; to attract their investment he assigned rights to them of lands that he expected to discover.

In June 1583, Gilbert's five vessels, carrying about 260 men, left Plymouth bound first for Newfoundland. His ultimate objective was to find Norumbega, like Saguenay a mythical city and region of great wealth that fanciful accounts said existed in the region of the Penobscot bay and river in Maine. This fictional tale of a land of fabulous riches had been spread by

LAMONT, EDWARD M., 1926-

FORTY YEARS THAT CREATED AMERICA: THE STORY OF
THE EXPLORERS, PROMOTERS, INVESTORS, AND SETTLERS
WHO FOUNDED THE...   Cloth   287 P.
LANHAM: ROWMAN & LITTLEFIELD, 2014

TITLE CONT: FIRST ENGLIGH COLONIES. EXAMINES
EARLY COLONIAL PERIOD, FROM 1585 TO 1625.
LCCN 2014014184
  ISBN 1442236590   **Library PO#** FIRM ORDERS

		List	38.00	USD
8395 NATIONAL UNIVERSITY LIBRAR	**Disc**	14.0%		
App. Date 12/10/14 COLS	8214-08	**Net**	32.68	USD

SUBJ: UNITED STATES--HIST.--COLONIAL PERIOD, CA.
1600-1775.

CLASS E162   DEWEY# 973.3   LEVEL GEN-AC

YBP Library Services

LAMONT, EDWARD M., 1926-

FORTY YEARS THAT CREATED AMERICA: THE STORY OF
THE EXPLORERS, PROMOTERS, INVESTORS, AND SETTLERS
WHO FOUNDED THE...   Cloth   287 P.
LANHAM: ROWMAN & LITTLEFIELD, 2014

TITLE CONT: FIRST ENGLIGH COLONIES. EXAMINES
EARLY COLONIAL PERIOD, FROM 1585 TO 1625.
LCCN 2014014184
  ISBN 1442236590   **Library PO#** FIRM ORDERS

		List	38.00	USD
8395 NATIONAL UNIVERSITY LIBRAR	**Disc**	14.0%		
App. Date 12/10/14 COLS	8214-08	**Net**	32.68	USD

SUBJ: UNITED STATES--HIST.--COLONIAL PERIOD, CA.
1600-1775.

CLASS E162   DEWEY# 973.3   LEVEL GEN-AC

*Sir Humphrey Gilbert claimed Newfoundland for Queen Elizabeth,
but failed to start a colony and was lost at sea.*
Courtesy of the Library of Virginia.

a cast-off English sailor who ended up in Maine and claimed to have been there before returning to England. Gilbert planned to leave a group of settlers there, including some miners and English Catholics seeking a new haven to worship free of Protestant harassment; they would establish a new colony for which he had drafted a detailed plan of governance.

Discipline in Gilbert's fleet broke down again, and one vessel soon deserted, probably to engage in piracy. Sailing west past giant icebergs, the fleet reached Newfoundland in seven weeks. Gilbert was surprised to find thirty-six fishing vessels from several European countries in St. John's Harbour. The fishermen must have been nonplussed to observe Sir Humphrey nail the royal coat of arms to a post, claim the land in the name of Queen Elizabeth, and announce that he was its governor. Anyone who spoke disrespectfully of the queen would lose his ears. Many of Gilbert's colonists, some of whom were released convicts, were a sullen lot, and some now wished to abandon the project and go home. Others had been struck down with dysentery. He was finally forced to send one of his ships with the sick and troublemakers back to England.

After enjoying the fishermen's convivial company for a couple of weeks, Gilbert's little fleet left Newfoundland bound for the mainland to plant the new settlement. Then, probably off Sable Island, disaster struck when one of his ships, in a thick fog, ran aground hard on a reef and sank, drowning around eighty-five prospective colonists. Fifteen escaped in a small boat and were saved. Gilbert, his captains, and crews had had enough exploring unknown and often fogbound waters. Gilbert, on board the frigate *Squirrel*, with his other ship, the *Golden Hind*, turned around and headed for England and home.

Gilbert was a soldier, not a sailor. Captain Edward Hayes of the much larger *Golden Hind* warned Gilbert that his small frigate was overburdened with cannon and unsafe, but he chose to remain on board. In response to Hayes's entreaty urging him to stay on the *Golden Hind*, he declared, "I will not forsake my little company going homeward with whom I have passed so many storms and perils," reported Hayes.

However, Gilbert's bad luck persisted. North of the Azores the ships encountered "very foule weather and terrible seas," wrote Hayes. On September 9 when the two ships came within hailing distance, Gilbert, casually sitting in the stern of the *Squirrel* and reading a book, shouted out exuberantly, "We are as near to heaven by sea as by land!" Sadly Sir Humphrey's ringing observation proved fateful. That night his frail little vessel sank in heavy seas off the Azores, and Sir Humphrey and all hands were lost. While Sir Humphrey Gilbert's expeditions failed to achieve their goals, his message promoting the benefits of English colonization and his bold efforts would spur on his queen and countrymen to plan new ventures in the New World.

There were other events and influential persons shaping England's strategy to the same end. In 1522 a ship from Ferdinand Magellan's fleet returned to Spain, having completed the first circumnavigation of the world and providing solid proof that the earth was round and the American continents were not part of Asia. Magellan himself had been killed by natives in the Philippines, where he had stopped to obtain fresh food. In 1580 Sir Francis Drake, following the same route of Magellan's fleet around the southern tip of South America, completed his three-year voyage of circumnavigating the world. He returned laden with treasure captured from Spanish ships and towns along the west coast of South America and Mexico. His voyage, ranging as far north as northern California, confirmed the vast size and wealth of the New World continents and further hardened England's opposition to

Spain's claim to exclusive rights over these newly discovered lands. In gratitude for Drake's accomplishments, Queen Elizabeth knighted him on the deck of his flagship.

As a youth, Richard Hakluyt had been inspired by his older cousin, a well-connected lawyer, to study geography. His growing fascination and enthusiasm for the subject at Oxford led him to study whatever writings he could find on voyages of discovery around the world. He also consulted sea captains, merchants, and mariners to add to his knowledge and began compiling information from the reports of voyagers to America that would assist expeditions hoping to start new English settlements. Hakluyt dedicated his life work to this cause: he would be a "publicist and counselor for present and future national enterprises across the ocean." Hakluyt, who was an Anglican minister, had the ear of Queen Elizabeth, who appointed him to a clerical sinecure that gave him the income and time to pursue his passion.

In 1582 Hakluyt produced a history of these travel accounts, *Diverse Voyages Touching the Discovery of America*, and two years later *A Discource of Westerne Planting*, summarizing the reasons why English colonization in America was imperative. The Hakluyt writings promoted the benefits to be gained by establishing outposts in America that could supply England with the products, such as foodstuffs and timber, that she was forced to import from other European nations. New colonies would provide markets for woolen cloth, England's major manufacture. During Queen Elizabeth's reign, many landlords had converted their farmlands to pastures for sheep raising to supply the profitable woolen industry, and many tenant farmers, driven from their homes, became jobless paupers roaming the streets of London and other cities. The new colonies would provide a livelihood for the large numbers of unemployed, an unhealthy condition that led to disorder and crime. Furthermore, undesirable folk—debtors, beggars, convicts, Catholics, and other troublemakers—could be shipped off to the new colonies. Another important goal was to convert the natives to Christianity and persuade them to become Protestant allies in the ongoing confrontation with Catholic Spain. Furthermore, an English outpost closer to the Caribbean could serve as a base for English privateers preying on the Spanish ships returning to Spain with their plundered treasures. In 1585 England and Spain went to war with each other. The time had come, Hakluyt declared, for England to take its share, along with Spain and Portugal, of the bountiful resources of the New World. The time had come to end Spanish domination everywhere.

In a paper published in the 1589 edition of *The Principall Navigations, Voiages, and Discoveries of the English Nation*, Hakluyt declared that he had read of "other nations miraculously extolled for their discoveries and notable enterprises by sea, but the English of all others for their sluggish security and continual neglect of the like attempts." They were "either ignominiously reported or exceedingly condemned." Richard Hakluyt was a major force until his death in 1616 in promoting English colonization in America.

Sir Walter Raleigh, another Devonshire man, was like his half-brother, Sir Humphrey Gilbert, in many ways. He was bright, sophisticated, outspoken, and ambitious. He told his son that life was a "troublesome bark," and each man should strive to gain his "station on the upper deck; those that live under hatches are ordained to be drudges and slaves." Raleigh was also a brave man of action. His military service in Ireland fighting against an Irish rebel uprising and his critical comments on English policy in Ireland had caught the eye of Queen Elizabeth. Handsome and charming, witty and impudent, and elegantly attired, he soon became one of her favorites at court. She rewarded him with valuable properties and lucrative appointments and made him captain of the Queen's Guard. However, Raleigh was roundly envied and

The enterprising and colorful Sir Walter Raleigh sponsored expeditions to start a colony on Roanoke Island, North Carolina.
Courtesy of the Library of Virginia.

disliked by many in the court and London for his close and rewarding relationship with the queen, his arrogant nature, and his luxurious lifestyle. His affair with Elizabeth Throckmorton, one of the queen's ladies-in-waiting, resulted in her pregnancy, and the two got married, without the queen's permission. The imperious Elizabeth ran a tight court: she imprisoned both lovers briefly in the Tower of London, and Raleigh's standing at court was considerably diminished.

Perhaps Sir Humphrey Gilbert's greatest legacy to his half-brother was the patent that the queen granted Raleigh, the same one that Gilbert had received—to acquire, settle, and develop new English territories in America (except those far northern lands already claimed by Gilbert). In 1584 Raleigh dispatched two ships, commanded by Philip Amadas and Arthur Barlowe, gentlemen from his household staff, to scout the east coast for a suitable location to establish a settlement. They chose to explore Pamlico Sound on the coast of North Carolina between the northern end of Cape Hatteras and Cape Lookout. The local Indians greeted them in friendly fashion and introduced them to the brother of Wingina, the chief of the Roanoke tribe. There was a harmonious exchange of gifts: the Indians gave them food—fresh fish, venison, rabbits, pumpkins, and corn—and the English reciprocated with items of clothing, trinkets, and a copper kettle. On a visit to the tribal village on Roanoke Island, the English guests were treated with warm hospitality and given a sumptuous meal.

Upon their return the captains presented a glowing account of the prospects for a new settlement where they had been—fertile land, plentiful game, fowl, fish, and forests to provide cedar, sassafras (for medical uses), and good timber for building houses and ships. Arthur Barlowe declared, "We found such plenty . . . that I think in all the world like abundance is not to be found." The climate was favorable and mild in the winter. Barlowe was effusive in his praise of the natives. "We were entertained with all love and kindness," he wrote. "We found the people most gentle, loving, and faithfull, void of all guile and treason."

Raleigh's captains brought back two Indians, Manteo and Wanchese, who stirred up considerable curiosity among Londoners about life in America. They also brought back some Indian tobacco, and Raleigh must have caused quite a stir at court when he first filled his clay pipe and smoked the Indian leaf. Over time the new diversion caught on famously. When Raleigh chose to honor his sovereign by naming the new territory *Virginia* after the Virgin Queen, Queen Elizabeth was so pleased with his accomplishment and the compliment that she knighted him.

Raleigh was an enthusiastic and bold advocate for establishing an English foothold in America. Encouraged by Barlowe's good news about prospects for starting a new colony, he planned to lead a new expedition to the North Carolina coast himself. However, Queen Elizabeth refused to let her favored courtier go, perhaps bearing in mind the imminent confrontation with Spain; instead she backed the project by lending Raleigh the *Tiger*, a Royal Navy ship that would serve as the fleet's flagship. So in 1585 Raleigh organized the enterprise under the command of his cousin Sir Richard Grenville, a daring naval commander and exploration devotee, who had fought the Irish like his kinsman. Six ships carrying 600 men comprised Grenville's fleet. It departed Plymouth on April 9, 1585. Grenville took a southerly route to the Caribbean, intending to assure a profitable venture for Raleigh's investors by seizing and looting Spanish treasure ships en route to his destination.

There were 108 colonists on board Grenville's flagship who would remain in Virginia to build a permanent settlement; the rest were crewmembers and soldiers. The two Indians taken by Barlowe to England, who would serve as interpreters, were also on board; so were Thomas Harriot, a scientist and reporter for the expedition, and John White, an accomplished artist and explorer, who had sailed to America on Frobisher's expedition in 1577. Simon Fernando, who had made three previous voyages to America, the last with Barlowe and Amadas to Roanoke, was named the chief pilot of the expedition.

Roving through the West Indies on his treasure hunt, Grenville captured several Spanish ships, which he ransomed for money and supplies (including cattle and swine) while keeping a good share of the booty for the ship's officers and crew and the expedition's investors. After wending their way north, the fleet finally reached the Outer Banks of Hatteras Island. Close to their destination, disaster struck. While attempting to enter Pamlico Sound through a narrow and shallow inlet, the *Tiger* and other ships ran aground. Before the crew was finally able to free the *Tiger*, the hull had taken a pounding and sprung a leak. Much of the food and other provisions were spoiled by seawater.

During July Sir Richard and a party ventured by boat north of Roanoke Island to explore the region. Grenville was a hotheaded soldier; diplomacy was not his strong suit. When a silver cup left in one of the boats near an Indian village disappeared, Grenville accused the Indians of stealing it. When they didn't produce the cup, he burned their village and destroyed their corn. This was the way he had treated Irish rebels. It was a cruel and stupid blunder that would prove to be very costly to the colonists later on.

The colonists settled on Roanoke Island on July 29, 1585. Located at the northern end of Pamlico Sound, the island was about ten miles long and two miles wide. There they erected a small fort and palisades surrounding their thatched roofed houses. It was the first English outpost in the New World, and the colonists soon faced unexpected challenges. The settlers, lacking the skills needed to live off the land or catch fish in a weir, would be forced to rely on the Indians for their food supplies, especially corn and game. On

In 1585 Sir Richard Grenville led the first two expeditions bringing settlers to Roanoke. A third expedition brought over a hundred new colonists including women and children.
Courtesy of the Library of Virginia.

August 25 Grenville departed for England, leaving the governor, Ralph Lane, another military veteran from the Irish campaign, in charge. Sir Richard promised to return with more supplies the following spring.

Many of the colonists, all men, were former soldiers and adventurers eager to enrich themselves by finding gold, silver, and pearls. There even was a miner and a jeweler in the company, and Governor Lane led an expedition searching in vain for gold mines and a route to the South Sea (Pacific Ocean) and the Orient. The colonists survived the winter; however, by the following spring the natives were no longer so friendly. While they had warmly greeted the first party of English visitors, this large new group had occupied their lands, set fire to a native village, and were constantly demanding more food from them. The English colonists were endangering their way of life and were no longer welcome.

Governor Lane felt threatened, and, after hearing that a large body of Indians planned to attack the English fort, he decided to take preemptive action. At night he led twenty-five soldiers, armed with muskets, to the village of Wingina, the Roanoke chief, where in a surprise attack they killed a number of natives including Wingina. Sir Richard Grenville and Ralph Lane were veteran soldiers who had won their spurs in Ireland by brutally subduing the Irish rebelling against their English rulers. English soldiers and their commanders had laid waste to vast areas and tortured, starved, and beheaded hundreds of men, women, and children. They looked down on the Irish as a wild bunch of barbarians, and many, including the Roanoke governors, viewed the American Indians in the same way.

After the brutal attack on the native village and murder of its chief, the Indians stopped supplying food to the colonists, leaving them in dire straits. The hungry colonists had had enough. Sir Francis Drake's fleet, following the queen's orders, came by to check on the colony in June 1586, after raiding Spanish possessions and shipping in the Caribbean and sacking St. Augustine in Florida. The remaining 103 colonists implored him to take them home to England, and he did. In mid-July Grenville came back from England with more provisions and to his surprise found the little settlement deserted. To maintain England's claim to the region, he left fifteen men before departing for home.

Sir Walter Raleigh, with the persuasive backing of Richard Hakluyt, refused to abandon his project to plant the first English colony in the New World. During the previous winter at Roanoke, Thomas Harriot and John White, sailing north with a crew in a pinnace, had reached the lower part of Chesapeake Bay. It was a superior location for a colony than Roanoke, which, on an island in shallow Pamlico Sound, lacked any deepwater port for ships. Governor Lane had praised the bay region's attributes, as had earlier explorers, reported Richard Hakluyt, who recommended to Raleigh that he start his new colony there. Raleigh agreed and this time sent three ships carrying a large group of colonists, who would be led by the new governor, John White. The company included women and children for the first time. Leaving Portsmouth in May 1587 on a course via the West Indies, they reached Roanoke in July. However, the fleet captain, Simon Fernando, who had been Grenville's chief pilot, now refused to take them any farther, saying it was too late in the year to proceed to the Chesapeake. He probably wished to return to the West Indies to plunder Spanish treasure ships. Spain and England were now at war, so privateering was officially sanctioned.

What the latest group of colonists found upon landing at Roanoke was ominous. The fort had been razed, and there were no signs of Grenville's men anywhere. The 117 bold colonists, including seventeen wives and eleven children, elected to stay and build their little houses on the ruined site of the old settlement. They would farm on land allotted to each settler by Raleigh and raise their families in their new home. Eleanor, the daughter of John

White and wife of Ananias Dare, gave birth to the first English baby born in America, Virginia Dare, shortly after their arrival. However, the promising hopes for the community were soon dimmed by an act of Indian violence: the body of settler George Howe, who had gone off fishing for crabs, was found dead with sixteen arrow wounds and his head bashed in.

Governor White, in an effort to restore good relations with the Indians, dispatched twenty-one men by boat about sixty miles south to parley with the Indians who lived on Croatoan Island. They were accompanied by Manteo, one of the Indians who had been brought to England on the first Raleigh-sponsored voyage and returned to his home on the next. He had already been helpful to the English and belonged to a Croatoan family on the island. White hoped that he would allay the fears of the natives toward the English, and he did. After an initial tense encounter the Indians accepted the colonists' wish that the two sides live together in harmony. In response to their plea, the colonists assured the natives that they would not destroy their cornfields. The Croatoans told them that a band of Roanoke warriors had surprised the small group of settlers Grenville had left behind at the fort and, after an intense fight, had driven them from the island in their boat. The Indians had either killed them later or perhaps they had perished at sea. The Croatoans hosted a feast for their guests, and both sides agreed that they would meet again in a week at the Roanoke village to try to restore peaceful relations between the colonists and the tribe of the slain Roanoke chief, Wingina.

The plan failed miserably. The Croatoans did not show up on time, and Governor White felt that the colonists must take action to avenge Howe's death and the killing of Grenville's men. A company of English attacked Wingina's village in the early morning darkness. Unfortunately, the natives that the colonists assaulted were the Croatoans, the very same group that they were supposed to meet but which had been delayed in getting to the rendezvous. Before they realized their mistake, the English had killed one of them as the others fled. The Roanokes had left the village earlier, fearing an English reprisal for Howe's death. Manteo, who trusted the English and was baptized into the Christian faith a few days later, forgave them for their tragic blunder and defended their action with his fellow Croatoans.

The Roanoke settlement was not adequately provisioned. The colonists still lacked enough essential supplies such as seed, livestock, ironware, and other items to endure. The colonists had great confidence in Governor White, who had been a member of the first group of settlers at Roanoke in 1585 and returned to England with them. They decided that White should sail to England and bring back the needed supplies plus additional colonists. They pleaded with him to go, and reluctant at first, he agreed. On August 27, 1587, White sailed for England. A terrible northeast storm drove his ship way off course, but it finally reached the Dingle Peninsula in Ireland, and White made his way back home to Southampton. He was determined to return to Roanoke to bring relief to his fellow colonists, friends, and family, as soon as he could.

As it turned out, three years would pass before White was able to go back to Roanoke. When Raleigh put together a relief expedition in March 1588, the Privy Council ordered it to stand down. The country was preparing for a Spanish invasion, and Queen Elizabeth intended to keep English ships and men in England to defend the homeland. John White also made an attempt to bring relief to Roanoke. However, after leaving port the captain and crews of his ships promptly turned to privateering—quite unsuccessfully, as it turned out: they were captured by some French privateers. White, wounded in the fray, made it back to England in his badly damaged ship. It was not the first time, nor would it be the last, that undisciplined crews by engaging in privateering disrupted voyages to start or support new colonies.

In 1590, two years after the English fleet under the command of Sir Francis Drake defeated the Spanish Armada, White was finally able to return to Roanoke. A ship from a fleet that had been plundering Spanish galleons throughout the Caribbean delivered White and a store of supplies to Roanoke Island. On August 17, when White and his party went ashore at the island, they were stunned by what they found. While the palisades of the fort remained, the colonists' little houses had been destroyed and ransacked, and the settlement was deserted. The only footprints on the ground were those of bare feet. The ruins were overgrown with grass and vines. The colonists' small cannons and boats were missing. Carved on a tree were the letters "CRO" and on a post by the fort entrance "CROATOAN."

White and his men searched the island in vain. A bugler played English songs in the event the colonists had gone into hiding in fear of marauding Indians. There was no answering sound. The colonists, including White's daughter and granddaughter, had completely disappeared. White desperately wanted to sail south to Croatoan Island, where the tree and post carving indicated the colonists might have gone and where the friendly Manteo was now the tribe's leader. To White it seemed likely that the English colonists had fled there to get away from the Roanokes, undoubtedly still furious over the murder of their chief, Wingina. However, his ship's captain refused. His ship had fouled and lost two anchors and had only one left; they were low on food and water. They headed toward the Caribbean islands to replenish their provisions, and then with the favorable westerlies backing them, they altered course and sailed back to England.

Given the previous bitter relations of the Roanoke colonists with the hostile local natives—especially the burning of the Roanoke village and the

A relief expedition arrived in 1590 and found the Roanoke settlement deserted and ransacked. Croatan, the name of an Indian tribe in Pamlico Sound, was carved on a post.
Courtesy of the Library of Virginia.

killing of their chief by English soldiers—the most likely theory to account for the missing colonists was that Roanoke warriors slaughtered all the English settlers. Some have believed it possible that the Roanoke colonists did indeed join and intermix with the Croatoans, whose tribe later migrated into the interior of North Carolina. The disappearance of the inhabitants of "The Lost Colony" of Roanoke remained clouded in mystery.

As the sixteenth century drew to a close, England had still not succeeded in planting a lasting colony in the new world. The French efforts had proven equally unsuccessful. However, the defeat of the Spanish Armada in 1588 had strengthened English resolve to ignore the overblown Spanish territorial claims in the New World and embark on colonial schemes of their own. Moreover, the propagandists, Richard Hakluyt and Sir Walter Raleigh, continued to stir the imagination and ambition of their fellow countrymen, both merchants and common folk, in promoting the significant benefits from establishing new colonies in America. Hakluyt updated and published his book, *Principal Navigations, Voyages, and Discoveries of the English Nation*.

Thomas Harriot, a member of the first Roanoke expedition, wrote a descriptive account of the colony, *A Briefe and True Report of the New Found Land of Virginia*, that contained engravings based on artist John White's

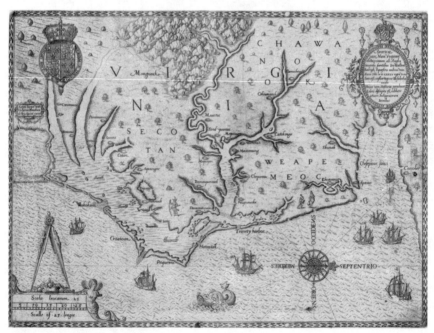

Engraving by Theodore de Bry of map of "The Lost Colony of Roanoke."
Courtesy of the Library of Virginia.

excellent watercolor drawings of the local Indians, their way of life, and flora and fauna. His drawings provided the Elizabethan court with its first real view of life and nature in America, which would inform England's future colonization initiatives. The Harriot book put forward very attractive prospects for future colonies in Virginia. He listed the valuable products that were available—cedar (for furniture making), sassafras (to cure venereal diseases and other ailments), ship supplies (tar and turpentine), fabric dyes, and more. He described the Indians, their villages, foods, and pleasure in smoking their pipes. He said little about the tense and sometimes violent relations between the natives and colonists, except to note that "some of our companie towardse the ende of the yeare, shewed them selves too fierce, in slaying some of the people." Harriot was right, but his observation generally fell on deaf ears.

Some of the returning colonists from the Grenville expedition had complained bitterly about their experience in Virginia and scorned its suitability for future settlement. Thomas Harriot had this to say about these critics:

> Many that after gold and silver was not soon found . . . had little or no care for any other thing but to pamper their bellies, or of that many which had little understanding, lesse discretion, and more tongue then was needful or requisite. Some also were of nice bringing up, only in cities or townes, or such as never . . . had scene the world before. Because there were not to bee found any English cities, nor such faire houses, nor at their owne wish any of their olde accustomed daintie food, nor any soft beds of downe or feathers, the country was to them miserable & their report thereof according.

Sir Walter Raleigh was a skilled naval captain and soldier who had fought bravely against the Spaniards, England's archenemy during Elizabeth's reign, and he participated in the great naval victory over the Spanish Armada and the capture of Cádiz. He was a passionate advocate of English colonization in America and had led the way in organizing and financing the Roanoke settlement. He was also quick-witted, arrogant, and vain, and enjoyed an extravagant and flamboyant lifestyle, which did not endear him to many in the court. However, his writings revealed a thoughtful, gentler side of Raleigh, less frequently exposed. He was a venturesome explorer, historian, and talented poet. One of his poems was "The Nymph's Reply to the Shepherd" written in reply to Christopher Marlowe's "The Passionate Shepherd to His Love." No modern-style free verse for Sir Walter. His graceful rhythms and sweet phrasing are a fine example of the popular pastoral and romantic poetry of the Elizabethan era.

While he had launched the Roanoke expeditions, Raleigh never set foot in Virginia, as he had named the region. However, in 1595 he led the first of two expeditions up the Orinoco River in South America seeking gold and the mythical golden city of El Dorado that some Indians and Spaniards had heard existed in the deep interior of the continent. The sons of Sir Humphrey Gilbert and Sir Richard Grenville, eager explorers like their fathers, accompanied Raleigh. They observed magnificent scenery, but not the fanciful city of gold. Upon Raleigh's return he published a journal describing his expedition, which greatly exaggerated the potential riches for daring adventurers that lay in store in Guiana.

Queen Elizabeth did not live to see the creation of an English colony in America. After her death in 1603, Raleigh's enemies at court accused him of plotting to overthrow her successor, King James I of Scotland, the only son of Mary, Queen of Scots. In his trial, presided over by England's chief justice, Sir John Popham, Raleigh professed his innocence of the trumped-up charges in vain. He was sent to the Tower of London to await execution, remaining fairly comfortably imprisoned there. His extensive patent to develop all of Virginia (the full length of the American east coast) was terminated. King James's bright and popular son, Prince Henry, declared disdainfully, "Only my father would keep such a bird in a cage." King James, an awkward man with a speech impediment, may not have taken to the elegant, outspoken Raleigh, who had introduced smoking Virginia tobacco to his countrymen. The king, displaying admirable good sense, roundly condemned smoking as an unattractive and unhealthy habit.

Nevertheless, James released Raleigh in 1616 to embark on his second expedition up the Orinoco. His band once again sought the golden city in vain. However, under the command of a subordinate officer his men burned down a small Spanish outpost on the Orinoco, against the strict orders of King James, who did not want to provoke the Spanish. The sixteen years of Anglo-Spanish warfare had ended with the Treaty of London in 1604, and King James was determined to maintain peaceful relations with England's former foe. Upon his return, Raleigh was imprisoned again in the Tower on the original conspiracy charge (and to placate the Spanish for the attack on their outpost in Guiana).

The Tudor monarchs had often sentenced offenders to the Crown to death by beheading. Henry VIII rid himself of two unwanted wives in this manner and dozens of suspected troublemakers. The Protestant Queen Elizabeth sent Mary, Queen of Scots, judged as a Catholic threat to the throne, to the executioner's block. Robert Devereux, the Earl of Essex, her erstwhile bosom companion who had replaced Raleigh in her affections, suffered the same fate in 1601 for conspiring against the queen in his determined pursuit of political power. Raleigh had witnessed Essex's execution on Tower Hill, looking down on the melancholy scene from the White Tower. In battles on land and at sea against the Spaniards, he and Essex had been fierce rivals in gaining victories to win the praise of their countrymen and their queen. In 1601 Raleigh had no reason to think that he would meet the same fate as Essex. He was wrong.

In 1618 King James I ordered the traditional form of royal punishment for Sir Walter Raleigh, and he was beheaded at Tower Hill, an execution that was seen by many to be quite unjust. When Raleigh saw the executioner's axe he observed, "This is sharp Medicine, but it is a Physician for all diseases and miseries." According to biographers, Sir Walter's last words, as he was kneeling waiting for the ax to fall, were "Strike, man, strike!"

Raleigh's death truly marked the end of the Elizabethan age. It was a sad ending for a man who throughout Elizabeth's reign had courageously defended his country and been a staunch and influential advocate for planting English colonies in the New World. In his writings he had declared his goals and motivation: "To seek new worlds for gold, for praise, for glory." Sir Walter was very quotable: "What shall we be," he asked. "Travelers or tinkers; conquerors or novices?" He also once said of Virginia. "I shall live to see it an English nation." And he did. Sir Walter Raleigh's contribution to America's history was later recognized in different ways: a minor brand of cigarettes was named after him, and so was the state capital of North Carolina.

The Roanoke experience offered valuable lessons for future English colonization initiatives, lessons which by and large would be ignored. First, the natives, if provoked, could quickly turn hostile toward intruders. While the English arrogantly regarded themselves as superior beings to the "savages," as they referred to them in their writings, it was foolish to treat them as such. The Indians deeply resented the invasion and occupation of their land by armed foreigners, and dealing with them obviously called for a diplomatic and respectful approach. Second, people with skills to enable a colony to be self-sufficient—farmers, carpenters, hunters, and fishermen, and not spoiled and lazy, gold-seeking gentlemen—should man the new colonies. The colony's sponsors should provide them with the necessary tools and provisions to enable them to sustain themselves, especially during the early years of building their new community, with regular relief expeditions from England to supply their needs. The colonists that were selected, both men and women, must be people who were motivated to succeed and willing to face hardship and arduous labor.

The search for the Northwest Passage, a short trade route to the Orient, would continue. It would be a huge advantage for England or any nation to find a way to avoid the overland caravan or sea route, around Africa's Cape of Good Hope, which were long, dangerous, and costly. While looking for gold and silver mines along the east coast of America did not appear promising, finding these precious metals and the fabulous wealth it would bring remained a primary objective of the elite lords and merchants who financed overseas ventures. The lure of gold even led some to decide that the fanciful tales of golden cities, first spread by the Indians, were worth pursuing. According to these legends there were silver palaces and houses with gold-leafed roofs in these places, and the inhabitants wore clothing adorned with precious jewels. The French king had sent explorers Cartier and Roberval to find the mythical land of Saguenay in Canada. Sir Humphrey Gilbert had set out to find the fabled wealth of Norumbega in Maine. Sir Walter Raleigh and the Spaniards searched in vain for the golden city of El Dorado in the heart of South America.

More profitable pursuits for the English would be gathering and exporting local commodities such as sassafras, furs, and timber. Furthermore, each year some two hundred European fishing vessels were now coming to America. For years West Country English fishermen had supplied English fish markets with catches taken from the bountiful waters off Newfoundland and Nova Scotia. Now they were moving on down to the coast of Maine where some said that the fishing was even better. These fabulous fishing grounds were the real silver mines.

• *3* •

Probing the Forbidding Shores

*B*y 1600 the Spaniards had been building bases and exploiting the riches of the New World for over a hundred years. Yet while English fishermen had ventured ashore in the Gulf of Maine to cure their fish and trade for beaver pelts from the Indians, at the start of the new century not a single Englishman was living in all of America. Nevertheless, English merchants were keenly interested in establishing trading posts and permanent settlements to profit from the rich resources in the New World that were reported by mariners sailing along the Atlantic coast. Some also harbored the lingering hope of discovering a northern river route to the Pacific Ocean or finding gold or silver deposits.

Bartholomew Gosnold, the son of an English country squire living at the family seat of Otley Hall near Ipswich, had graduated from Cambridge, studied law at the Middle Temple, married, and settled down in Bury St. Edmunds. He was an able sea captain who had joined the Earl of Essex and Sir Walter Raleigh on the Essex-led expedition to the Azores in 1597 to capture Spanish treasure ships and in other privateering raids against Spanish shipping. Gosnold had become acquainted with Richard Hakluyt, the first and highly respected professor of geography at Oxford, and his lectures at the Middle Temple promoting English colonization of the New World had undoubtedly inspired Gosnold. Hakluyt's prolific and informative writings and advice were instrumental in influencing the country's leaders to press forward with English colonization in America. Gosnold also was intrigued by the prospect of obtaining profitable cargoes and establishing new settlements in northern Virginia, as his countrymen referred to the northern part of the east coast of America.

Henry Wriothesley, the Earl of Southampton, was a prominent figure at the court of King James and a generous patron of William Shakespeare and other writers. He also was attracted by the lure of profitable ventures in the New World and outfitted the barque *Concord* for the thirty-one-year-old Gosnold to command in a voyage of exploration. Gosnold was accompanied by Bartholomew Gilbert, the son of Sir Humphrey, who had inherited his father's zest for exploration and building new colonial outposts in America. There were thirty-two men on board, of which twenty, led by Gosnold, were designated to remain in Northern Virginia to man a new settlement.

The *Concord* sailed from Falmouth on March 26, 1602, following a direct route from the Azores, a voyage that took seven weeks. It made its first landfall near Cape Elizabeth in southern Maine. The rockbound coast with its fog, treacherous reefs and ledges, and dense, forest-covered shores was not inviting. Sailing off the coast they were startled to see "a Biscay shallop with sails and oars" approaching them, and furthermore, when it got closer, that the eight men on board were all Indians! Moreover, the man who appeared to be their leader was wearing European clothing—a waistcoat, breeches, shoes, and hat, and others had some European articles, reported Gabriel Archer, a passenger on the *Concord*. After the Indians had made signs of peace, Gosnold let them board his ship. They spoke "divers Christian words," indicating that they had been in contact with French Basque fishermen, who had been fishing the waters off Newfoundland for years. Now they had started moving southwest to the Gulf of Maine, where cod and other fish were plentiful and closer in. Gosnold did not know whether the Indians had traded for the shallop, stolen it, or looted a shipwreck. He did not see a good harbor and sailed off, heading south. Gosnold hoped to find Narraganset Bay, whose pleasant environs and friendly Indians had been reported by Giovanni da Verrazzano after his 1524 voyage.

A day later, according to John Brereton, a minister on board who wrote a journal of the voyage, the *Concord* anchored in Cape Cod Bay, looking out on "a mighty headland" with "a white, sandy and very bold shore." When Gosnold and his men set foot on the inner shore, it was the first officially recorded landing by an Englishman on the New England coast, although English fishermen were already drying and salting their catches on islands off the coast of Maine. The waters close to shore off the cape were teeming with cod, and after hauling in a huge catch, Gosnold named the giant hooked peninsula Cape Cod. Rounding the cape, they next headed down the outer shore and explored the nearby island of Martha's Vineyard. Gosnold was impressed by the vast amount of grapevines growing everywhere, and in memory of his deceased infant daughter, Martha, Gosnold gave the island its name.

The *Concord*'s next stop was the island of Cuttyhunk, the southernmost of the Elizabeth Islands, named by Gosnold, in Buzzards Bay, where the company built a small fort. The main purpose of the expedition was to collect sassafras roots, which were in great demand in England for allegedly curing a number of physical ailments from rheumatism to the "French poxe," namely syphilis. Gosnold's encounter with local Indians went well in a trading session with a group of about fifty that came over from the mainland in nine canoes. They exchanged furs for the white man's knives, axes, and articles of clothing, which were very popular with the natives, and the two groups feasted and smoked together. Gosnold, wishing to view the mainland, sailed across Buzzards Bay, where the natives, probably Narragansetts, greeted his party with gifts of furs and tobacco. Later on at Cuttyhunk, however, four Indians assaulted two of Gosnold's men gathering food, and one suffered an arrow wound. They escaped, but the incident sent a chill through the group assigned to stay and man the little fort as a trading post. Furthermore, they had insufficient provisions to make it through the winter until they could be resupplied the following spring. Gosnold was forced to abandon the plan to start a new settlement at Cuttyhunk, and he sailed home to England, making port in Exmouth on July 23.

The seventeen-week expedition, with only just over a month on land, was not a complete failure. The *Concord* returned laden with a valuable cargo of sassafras, cedar, and furs. Gosnold had failed to obtain Sir Walter Raleigh's permission for the expedition, as required by the royal patent held by Raleigh, and he was forced to negotiate a compensation settlement with him. A Raleigh vessel had recently returned from Virginia with a shipload of sassafras, and Sir Walter feared Gosnold's added cargo would depress prices in the market. Added to the evidence of the abundance of profitable commodities in Northern Virginia, John Brereton provided a descriptive account of the expedition, *Briefe and True Relation of the Discoverie of the North Part of Virginia in 1602*. In it he described the natives as "exceeding courteous, gentle of disposition," but added that there were "some of the meaner sort, given to filching." The outcome of the Gosnold expedition and Brereton's enthusiastic report on the natural assets of the region would stir other merchants and adventurers to action. Nor would Bartholomew Gosnold forget his dream of establishing settlements in the New World.

Several Bristol merchants, town officials, and Richard Hakluyt were well impressed by the commercial prospects revealed by the Gosnold expedition and decided to launch their own venture. They chose Martin Pring, another Devonshire sea captain, only twenty-three years old, to command two ships, *Speedwell* and the smaller barque *Discoverer*, on an expedition to the northern Virginia coast; this time Pring obtained Raleigh's consent. The two vessels

Bartholomew Gosnold landed on Cape Cod in 1602. His was the first recorded landing of an Englishman in New England, although English fishermen had often dried their catches on these shores before returning to England. Courtesy of the New Bedford Whaling Museum.

with a crew of forty-three men left Bristol on April 10, 1603. Their mission was to return with a shipload of sassafras and explore other commercial opportunities along the coast. They were well supplied with a store of goods for trading with Indians—varied articles of clothing, shovels, axes, knives, and trinkets. They made their first landfall among the islands in Penobscot Bay, Maine, where Captain Pring, observing numerous foxes on today's islands of North Haven and Vinalhaven, named them the Fox Islands.

Heading southwest down the coast, they passed by the mouths of the Kennebec, Saco, and York rivers, which Pring decided did not extend far enough inland to warrant exploration. The Piscataqua, which reaches the sea near present-day Portsmouth, looked more promising, and in the *Discoverer* they ascended the river for about a dozen miles, noting the "goodly groves and woods," but they found no sassafras. So Pring continued down the coast, visiting Plymouth Harbor, and then landing near the present-day town of Truro on the northern arm of Cape Cod. A member of the Gosnold expedition, Bristol merchant agent Robert Salterne, was accompanying Pring on the voyage and helped guide him to the Cape Cod area. Pring's men erected a small stockade and began gathering sassafras roots to bring home to their merchant backers in Bristol. They also growth-tested wheat, barley, oats, and various garden seeds that showed good results after seven weeks.

Pring's experience with the local Indians echoed a pattern of conduct other explorers had experienced. They appeared to be friendly, especially when trading for goods they desired, like articles of clothing and metal tools, but they could quickly turn angry and violent toward the foreign intruders. Eager to trade, a group of Indians gathered at the little wooden barricade one day were delighted to listen to one of Pring's sailors playing tunes on an instrument similar to a mandolin. The Indians gleefully danced around the musician in a circle, making gestures and chanting. They rewarded the sailor later with gifts—tobacco and a pipe, and a six-foot dried snakeskin. However, the natives' mood changed on another day when more than one hundred braves armed with bows and arrows appeared to threaten the sassafras gatherers. Warning blasts from the ship's cannon and the crew's two giant English mastiffs, Fool and Gallant, scattered the Indians, who were terrified of the dogs.

Pring dispatched the *Discoverer* first on its homeward-bound voyage with a cargo of sassafras. A number of Indians in canoes came out to the *Speedwell* at anchor, but the two watchdogs' barking alerted the crew in time to defend the ship. As the *Speedwell* weighed anchor for home, the Indians along the shore shouted angrily at the departing crew. The two ships reached England by early October 1603 and delivered their profitable cargoes of sassafras and cedar, which was popular for its fragrance, to the Bristol merchants.

Martin Pring's expedition, similar in scope to that of Bartholomew Gosnold, did not break any new ground for promising exploration. He brought back an Indian birch bark canoe, and his compatriots were fascinated by the little craft built by the native inhabitants of the New World. His detailed account of his findings provided an excellent description of the region. Richard Hakluyt, the energetic promoter of English colonization, obtained a copy of Pring's report, and while it was not published until 1625, it is likely that its message got around earlier to prospective venturers and colonists. "The land is full of God's good blessings," and so was the sea, reported Pring. There was an abundance of fish in the northern coastal waters, "better than those of Newfoundland." The cod were especially plentiful, although there were many others—mackerel, herring, crabs, halibut, lobsters, seals (for making oil), and more, but cod was king.

Another French attempt to establish a colony in New France had also failed miserably. It was doomed from the start. Its sponsor, the Marquis de la Roche, a Breton nobleman, apparently was not aware of the age-old maxim regarding the importance of location in real estate ventures. In 1598 he landed sixty convicts selected from French prisons on Sable Island, an isolated, narrow, twenty-mile-long strip of barren land about a hundred miles southeast of Cape Breton Island. Fortunately there were wild cattle on the island left by the Portuguese years before, and a French ship delivered some provisions each year. Five years later, having succumbed to the usual misfortunes, there were only eleven settlers left alive, and the ship captain on his regular visit took pity on them and brought them back to France.

During the sixteenth century the French attempts to establish colonies in New France had all collapsed, as had their efforts in Florida. Nevertheless, with the strong backing of King Henry IV, the quest continued, invigorated by the determination of Samuel de Champlain, a master mariner, navigator, and explorer. Champlain had been trained in seamanship by his father, a ship's pilot, with whom he had sailed many times. Now, in his early thirties, in preparation for exploring the region known as La Nouvelle France, the St. Lawrence River valley, he visited French seaports to gather information from Breton, Norman, and Basque fishermen, who had been fishing the waters of the Grand Banks and Nova Scotia throughout the sixteenth century. Trading with the Indians, the French ships brought back beaver skins and other furs, which were becoming increasingly popular in Europe for making hats.

In 1603 Champlain joined an expedition that explored up the St. Lawrence River as far as Montreal. He gathered considerable information about the terrain and geography of the region with the help of friendly local Indians and traded with them for furs to bring back to France. On his return Champlain produced a journal describing his findings, which he reported to Henry

IV. The king decided to send another expedition to New France under the command of the Sieur de Mons, a wealthy nobleman and veteran soldier, who shared Champlain's vision for the region and had also visited it on an earlier voyage. De Mons invited Champlain, whom he knew well, to join the expedition as a trusted advisor, who would report their discoveries directly to the king. Henry IV also granted de Mons a monopoly of the fur trade in New France, enabling him to raise the necessary funds to back the project from a group of French investors, as well as authority over the French territorial claims of the regions north of present-day New Jersey.

While de Mons and Champlain still hoped to discover a northern river route to the Pacific, their highest priority was to plant the first permanent French outpost in the New World. Their preferred site for the new colony was Acadia, the coastal regions of present-day New Brunswick and Nova Scotia. They expected to encounter a more benign climate than that of the St. Lawrence River valley further north, where severe winter weather had brought down earlier French outposts. De Mons recruited more than a hundred men with the range of skills needed to build and maintain the new settlement. No women or families joined the venture; that would come later assuming the first attempt succeeded. In April 1604 the expedition's two ships, well manned and equipped for the enterprise, departed Le Havre bound for Acadia.

After making their first landfall on the Atlantic coast of Nova Scotia, de Mons and Champlain sailed around the southern end and up the western shore exploring bays and harbors that might be suitable for a settlement. They were impressed with the present-day Annapolis Basin off the Bay of Fundy, which they named Port Royal. However, they eventually chose a five-acre island up the small St. Croix River on the mainland side of the bay, which they named Isle St. Croix. The island site would be easy to fortify and defend against attacks from hostile Indians or even English or Spanish forces.

During the summer while a settlement was being built, de Mons dispatched Champlain on an exploratory voyage southwest down the coast of Maine to seek other promising sites for French settlements in a warmer climate. In a two-masted vessel, about forty feet long, Champlain and twenty men, including two Indian guides and translators, started down the coast. He relied heavily on his lead line as he sailed through uncharted waters along shorelines with protruding rocks and ledges, sometimes shrouded in dense fog. Passing by Mt. Desert Island with its barren mountaintops, Champlain gave the island its name, L'Isle des Montes Deserts, as he did for another island with a prominent hill, Isle au Haut. After entering Penobscot Bay he ascended the Penobscot River as far as present-day Bangor. A large band of Indians, led by the sagamore or chieftain of the region, Basheba, gave a warm welcome to the French explorers. Champlain's straightforward, respectful, and nonthreatening approach to them served the French well, as they feasted and traded for beaver pelts with their hosts. Champlain and his men then continued on down the bay past today's Camden and Rockland. Running short of provisions, they turned around near the Kennebec River and returned to St. Croix in ten days.

At St. Croix the settlers had built a barricade, a cannon emplacement, housing, and other buildings. Seventy-nine men remained in the outpost, including de Mons and Champlain, when the expedition's two mother ships departed for France. As it turned out, they had made a catastrophic decision in their choice of location. It started snowing early in October, and the weather became bitterly cold. On the St. Croix River a jumble of ice flows and jagged slabs imprisoned the settlers on the island much of the winter. Their wine and cider froze, and they were reduced to melting snow for drinking water. They had no fresh food and existed on bread and salted meat. As the winter dragged on, most of the men succumbed to scurvy, and by spring thirty-five men had died from malnutrition and the debilitating disease. Recognizing the obvious—that the St. Croix site was completely unsustainable—de Mons and Champlain decided to abandon the island outpost in the spring of 1605 and look elsewhere to build a settlement. The brutal winter weather in Acadia, along with poor judgment and planning by the expedition leaders, had finished off another French settlement in America.

De Mons still hoped to find a suitable site for a French colony in a warmer clime than Arcadia. With Champlain at his side and about thirty men he sailed down the coast, mainly retracing Champlain's earlier route, until they reached the Kennebec River, which they explored. They continued following the coast past Casco Bay and on to Saco, where Champlain for the first time observed cultivated fields of corn, squash, and beans in a permanent Indian settlement. They sailed past Massachusetts Bay down the coast into Plymouth Bay, where Champlain noted the thriving Pokanoket village of Patuxet, and then down the outer shore of the cape to a small harbor near the elbow of Cape Cod. Along their route, bands of Indians in canoes came out to greet the French in friendly fashion, as did the Cape Cod Nauset Indians, one of the Pokanoket tribes. However, when an armed French landing party led by de Mons made off with some of the Indians' crops from their gardens, the Indians' attitude understandably changed sharply. When another French party went ashore to collect fresh water, an Indian tried to steal a metal kettle from a sailor. A fight broke out between the two groups, arrows and musket shots were exchanged, and a sailor was killed. After that violent confrontation there was no possibility of restoring peaceful relations, and the French ship headed back to St. Croix.

Even though de Mons, along with Champlain, had spotted some promising sites for French settlements, the hostility of the Indians that they encountered led him to give up the idea of starting a settlement south of Acadia. Instead, de Mons would proceed with his plan to dismantle the St. Croix outpost and move it across the Bay of Fundy to Port St. Royal on the western shore of Nova Scotia, at today's Annapolis Basin. They had admired the area with its fertile land and excellent harbor on their stopover a year before. Moreover, the local Indians, the Mi'kmaq, were friendly to the French settlers, hoping to enlist their support in conflicts with a rival tribe.

The settlers went to work building the fortified hamlet where forty-five of them would live. Port Royal would become the first permanent European settlement in North America since St. Augustine in Florida. It was surrounded by gardens, community lands, and individual plots for the men to cultivate for their own use. In the fall of 1605 they were better provisioned for the winter than they had been a year before at St. Croix. Nevertheless, as the winter wore on, the dreaded scurvy reappeared and spread through the hamlet; twelve men died from the disease. When spring finally came, the French were desperately short of provisions, and when the expected supply ships failed to arrive, they decided to abandon Port Royal. They were on their way by sea to the Atlantic coast to seek passage home when they met the supply ship commanded by the new governor, the Sieur de Poutrincourt, a nobleman associate of de Mons. Fifty additional men accompanied Poutrincourt, and Champlain's group joined them in returning to Port Royal.

In September 1606, Champlain made his third exploratory voyage down the coast from Acadia in an expedition commanded by the Sieur de Poutrincourt. Poutrincourt's approach to the Indians that they met en route to Cape Cod was, like that of de Mons, quite different from Champlain's sensible diplomatic dealings with the natives. At Cape Cod he marched his armed musketeers through the countryside and Indian villages in a manner that the Indians clearly perceived as threatening. They undoubtedly knew of the violent Indian confrontation with the de Mons's crew a year before. Near today's Chatham on the cape the Indians attacked some French crewmembers on the beach and killed four of them in a hail of arrows. The French fired back, and in another skirmish more of them were killed, before Poutrincourt retreated back to Port Royal.

Back at Port Royal the settlers harvested their crops, hunted, and fished. They continued to cultivate good relations with the local Indians, joining them for feasts as hosts and guests. Provided with fresh food and ample provisions throughout the winter, they were able to ward off the dreaded scurvy. With the arrival of spring in 1607, the colonists were in good spirits. Their morale was high: Poutrincourt's men had passed their first winter in

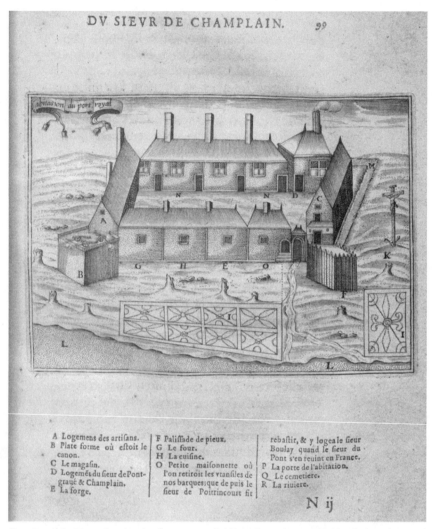

Acadia without undue hardship. They planted their crops in the fertile soil and enjoyed excellent fishing in the local streams and bay. The prospect of maintaining a flourishing colony at Port Royal was promising.

Then in May a ship arrived that brought bad news for the settlers from the Sieur de Mons, who had returned to France. Fashionable men's attire in Europe called for felt hats made from beaver pelts and fur collars and trim adorning clothes. The growing demand for beaver and other furs in Europe

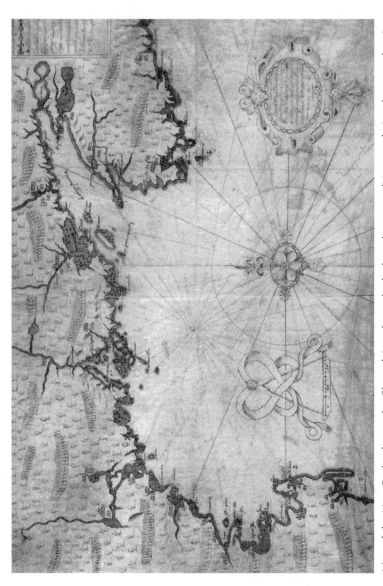

Map of the New England coast by Champlain, who embarked on three expeditions exploring the coastal region from Nova Scotia to Cape Cod. Library of Congress, Geography and Map Division.

had led de Mons's rivals to persuade the king to cancel de Mons's monopoly control of the fur trade. His investors would no longer back his company, and de Mons in turn could no longer support the colony in Acadia. He ordered the settlers to abandon Port Royal and return to France, and they did, some quite reluctantly.

The last two French expeditions down the coast from Acadia to Cape Cod had run up against the hostility of local Indians, dashing French hopes to establish colonies south of the Penobscot River. Champlain's detailed account of his explorations, *Les Voyages du sieur de Champlain*, and his excellent map of the coast, based on his three expeditions through the region, was published in 1613. It would prove to be very useful for explorers and colonists in future years. While the French had withdrawn from St. Croix and Port Royal, Champlain's explorations and colonization plans in America were just beginning.

The English Are Coming

When Champlain and de Mons were returning from their expedition along the New England coast in July 1605, they met the local Indian chief near the Kennebec River, who gave them some startling news. He reported, according to Champlain, that about thirty miles to the east the crew of a ship had enticed five local Indians on board and killed them. "From his description we judged that they were English," wrote Champlain, and indeed they were. It was Captain George Waymouth and his crew on the *Archangell*, who had kidnapped (not killed) five Indians to take them back to England.

When Sir Walter Raleigh was imprisoned in the Tower, his patent for exploration and colonization in America reverted to the Crown. While a few expeditions to Virginia organized by Raleigh to collect sassafras and other products had been profitable to Raleigh, he had not succeeded in starting a single permanent settlement in America, England's strategic goal. King James now felt a heightened sense of urgency to accomplish this objective. He had anxiously observed the efforts of the French to establish outposts in the St. Lawrence River valley and Acadia and the Spanish settlement in Florida. He would encourage English expeditions attempting to find suitable sites for building new settlements on America's east coast.

In 1602 two vessels under the command of Captain George Waymouth explored the coast of Labrador and went on to the mouth of Hudson's Bay, seeking the elusive Northwest Passage. Under pressure from his crew, they turned back and headed home to England. After the voyage Waymouth wrote *The Jewell of Artes*, a treatise on navigational instruments, ship building, and related topics and presented copies to King James. The book, his experience as an explorer, and his reputation as a naval architect and navigator impressed the sponsors of a new expedition to America's east coast.

*The first successful English colonies in America were founded during
the reign of James I.*
Courtesy of the Library of Virginia.

In 1605 three noblemen, Lord Thomas Arundell, the Earl of Southampton, and Sir John Popham decided to back a reconnaissance voyage to
explore the northern Virginia (New England) coast under the command of
Captain George Waymouth. Arundel was a wealthy Catholic and military
veteran from a noble family, well regarded by King James. We have met
the Earl of Southampton before. He was Arundell's rich brother-in-law,
keenly interested in New World ventures and the sponsor of the Gosnold
expedition to Cape Cod in 1602. Sir John Popham, who has been described

by contemporaries as a bullying "huge, heavie, ugly man," was England's chief justice, who had presided over the kangaroo court that had sentenced Sir Walter Raleigh to death. He was especially interested in finding a place where the English courts could transport convicts from their overcrowded prisons.

The primary purpose of the expedition was to locate suitable sites to establish new English colonies. The idea to form a settlement for English Catholics living uncomfortably in Protestant England had been raised in court circles before. With the end of the war with Spain in 1604, Catholics exiled from England during Elizabeth's reign were returning home, and Thomas Arundell put forward the suggestion again. However, his fellow Protestant sponsors of the voyage rejected the notion, and King James appointed Arundell to a military assignment in the Netherlands, separating him from the venture.

On March 31, 1605, the ship *Archangell* sailed from Dartmouth commanded by Captain George Waymouth with a crew of twenty-eight men including James Rosier, from whose journal of the expedition one can trace the ship's voyage. The routes and places visited by Waymouth after his landfall off Nantucket have been identified by Rosier's physical description of the islands, mainland, bay, and river and not by specific navigational terms. He suspected that Spanish spies were eager to gain information about England's attempts to start colonies in Virginia. He would not disclose the location of the bountiful area Waymouth had discovered to the nation that had been England's chief antagonist just a few years earlier, or, for that matter, to the French, already active in New France. "And this is the cause that I have neither written of the latitude or variation most exactly observed by our Captaine with sundrie instruments," wrote Rosier. His journal also provided a detailed account of the expedition's activities, including their encounters with the Indians on the coast of Maine and a full description of the flora and fauna in the region they visited.

The *Archangell* made its first landfall near the Nantucket Shoals at the southern end of Cape Cod on May 14. Captain Waymouth had intended to sail south of Cape Cod in seeking a good site for a colony, probably to the general area where Gosnold had landed. However, adverse southwest winds forced *Archangell* to leave those dangerous waters filled with reefs and shoals, and they sailed north across the Gulf of Maine to Monhegan Island. There some of the crew went ashore to gather firewood; others threw their fishing lines overboard and soon caught thirty large cod and haddock. Seeking a more sheltered anchorage, Captain Waymouth steered his ship toward the mainland. The new anchorage that he chose to be his base lay at the northern end of Allen Island south of present-day Port Clyde.

On Allen Island the crew dug wells to obtain fresh water, planted a garden plot to raise peas and barley, and erected a cross signifying England's claim to the territory. They also began building a shallop, which would enable them to sail or row close to shore. It was constructed from sections stored in the hold of the *Archangell* and was probably about thirty-five feet long.

The fishing in the bay waters was fabulous, as earlier voyagers to the region had reported. At Allen Island Rosier wrote, "Our men took Cod and Haddock by the ship side, and lobsters very great, which before we had not tried." Another time a fishing party took the shallop out about a mile and soon caught enough fish to feed the whole crew for three days. The crew was astonished by the plentiful amount of fish wherever they dropped their hooks or nets and was amazed at their huge size; some cod were as long as five feet, Rosier reported.

On May 30 Captain Waymouth and thirteen men sailed off in the shallop to explore the nearby coastal region, leaving the remaining half of the crew on the *Archangell*. That afternoon they encountered Indians for the first time when three birch bark canoes, each manned by several Indians, came into view. At first they warily kept their distance from the ship. However, when the crew displayed some items that they had brought to give to the natives—knives, bracelets, pipes, and other trinkets—two canoes approached and happily received the presents before returning to the nearby shore to spend the night.

Early the next morning a canoe came alongside manned by three Indians, whom Rosier and the crew welcomed on board. They led the natives below deck and fed them a meal of pork, fish, bread, and peas, which the Indians heartily enjoyed. When a crewmember shot off a musket, they fell flat on the deck in fright. The leader of the Indians understood Rosier's signs that he would like to trade for beaver and other furs with the Indians and agreed to return later in the day with skins and furs for trading.

On May 31 Captain Waymouth and his men in the shallop returned from their excursion along the Penobscot Bay coastline. Passing the harbors of today's Rockland and Camden and sailing up the passage between Isleboro and the mainland, Waymouth had sailed as far north as today's Stockton Springs at the mouth of the Penobscot River. However, because the river that lay directly ahead became quite narrow, a boat passing through would be exposed to an attack by Indians on shore with bows and arrows. Before proceeding further, he decided to return to his base to install protective canvas armor designed for the shallop, which was called a Light Horseman when used for military purposes.

During the following twelve days, Waymouth, Rosier, and the *Archangell* crew would have a number of exchanges with the local Indians. The apparent harmonious relations with the natives concealed a wariness and sometimes fear that was felt by both groups. The Indians returned in their canoes around one o'clock, as promised. Two of them, who had ventured aboard the ship before, brought with them another native, who appeared to be their leader. When the three Indians came on board, Waymouth gave the chief a shirt, a large knife, and other gifts; he gave some smaller trinkets to his companions, including some little mirrors. The Indians laughed with delight in seeing the reflection of their images. Waymouth then fed his guests, who especially savored sugar candy, and gave them food to take to their companions on shore. Rosier noted in his journal that they were treating the natives as kindly as possible. Judging the place to be "fit for any nation to inhabit," the English hoped to ensure a warm welcome for their countrymen who might come to settle in the area later.

The next day Rosier went ashore where some twenty-eight Indians had gathered either to trade or enjoy the newcomers' hospitality that they had heard about from their companions. For some knives, combs, mirrors, and other trinkets worth four or five shillings, Rosier obtained forty beaver pelts, otter, sable, and other skins. Captain Waymouth then invited some of the Indians on board the *Archangell*, where they enjoyed themselves eating and making merry.

When Captain Waymouth went ashore that evening, the Indians gathered around. They "marveled to see us catch fish with a net" and were astonished at the little tricks that the captain performed with a small magnet, used on the ship for adjusting the compass. He invited two Indians to have supper with him and Rosier in his cabin and gave them some peas and other foods to take back to their women. After supper Rosier and some crewmembers joined the Indians on shore where they sat on deerskins before a fire and smoked the Indians' tobacco with them, the customary way in which Indians expressed their welcome and gratitude for the gifts they had received.

A curious negotiation then took place. Captain Waymouth invited the two Indians who had dined with him to sleep on board the *Archangell*, and they were quite willing. However, the other natives felt uneasy about the idea. After some discussion they proposed by signs that if an English crewmember slept on shore with them, they would permit three of their people to sleep on board the ship. So Waymouth sent Owen Griffin to spend the night ashore, and he provided bedding from old sails for the Indians, who would sleep on the lower deck.

The next day around four o'clock three canoes came alongside presenting a large quantity of tobacco as a gift to the ship. Captain Waymouth in turn gave the Indians some peas and bread, which they took ashore. After supper Rosier and some crewmembers went ashore for another pipe-smoking session. When it was time to go back to the ship, the Indians again proposed an exchange of guests. Two of the crew remained on shore to sleep, and Rosier took back three Indians to sleep on the ship.

The following day the Indians came up with a new proposal: they earnestly urged Captain Waymouth to follow them by boat to their encampment on the mainland where they had supplies of furs and tobacco to trade. Waymouth agreed, and with Rosier and fifteen men they set out rowing in the Light Horseman behind their Indian guides in two canoes. When they reached their destination, probably the tip of Point Pleasant in present-day Cushing, the Indians, instead of greeting them on shore, slipped off to join a group of natives nearby. Waymouth, now uneasy about the Indians' intentions, decided to stand off nearby Davis Point with his boat. While awaiting the natives' next move, Thomas King, the ship's boatswain loitering on shore, carved his name, a cross, and the year, 1605, in the shore bedrock.

The next negotiation with the natives' leader continued the nervous chess game between the two parties with another exchange of pawns: Waymouth agreed to send Owen Lattimore ashore to survey the situation and plans for trading if the Indians left one of their men on board the Light Horseman as a hostage for his safe return. Upon his return Lattimore reported his estimate that 283 Indians were gathered nearby armed with bows and arrows. They wanted the Waymouth party to follow them up a small, narrow river to the place where they had a supply of furs for trading. However, the English suspected a trap, remembering the pattern of Indian behavior reported by previous expeditions. Landing upriver would expose the English to an overwhelming Indian assault, and they returned to Allen Island.

It appears from Rosier's account that Captain Waymouth's earlier charm offensive with the Indians had had another more sinister motive all along. "We determined as soone as we could to take some of them, least (being suspitious we had discovered their plots) they should absent themselves from us." The expedition had apparently planned from the beginning to capture some Indians and bring them back to England, and the next morning Waymouth carried out the plan.

When two canoes carrying six natives came alongside the ship, the crew enticed three of them to come on board, probably with the offer of a meal of peas and bread, and then took them prisoner. Rosier and seven or eight men then went ashore on Allen Island to capture the other three natives, bringing some items for trading and a platter of peas. Two of the Indians were willing to meet them, but the other, obviously fearful of their intentions, ran off into the woods. Rosier's men then seized the two natives. They put up a stiff struggle before the crew members, seizing them by their long hair, overcame them and brought them back to the *Archangell*, where they were locked in below the main deck with their three companions. Capturing the five Indians, along with their two canoes and bows and arrows, was "a matter of great importance for the full accomplement of our voyage," reported Rosier.

Over the next few days Captain Waymouth in the Light Horseman cruised about the local islands and harbor where *Archangell* was anchored, taking soundings with the lead line. He wanted to provide a good description of the harbor and water depths for ships visiting the region in the future. Rosier also recorded a description of Allen Island: it had a sandy cove for small boats to land, a freshwater pond and stream, and tall spruce trees providing excellent timber for ship's masts. He added, "How great a profit the fishing would be, they being so plentifull, so great and so good, with such convenient drying as can be wished, neere at hand upon the rockes."

On June 8 two canoes approached the ship containing seven Indians, including the native leader from Point Pleasant. The Indians, who had painted faces with red, black, and blue stripes, indicated that they were emissaries from Basheba, the great sagamore or chieftain of the Penobscot region (whom Champlain had met the summer before). Basheba invited the English to come to his encampment on the mainland where the Indians were ready to exchange furs and tobacco with them. Waymouth declined the invitation, again worried that the plan presented too great a risk of exposing his men to an Indian assault. The Indians probably suspected that five of their companions were prisoners aboard the *Archangell*. Instead, Waymouth replied that the English would be glad to receive Basheba if he came to the ship.

On June 11 the *Archangell* sailed up the western entrance to Penobscot Bay to a spot near present-day Rockport, and on the following morning Waymouth went ashore. Leaving six men behind with the Light Horseman, he led ten men armed with muskets on a four-mile march inland where they climbed today's Ragged Mountain in the Camden Hills to gain an overall view of the region. Rosier was greatly impressed with the area. There was "as much diversitie of good commodities, as any reasonable man can wish, for present habitation and planting," he reported.

After their trek, as the Waymouth party rowed back to their ship, a canoe, manned by the same Indian they knew from Point Pleasant and two companions, approached with another message: Basheba invited one of the crew to spend that night on shore with him, and he would come out to the ship the next morning with furs and tobacco to trade with the English. Again Waymouth rejected the idea, suspecting that the Indians wished to hold an Englishman hostage to obtain the release of the Indian captives on the *Archangell*. After this brief exchange, the *Archangell* weighed anchor and sailed up the western shore of the bay to the spot just inside the mouth of the Penobscot River that Waymouth had reached on his first cruise up the coast. Rosier marveled at the well-protected harbors that they passed en route, possessing good water and large enough to accommodate many vessels. (Starting with today's Rockland in the south and moving up the bay, the string of harbors along the mainland coast well matches Rosier's description.)

Early the next morning, Waymouth and a group of well-armed men rowed the Light Horseman on the incoming tide up the river to the place now known as Fort Knox; after a brief stop, they continued upstream to present-day Bangor. They were impressed with the suitability of the river for shipping and with the fertile land and meadows on both sides. On their return downstream, they erected a cross to mark their claim to the territory for the English Crown.

While the *Archangell* had enough provisions to stay longer to explore and trade with the Indians, Captain Waymouth decided to end the expedition and return to England. Rosier's account expresses concern for their safety, apparently fearing that the Penobscot Indians might attack and overwhelm their small crew to free the five Indians captive on the ship. In identifying a favorable area for establishing English settlements, they had honorably accomplished their mission. Rosier believed that the expedition's report of the voyage would be of great value to those undertaking new colonies on the Maine coast. On June 14 the *Archangell* headed back down the coast to the Rockland harbor area, returning the next day to the anchorage at Allen Island, which they had named Pentecost Harbor.

On June 16 the *Archangell* weighed anchor and sailed for England. Captain Waymouth took regular lead line soundings, and two days later, when they indicated a depth of only twenty-four fathoms, the crew lowered the sails and began fishing with hook and line. The *Archangell* had probably reached the northern edge of Georges Bank, the great cod fishery off Cape Cod. They were amazed at the ease with which they hauled in numerous giant codfish. Rosier noted that fishing these waters could yield a more profitable return than fishing off Newfoundland, "the fish being so much greater." Then, directing their course for England, the *Archangell* set sail and in a quick passage entered Dartmouth harbor on July 18, 1605.

Rosier's opinion regarding the Indians' way of life was contemptuous and mean-spirited. In his journal he referred to them as "a purloin generation whose understanding it hath pleased God to so darken" that they did not appreciate and make use of the rich resources where they lived that were given to them by the grace of God. Displaying an arrogant English attitude of racial superiority, the crew had deceitfully kidnapped five Indians to show off as trophies back home in England. Seizing Indians and taking them back to Europe was not an uncommon practice by New World explorers, starting with Columbus, who had taken thirty natives back to Spain on his first voyage and more on his subsequent expeditions. They were sold into slavery. The English had a more humane plan for their prisoners. Nevertheless, the natives of the Maine coast would not soon forget this act of treachery, sowing distrust and enmity toward future English arrivals on their shores.

According to Rosier, the Indians' initial shock and fear subsided when they realized that the crew intended to treat them kindly and do them no harm, and they tried to please their captors by responding to their questions about their country and way of life. They learned some English words and taught Rosier and others some Wabenaki words. Clearly the Indians had decided to make the best of a bad situation.

Upon their arrival in England, three of the Indians were taken to the fort at Plymouth, which was commanded by Sir Ferdinando Gorges. Gorges was another West Country nobleman and a cousin of Sir Walter Raleigh and Sir Humphrey Gilbert. He had fought with the Huguenots against the Catholics in France and against the Spanish in the Low Countries. As a naval commander he had served in the victorious sea battle against the Spanish Armada. He had been knighted by Queen Elizabeth for his military service and awarded his prestigious post at Plymouth. In 1605, at age thirty-nine, he strongly backed the idea of royal sponsorship of new English settlements in America. From his post at the fort he had watched the fishermen and explorers come and go, and he dreamed one day of acquiring and developing a large domain in Northern Virginia (New England). The other two Indians were placed in the household of Chief Justice Sir John Popham, whom we have already met.

Their masters hoped that they would become useful guides and translators for future English expeditions to America, which would return them to their homeland. The Indians were well treated in their new homes and learned acceptable English. They even gave talks extolling the virtues of their country as a bountiful place to settle, and their dignified presence and demeanor favorably impressed the court and people of London. They played a promotional role similar to that of the two Indians brought back to London by the first exploratory voyage sponsored by Sir Walter Raleigh to Virginia in 1584.

In 1605 James Rosier's narrative of the expedition was published: *A True Relation of the most prosperous voyage made this present year 1605 by Captaine George Waymouth, in the Discovery of the land of Virginia; where he discovered 60 miles up a most excellent River; together with a most fertile Land. Written by JAMES ROSIER, a Gentleman employed in the voyage.* The book provided a glowing picture, a virtual paradise, of the Penobscot Bay area as a good location for new English settlements. (The fine summer weather undoubtedly contributed to the writer's optimism. He had not spent a winter in that part of Maine.)

Spain, by now at peace with England, was not actively opposing English colonization efforts in the vast, unsettled areas of the American east coast, although Spanish spies were keeping a close watch over the English moves. The Waymouth expedition had only spent twenty-nine days exploring a small part of the Maine coast. Nevertheless, their discoveries, territorial claims, and Rosier's account stirred a new surge of enthusiasm for starting English colonies in Northern Virginia. The war with Spain was over, and English raiders could no longer legally go after Spanish treasure ships to seize their precious cargoes. The government lacked the funds to finance a large-scale colonization effort, but there were wealthy English merchants, nobles, and other investors with connections to the court who were more eager than ever to launch profitable commercial ventures in America—such men as Sir Thomas Gates, Richard Hakluyt, Raleigh Gilbert, George Popham, Edward Wingfield, Sir John Popham, Sir Ferdinando Gorges, and Sir Thomas Smythe, a prominent businessman who had led the successful six-year-old East India Company in developing trade with Russia.

On April 10, 1606, King James, petitioned by this group of prominent colonization advocates, issued a royal charter providing for the establishment of two companies to form colonies in Virginia, a vast territory encompassing all of the Atlantic coastal regions stretching from Nova Scotia to North Carolina. They would be under the overall supervision of the Council of Virginia, thirteen members appointed by the king. The companies would be joint stock enterprises financed by "adventurers" or private investors. The Council would appoint members of local resident councils who would govern the colonies in accord with English law. The Virginia Company of London, or simply the London Company, composed of merchants, knights, adventurers, and other prominent folk from London, was granted rights to colonize an area running roughly from today's Cape Fear, North Carolina, to eastern Connecticut. The Plymouth Company's rights, granted to similarly prominent citizens from Bristol, Exeter, Plymouth, and other West Country towns, extended approximately from Chesapeake Bay to today's Eastport, Maine, across the Bay of Fundy from the French in Nova Scotia. Both companies were permitted to build settlements between Chesapeake Bay and Connecticut, which could be no less than one hundred miles apart. The charter granted exclusive trading rights to the new colonies. Two powerful colonizers acted quickly under the authority of the Plymouth Company.

Sir Ferdinando Gorges and Sir John Popham dispatched two vessels in 1606 to start a settlement in the area in Maine discovered by Waymouth. The *Richard* left first in August, commanded by Captain Henry Challons, with John Stoneham, who had sailed with Waymouth, acting as pilot. Two of the Indian captives held by Gorges, Sassacomoit and Mannedo, would assist as guides and interpreters, and then be returned to their homes. There was also a group of colonists on board who would remain to start the new settlement.

Sir John Popham, England's Lord Chief Justice, and Sir Ferdinando
Gorges sponsored the first English attempt to found a colony in New
England. The settlement in Maine collapsed within a year.
Historical & Special Collections, Harvard Law School Library.

The *Richard* never reached America. Starting on a southerly course to the West Indies, it was captured by a Spanish squadron (despite the peace treaty between the two nations), and the ship and crew were taken to Seville and imprisoned. After official legal proceedings, they were repatriated to England in 1608, and Sassacomoit returned to the household of Ferdinando Gorges. An English vessel brought him back to his homeland in 1614. (There is no record of what became of Mannedo.)

The second vessel left England soon after the first, commanded by Captain Thomas Hanham, son-in-law of Sir John Popham, with Martin Pring, who had cruised the coast of Maine in 1603, as master. One of Popham's captive Indians, Nahanada, and probably his brother, Amoret, and a second group of settlers were on board. They reached the Maine coast. However, when the *Richard* with the one person, Stoneham, who had firsthand knowledge of the location for a colony recommended by Waymouth, didn't appear, they abandoned the plan to remain and build a settlement. The loss of Stoneham was critical, because Waymouth had not provided a map of his findings, and he and Rosier were no longer involved in the project. Captain Hanham scouted the area for a few days, released the Indians in their homeland, and returned to England.

Sir John Popham and Ferdinando Gorges were determined to try once again to plant a colony in that part of the Maine coast discovered by Waymouth and Rosier. They had received another favorable report about the region from Captain Hanham, who had "found the Coasts, Havens, and Harbours answerable to our desires." In May 1607 the Plymouth Company dispatched two ships from Plymouth bound for the coast of Maine. The *Gift of God* was commanded by the colony leader, George Popham, who was a nephew of Sir John Popham. The *Mary and John* was under the colony's second-in-command, Raleigh Gilbert, son of Sir Humphrey Gilbert; the captain of the *Mary and John* was Robert Davies. There were about one hundred colonists on board the ships, including gentlemen, traders, and carpenters. Three months before a London Company expedition had departed to establish a settlement in southern Virginia. Now the race was on between the Plymouth Company and the London Company to determine which would establish the first English colony in America.

The two ships became separated during the ocean crossing, but they reunited near Allen's Island, Waymouth's base two years earlier. The *Mary and John* had come from Nova Scotia, where it had made its first landfall. Anchoring off Allen's Island, Gilbert went ashore and found the cross Waymouth had placed there two years before. Gilbert delivered Skidwarres, the last of the Waymouth captives, to his nearby home at Pemaquid. However, when Gilbert and Popham met with Nahanada, the local sagamore whom Hanham had brought back to the area, they received a chilly reception. It was not a good sign.

The *Mary and John*, after scouting the nearby islands, joined the *Gift of God* at the mouth of the Kennebec River, then called the Sagadahoc. The colony leaders chose a poor location for their settlement. There were far better spots up the river. The site was on a barren, windswept, rocky point, fully exposed to winter storms, not far from the river's mouth. Probably, with no map or navigational coordinates, the expedition leaders had mistakenly assumed that the Kennebec was the great river with its pleasing surroundings that Waymouth and Rosier had praised as a fine site for a settlement, namely the Penobscot, some sixty miles to the northeast. On August 19, 1607, the colonists disembarked from the ships and held a church service to ask the Lord's blessings on their enterprise.

The settlers set about building a sturdy, star-shaped fort with ramparts and ditches and various buildings inside the palisades, including a large storehouse, chapel, houses for the colony leaders, and huts for the men; they named it Fort St. George and completed the construction in two months. The leaders' decision to build a strong fort at that location reflected their concern over the possibility of an attack by the French, who had surveyed the area earlier on the voyages led by Champlain. Raleigh Gilbert explored the upper reaches of the Kennebec and the surrounding area in a shallop. Shipwrights on the expedition also built a fifty-foot vessel, called a pinnace. It was named *Virginia*. The leaders wanted to demonstrate that shipbuilding could be a profitable enterprise in the colony. It was the first ship built by the English in North America (and a forerunner of the later large-scale wooden ship construction in Maine and the modern shipbuilding industry up the Kennebec at Bath). On October 8 the *Mary and John* sailed back to England with a report for Gorges.

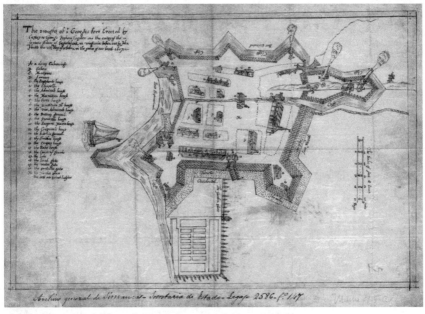

Design of Popham colony fort at the mouth of the Kennebec River in Maine.
Collections of Maine Historical Society.

The settlement soon faced unexpected setbacks. Relations with the Wabenaki Indians were often tense; the memory of Waymouth's treachery remained fresh in their minds. The late summer arrival ruled out raising crops for fresh food. The most serious drawback was the bitter discord between George Popham and Raleigh Gilbert, which divided the colony into two partisan camps. Popham was the president of the colony. Aging, overweight, and incompetent, he was later described by Gorges as "timourously fearful to offend or contest with others that do oppose him." Popham had high hopes that the colony would become a profitable trading enterprise. He reported to King James, quite fancifully, that he had heard that a huge body of water could be reached in a seven-day's journey. "This cannot be any other than the Southern Ocean, reaching the regions of China." Fine woods, tropical spices like cinnamon and nutmeg, and other good products would be abundant in the region. There was no limit to his fabrications: "I have thought it should be made known to your Majesty that here among the Indians, that there is none on the world more admired than King James."

Raleigh Gilbert, holding the title of admiral at the age of twenty-five, was "desirous of supremacy and rule, a loose life, prompt to sensuality, little zeal in religion, humorous, headstrong and of small judgment and experience, other ways valiant enough," according to Gorges. Gilbert had little respect for Popham and longed to take over command of the colony from him. Lacking discipline, many of the men were lazy and quarrelsome with little enthusiasm for the enterprise. In December about half of the colonists returned to England on *Gift of God*. Only forty-five men were left to pass the winter in the newly erected Fort St. George.

The winter weather was unusually severe, extremely cold with heavy snows, and the Kennebec froze over. A fire destroyed much of the storehouse and some provisions stored inside it. George Popham was dying. He knew it and wrote, "I die content. My name will always be associated with the first planting of the English race in the New World." Popham died in February 1608 in unpleasant circumstances, yet comfortable with his vision, not knowing that it would never be realized. Raleigh Gilbert became president of the colony. Food became short, and a few other colonists became ill and died. The Wabenakis remained hostile, and there may have been open conflict between the two groups. A colonist's diary, which was read by a London editor and later lost, reported that a fight had broken out between the settlers and Indians within the fort and a gunpowder explosion had killed some natives.

When spring arrived, a ship carrying fresh supplies brought the news that Sir John Popham, one of the colony's two main backers, had died. Gilbert sent her back to England with a cargo of sassafras and furs. The *Mary and John* returned in late summer with a message for Gilbert that his elder

The Virginia, *built by the Popham colonists, was the first ship built by the English in America. After bringing men back to England from the abandoned colony, the pinnace later delivered colonists to Jamestown.*
Maine Maritime Museum, Bath, Maine.

brother John had died, and Gilbert had become heir to a title and the family estate of Compton Castle in Devon. He decided to return to England to take charge of his family affairs. Unhappy with their lot and leaderless, the remaining colonists elected to go home as well. No one wanted to face another brutal New England winter. Some sailed with Gilbert on the *Mary and John*, and others sailed home on the boat that they had built, the *Virginia*.

The Popham colony had collapsed after just fourteen months; the Plymouth Company made no effort to revive it. Back in England one colonist declared that the region was "over cold, and in respect of that not habitable by our nation." Sir Ferdinando Gorges wrote, "All our hopes have been frozen to death." Another European settlement had succumbed to the harsh winter climate in northeastern America, the selection of a bad site, and incompetent leadership. However, the Popham colony debacle marked a turning point for English colonization efforts in America. There were other staunch advocates of building new colonies who were determined to succeed.

• 5 •

Soldier of Fortune

*T*hree months before the Popham expedition set sail for Maine in 1607, the London Company had launched its first enterprise to plant a settlement in southern Virginia, the area that the Company had received authority to colonize. Three ships took a southerly route, heading with favorable winds to the West Indies before turning north toward Virginia. John Smith, a twenty-seven-year-old, feisty, outspoken soldier of fortune, was a member of the company on the *Susan Constant*, the flagship of the little fleet. Short in stature, but physically fit and strong, Smith had already led a remarkable life of perilous adventure before embarking on this latest undertaking.

John Smith was born in 1580 in the little village of Willoughby in Lincolnshire. His father, George Smith, was a member of the yeoman class in England's social structure. He farmed his own lands and was also a tenant farmer on the estate of Peregrine Bertie, Lord Willoughby, the biggest landowner in the area. George Smith was a respected man of means in his village, and young John grew up in a comfortable, well-furnished home in Willoughby. He attended elementary school in nearby Alford before going on to boarding school in Louth, the King Edward VI Grammar School, about twelve miles from Willoughby. It was there that the yeoman's son, a farmer's boy, met the sons of gentlemen and others of higher rank in the English pecking order. Perhaps it was during those years that Smith developed his lifelong feelings of bitterness toward those ordained by birth to be his superior yet who lacked any record of accomplishment that justified paying deference to them. He believed that by right and dint of achievement he was at least their equal.

Long hours of study—Latin grammar, moral instruction, and penmanship—and the strict discipline imposed by the teachers, including

59

caning, were not for John, and he ran away once. When he was fifteen, his father arranged for him to serve as an apprentice to a merchant in Norfolk, a task too sedentary and dull for John's taste. When his father died in 1596 and his mother remarried, John inherited his father's farm and some pastureland. However, he knew the life of a farmer, and it was not for him. He recalled later that even then he was "set upon brave adventures," a boyhood longing that continued throughout his life.

Much of what we know about Smith comes from his own writings, although his books about Jamestown also contain his collection of accounts by other colonists. The story of his life is one of history's most amazing tales of adventure. There have been critics, his contemporaries, and later on, who questioned his credibility, but researchers have not uncovered any evidence to dispute the basic facts of his story. John Smith's goal in life was to earn the praise of his countrymen by accomplishing great things—to win battles against the enemies of Christianity, explore new places, and build English colonies in the New World. The main purpose of his prolific writings was to put forward his vision for starting new colonies and to provide a record of his role in these history-making endeavors. As his books reveal, he was very proud of his accomplishments and was by no means shy in telling about them. He was boastful and sometimes mistaken about dates and spelling in his writings. Nevertheless, John Smith wrote to record history, not to tell a trumped-up story. In a few parts of his tale, some written years after the incidents occurred, the chronology of events is confusing, and historians have reconstructed the story based on other accounts. These few murky passages do not affect the main thrust of the narrative. The story of Smith's life before the Jamestown expedition—his European adventures, battles in Hungary, enslavement in Turkey, and the rest is largely based on Smith's own account, *The True Travels*.

At the age of sixteen, "to learn the life of a soldier," he enlisted in a company of English soldiers sent by Queen Elizabeth to assist the Protestant forces fighting in France. When that conflict ended, the English troops joined the Dutch fighting to drive the Spanish army from the Netherlands. After enduring the rough life of a foot soldier for several years, Smith was happy to join the two sons of Lord Willoughby on a sightseeing tour through France, accompanied by a tutor and servants. John's father, the tenant farmer, had enjoyed a mutually respectful relationship with Lord Willoughby, and in his will he had left the noble lord a fine, two-year-old colt. George Smith had also commanded his son John to "honore and love" Lord Willoughby. Clearly the Willoughby family considered John Smith to be a promising young man, even though he was well below their social rank. Probably through this influential connection Smith was given letters of introduction to members of the court of King James VI of Scotland (who would become James I of England when Queen Elizabeth died in 1603), and Smith decided to pursue this new opportunity for advancement. He almost perished, however, when his ship, bound for Scotland, was wrecked off the English coast near Berwick. He made his way to Edinburgh and was well received by the Scottish gentlemen, but with "neither money or meanes to make him a courtier," he returned to Willoughby around 1600.

Smith received a warm welcome home from his neighbors and friends. After a while, tiring of "too much company," he withdrew to a small, isolated spot of pasture and forest where he built a small hutch of boughs by a stream. There he would study and plan his future course of action. He hired a local man to bring him food from town. Smith knew the life of a soldier; now he wished to learn the strategy of warfare, and he read Machiavelli's *The Art of War* and a translation of the meditations of Marcus Aurelius.

Although the customs of the knighthood era were no longer in fashion in England, Smith practiced jousting in his forest retreat—thrusting his lance time after time through a hanging ring as he galloped by on his horse. He accepted an invitation, probably arranged by Lord Willoughby or his sons, to visit Tatersall, the estate of the Earl of Lincoln, where he was tutored by Theodore Paleologue, an Italian gentleman, who was the Earl's riding master. Paleologue taught Smith horsemanship, and Smith probably practiced fencing and jousting as well. The worldly tutor also told him stories of the long-standing battle between the Christian nations and Islam. The Turks controlled parts of Eastern Europe, and plans were afoot to raise an army to drive them from these formerly Christian lands.

Smith's ambition was to move up the social ladder and earn the respect of his fellow citizens by his deeds. He was also eager to see more of the world, and joining the Christian armies fighting the Muslim Turks in Hungary would meet his goals. He got off to a bad start. Four French gentlemen he met in the Netherlands invited him to join them sailing to France; with their influential connections he would be introduced to an important general in Hungary. On reaching port in France the four confidence men, with the connivance of the ship's captain, made off with all of Smith's money and a trunk containing his belongings. With no more than the clothes on his back, Smith headed south. It was hard going, and sometimes he ended up sleeping on the ground in the forest. Smith was tough, persevering, and outgoing. Meeting new people who might assist him came easily to him, and a friendly farmer and a French noble, the Count of Plouer, provided him with shelter, clothing, and supplies for his arduous journey. Near Mont-Saint-Michel by chance he ran into one of the thieves who had stolen his belongings, and Smith severely wounded him in a sword fight. He finally reached Marseilles and boarded a ship for Rome.

Misfortune continued to dog his steps. In heavy weather the captain anchored close to shore near Nice to ride out the storm. His fellow passengers, Catholic pilgrims going to Rome, were angry at the presence of the English Protestant; they despised his religion and his country. He brought bad luck to the voyage, and they would never enjoy fair weather with him on board. The solution was simple—they threw him overboard. Smith swam ashore to the nearby island of Saint Mary, and the next day he hailed a ship anchored off the island. By a stroke of amazing good luck, the vessel's Captain La Roche from Saint Malo turned out to be a neighbor of the Count of Plouer, who had treated Smith so kindly earlier. He agreed to take Smith on board his ship as a passenger on his voyage to carry freight to Alexandria. After sailing along the North African coast, they delivered their cargo and continued on a course to the Adriatic Sea.

Captain La Roche was also a French privateer on the lookout for ships with valuable cargoes he could seize, and at the mouth of the Adriatic he spotted a promising prize, a large merchant ship from Venice. The French battered the Venetian ship with cannon broadsides, and then closed and boarded her. After a vicious battle (some thirty-five were killed on both sides and many more wounded), the French captured their prize and seized as much of the rich cargo as their ship could hold. Presumably Smith fought well alongside his French comrades, because when he left the ship in Antibes, La Roche awarded him five hundred gold coins and a small box, apparently containing some items of considerable value.

With his newly acquired wealth, Smith toured Italy. He wondered at the splendors of Rome and was excited to catch a glimpse of Pope Clement VIII. Sailing from Venice across the Adriatic, he made his way to Graz, the seat of Ferdinand, Archduke of Austria. When Smith arrived in Graz, most of Hungary was under Turkish rule, and the Christian armies were fighting to repel the Turkish invaders and drive them from Hungary. Smith first met an Irish priest, who, in turn, introduced him to the Count of Modrusch and other "brave gentlemen," including Lord Ebersbaught, the governor of the town of Oberlimbach. Modrusch commanded a regiment in the Hungarian army fighting the Turkish forces, and after hearing Smith's story, he enlisted him in his regiment.

The immediate objective of Modrusch's regiment was to end the Turkish siege of the walled town of Oberlimbach. The Turkish army surrounding the town had trapped governor Ebersbaught and its defenders inside with no way to communicate with their allies outside the walls. Now Smith put in place a plan that he had learned from his military studies at Willoughby and confided earlier to Ebersbaught. He sent a coded signal with flaming torches from a nearby hilltop informing the governor when and where the Hungarian forces would attack. He also implemented a diversionary tactic designed to mislead the Turks regarding the location of the coming attack. At night the Hungarian soldiers set out a long line of over two thousand burning musket fuses, which fooled the Turks into thinking that the assault would come from that direction and led them to focus their defenses there. The Hungarian attack came from another quarter, and, joined by the town's defenders, it was a success. The Turks fled, and the siege was ended. Smith's scheme had worked, and Modrusch awarded him with an officer's commission as captain of 250 horsemen. He would now be known as Captain John Smith. He was just twenty-one years old.

In its next engagement Smith's regiment joined a Christian force of thirty thousand in its attack to liberate the city of Stuhlweissenburg, held by the Turks. Smith again used the military expertise derived from his earlier studies to produce an explosive bomb. The soldiers filled some fifty pots with gunpowder; their exteriors were coated with inflammable tar and pitch and studded with musket balls. First set on fire, the flaming bombs were projected over the city walls with devastating effect, reported Smith. The Christian army then attacked, slaughtering many Turkish soldiers, and they retook the city. It was a great victory, for the Turks had held the city for more than fifty years.

The Christian and Turkish armies next battled on the plains of Girke in Hungary, "where began a hot and bloody Skirmish betwixt them," with thousands of men engaged on both sides, according to Smith. He did not escape unscathed—his horse was shot from under him, and he was wounded, although not seriously. After sporadic fighting over the next two weeks, both sides retired to winter quarters.

In the spring of 1602 Modrusch's force of six thousand men was assigned to Prince Zsigmond Bathory of Transylvania in Romania, who needed military support to fight the Turks occupying his domain. After engaging a renegade army of Turks and Hungarian mercenaries that had been plundering and slaughtering throughout Transylvania, the Christian troops surrounded them in a mountain fortress and placed it under siege. Joined by another large force under a Transylvanian general, they spent the next month preparing their entrenchments and mounting artillery batteries, slow work that drew taunts from the Turks on the town walls. They jeered that they were growing fat from lack of exercise, and a Turkish officer, Lord Turbashaw, dared any captain in the Christian army to "combat with him for his head." This was to be mortal combat. Several officers drew lots to determine which one would meet the challenge, and Captain Smith won.

The two opponents entered the arena on horseback, fully armored, to engage in a joust to the death before the soldiers of both armies. Though short of stature, Smith was strong and smart, and his hours of target practice with his lance and horsemanship and jousting lessons at Tatersall would prove their worth for him. At the sound of a trumpet the two antagonists spurred their horses toward each other. Smith knew his lance could not pierce the Turk's body armor. With careful aim Smith thrust his lance through the eye slit of Turbashaw's helmet visor. The Turk was killed instantly and fell to the ground. Smith dismounted, and following the protocol of the contest, he cut off his adversary's head and presented it to the Christian general. However, his work was not yet over. A friend of Turbashaw angrily challenged Smith to combat "to regaine his friend's head or lose his owne." This time, after shattering their lances, the contestants fought with pistols, and Smith's shot felled his adversary, whom he dispatched with his sword. Another Turk lost his head. Smith was confident in his ability to prevail in one-on-one combat. Some time later he issued a challenge to any enemy who wished to win back the two heads of their comrades. This time a skillful sword thrust by Smith killed his enemy. Thousands of Christian troops cheered their hero as he rode to present the third Turkish head to his general, who rewarded him with a handsomely furnished horse and valuable belt and scimitar.

Smith's deeds had given the army time to mount their cannons strategically to bombard the town. They pounded the walls, opening two breaches through which the Christian forces streamed, seized the town, and slaughtered all the Turkish soldiers. They went on to seize and sack three other towns held by the Turks. When Prince Zsigmond reviewed his victorious troops, he honored John Smith for his exploits by officially awarding him a coat of arms, a portrait of himself, and an annual pension of three hundred ducats.

Modrusch's force fought on, but on November 18, 1602, Smith's good fortune ended when the regiment met defeat at the hands of an overwhelming force of forty thousand Turks. The Christian soldiers took a heavy toll of the enemy but in the end were all killed or taken prisoner. Smith later described the vicious battle: "And thus in this bloudy field, neere 30,000 lay; some headlesse, armlesse, and leglesse, all cut and mangled, where breathing their last." Among them lay Captain Smith, groaning from his wounds and unable to help himself. The battlefield scavengers, impressed by his fine armor, decided to spare his life; he appeared to be an officer for whom they could seek a substantial ransom, recalled Smith. However, when his wounds were healed, his captors took him, along with other prisoners, to Axopolis, near the mouth of the Danube River, to be sold in the slave market. There, after a close examination of his physical condition, he was purchased by a slave trader who then sent him as a gift to a young lady in Constantinople. After a long journey, including a final hard march chained in groups of other slaves, Smith reached the home of his new mistress, Charatza Tragabigzanda.

When Charatza, whom Smith referred to as a "Noble Gentlewoman," talked with him with the aid of translators and learned about his background and deeds, "she tooke much compassion on him," Smith wrote. Fearing that her mother, who controlled the household, might sell him, she decided to send Smith to her brother, a Timor or official in a part of the Ottoman Empire controlled by the Tartars, north of the Caucasus Mountains in Russia. She told Smith that she had asked her brother to treat him well. He would remain there to "learn the language, and what it was like to be a Turke until time made her master of herself," when presumably she would send for him.

The Timor, who ruled the surrounding countryside from a huge castle, completely ignored his sister's request. Upon his arrival Smith was stripped naked, his hair and beard were shaved off, and an iron ring was riveted about his neck. He was given a raw sheepskin to wear and joined more than a hundred other slaves working on the Timor's estate, where they were "no more regarded than a beast." John Smith was not the kind of man to endure this brutal and hopeless life for long. One day Smith was threshing wheat in a field several miles from the castle when the Timor rode up and "tooke occasion so to beat, spurne, and revile him." The two men were alone, and Smith seized the opportunity to beat out the Timor's brains with his threshing bat.

Thus began the last leg of John Smith's amazing odyssey. Smith donned the fine clothes of the Timor, hid his body under a pile of straw, filled his knapsack with corn, and rode off into the desert on the Timor's horse, heading north toward Christian Russia. He was constantly on guard, avoiding contact with others. If recaptured, he would surely be executed for his crime. After several days he came to a crossroads with a sign post pointing out with symbols the routes to various destinations. Smith chose the road to Muscovy or Russia, marked by a cross. Sixteen days later Smith's fortunes rebounded—he reached a Russian garrison on the Don River, where the governor, after listening to his story, removed the iron ring from his neck and provided him with a safe conduct pass for his journey. Smith also met another generous woman: "The good lady Callamata largely supplied all his wants."

Refreshed and provided with clothing and money, Smith took to the road again, heading west through Russia, the Ukrainian steppe, and Poland to Transylvania. His pass assured him of a safe journey and friendly receptions en route. Smith was seeking Prince Zsigmond to obtain a document from him certifying the military honors that he had been awarded and his claim to a coat of arms, whose inscription chosen by Smith was *Vincere est Vivere*. Finally in Leipzig he tracked down the prince, who gave him the confirming paper that he sought and fifteen hundred golden ducats. Smith was an inveterate tourist, and with money in his purse, he toured Germany, France, and Spain. In Morocco, he became friendly with the captain of a French ship in the port of Safi, who invited him to pass the evening on board his vessel. A storm arose during the night that forced the ship to put out to sea to avoid being driven on to the shore. It turned out that the captain was eager to turn to piracy when a promising opportunity arose. With Smith on board, the ship captured several vessels of little value. John Smith, who had relished a life of adventure, never anticipated being caught up in the kind of violent confrontation that came next. His ship became engaged with two Spanish men-of-war in a ferocious running sea battle, with cannon broadsides and a boarding, which lasted two days. The French ship was badly damaged and suffered many casualties. It finally escaped, and with patched repair work it made it back to Safi. John Smith, at age twenty-four, had already seen much of the world and experienced a multitude of exciting and perilous adventures. He was ready to end his travels, at least for the time being, and in 1604 he returned to London.

· 6 ·

The First English Colony

$\mathcal{I}$n 1604 London was a bustling, overcrowded city of two hundred and fifty thousand; it was the nation's capital and by far the largest city in England. It spread out on both sides of the Thames, the great river teeming with all manner of vessels both at anchor or underway. Good Queen Bess had died a year before. One of her favorite courtiers, Sir Walter Raleigh, had been unjustly imprisoned in the Tower of London by her successor, King James I, who had also negotiated a peace treaty ending the war with Spain. The Globe Theatre was putting on some of William Shakespeare's greatest plays. After some seven years of perilous wanderings and soldiering, we can imagine that John Smith enjoyed a bit of rest and recreation during his stay over the next two years in London, perhaps socializing in some of the city's many taverns. We can also assume that he sought out captains and sponsors of exploratory expeditions to the New World, for along the way he met Bartholomew Gosnold, the first officially recorded English explorer to land in New England (or Northern Virginia as it was then known).

The well-connected Gosnold, age thirty-five, was a passionate advocate of colonization with its significant benefits for England, and for months he had sought financial backers for the London Company's project in southern Virginia. He recruited Smith and Edward Maria Wingfield, his aristocratic cousin who was also a colonizer, to join him in his effort. They finally were successful in gaining the support of wealthy merchants and nobles, although Smith's role, lacking the connections of his colleagues, was probably minor. King James granted a patent authorizing the project, and the royal Council of Virginia named seven men to serve as a local council to govern the colony. However, their identities would be kept secret, locked in a box entrusted to the fleet captain, until the expedition reached its destination. The royal

67

council directed the expedition to choose a spot for their settlement at the mouth of a navigable river; if they found a river flowing generally from the northwest, it might turn out to be the long-sought passage to the South Sea (Pacific Ocean) and Asia. The expedition should also seek trading opportunities with the natives and return with a valuable cargo of the commodities that they expected to find.

On December 20, 1606, three vessels—the *Susan Constant*, the fleet flagship, the *Godspeed*, and the pinnace *Discovery*—weighed anchor and headed down the Thames. On board, besides the crew, were 105 men, the group that would stay to form the new settlement. Captain Christopher Newport, forty-six years old, was in command of the fleet and would be in charge of the expedition until it reached its destination in Virginia. He was a seasoned officer who had led privateering voyages to the West Indies, losing his right arm in an engagement with a Spanish treasure ship. Bartholomew Gosnold was in command of the *Godspeed*.

Unfavorable winds and terrible weather forced the fleet to anchor off the Kent coast for over six weeks, imposing severe hardship on the passengers and crews. The fleet finally cleared the coast of England on January 29, 1607, bound for the Canary Islands, where it would replenish its depleted provisions before crossing over to the West Indies. Captain John Smith was one of the gentlemen passengers on the *Susan Constant*. He was still eager to "set upon brave adventures" and make a name for himself in creating a new English colony in Virginia.

During the voyage some of Smith's peers apparently developed a strong dislike for him, led by Edward Wingfield, a leader of the expedition. Wingfield was one of the four members of the London Company that had received the royal patent for colonization and the only one that was making the voyage. He was a veteran soldier, who had fought in Ireland and the Netherlands, and he was about twenty years older than Smith. He was proud of his distinguished family heritage and disdained Smith, the son of a tenant farmer, who now held the rank of a gentleman but lacked the birthright that automatically bestowed that elevated social standing. Wingfield also would have resented Smith's tendency to remind people of his valorous exploits. Smith may have been contentious and boastful, bragging about his record. He may have openly criticized the decisions of Wingfield and his associates and probably was reluctant to defer routinely to the older man's views. He was only inclined to show respect to those who by their actions, not their rank or birth, deserved it in his eyes. What we do know is that when the fleet left the Canary Islands, Wingfield charged Smith with plotting a mutiny to take over the colony's government, murder the governing council, and make himself king. This was a stunning accusation, and he did not produce any evidence to substantiate it. Nevertheless, Captain Newport ordered that Smith should be "restrained as a prisoner," probably below decks in chains.

In late March the fleet reached the West Indies and spent the next three weeks among the Caribbean islands, where the crews refreshed themselves enjoying the local fruits, fish, game, and fowl. According to Smith, when they reached the island of Nevis, his enemies planned to hang him. They did not succeed, perhaps because Bartholomew Gosnold and other allies intervened to save him.

Twenty years before, governor Lane and Richard Hakluyt had advised Sir Walter Raleigh that the Chesapeake Bay region in Virginia presented the most favorable place to establish a new colony, and Captain Newport now directed his ships toward this destination. On April 26, 1607, the little fleet reached Chesapeake Bay and anchored at the mouth of the bay off Cape Henry, which they named after the king's popular son. The sea-weary men were delighted to view their pleasant surroundings. However, their initial joy was dimmed when a shore party, led by Captain Newport, was met with a hail of arrows from a band of natives, wounding two men before they retreated to their ship.

That evening, in accord with his instructions, Captain Newport opened the strong box to reveal the names of the seven men that had been chosen to make up the governing council of Virginia—Captain Newport, who would soon return to England, Edward Wingfield, Bartholomew Gosnold, John Ratcliffe, John Martin, George Kendall; and, presumably to everyone's surprise, John Smith. The new council members were probably dumbfounded to learn that Smith had been chosen as a fellow member. Apparently, they still were suspicious of Smith's loyalty, or just plain disliked him, for they refused to officially accept him as a member of the council.

On the next day the crew assembled a knocked-down shallop they had brought from England. Over the next two weeks a party in the shallop, seeking a suitable colony site, explored the lower part of the southern river running inland from the bay, which they named the *James* after their king. This time their several encounters with local Indians were peaceful and generally friendly. On May 13 Wingfield and the other leaders selected a spot on the James River to build their settlement, which they named Jamestown. The site they chose was a peninsular of swampy land connected to the mainland by a sandy neck of land; it was about fifty miles from the mouth of the river. The deep river channel in that spot enabled their ships to tie up to trees on shore for loading and unloading supply ships. The leaders felt that location should make Jamestown easy to defend against an Indian attack by land or a Spanish attack by sea. However, it was also marshy, mosquito ridden, and lacked fresh water. Six council members were sworn into office, but not John Smith. They then elected Edward Wingfield to be their president.

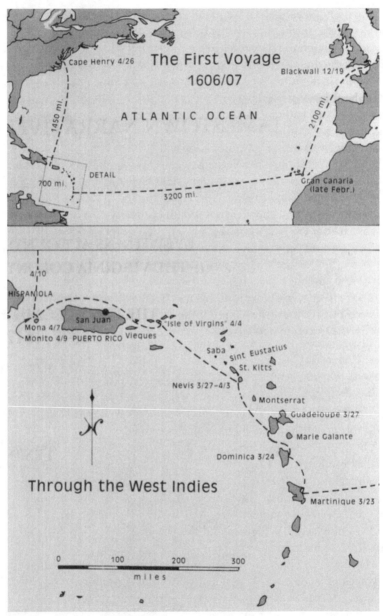

Map of the first voyage to Jamestown in 1607 by the Susan Constant, *the* Godspeed, *and the* Discovery. *Captain John Smith was on board the* Susan Constant.

© 1998 Jamestown Narratives, Edward Wright Haile.

The colonists unloaded the three ships, cleared the ground, and put up tents for shelter. The London Company instructions were to avoid offending the Indians, and Wingfield felt that building a fort might anger them and incite their hostility, so the men simply constructed a weak barricade of tree bows for protection. Several days later the chief of the Paspaheghs, the local native tribe, showed up at Jamestown with one hundred braves armed with bows and arrows. The colonists kept their muskets close at hand. The chief also brought a supply of food to have a feast of friendship with the colonists. However, according to the account of colonist George Percy, a scuffle occurred when a native tried to steal a metal hatchet. After a brief armed standoff between the two sides, the Indians withdrew angrily.

John Smith's prospects now grew brighter. Captain Newport, following the instructions of the royal Council of Virginia, planned to sail the shallop up the James River to determine if it might present a short route to the Southern Sea (the Pacific). On May 21 he selected Smith and a party of twenty-two men to go on this mission. The Indians they met as they progressed inland were remarkably friendly. On the first night the natives where they anchored entertained them "with Daunces and much rejoicing," related colonist Gabriel Archer. As they proceeded upstream, the word went out that Captain Newport was very generous in handing out gifts—trinkets like little knives, bells, and beads—and the English were welcomed with feasts and pipe-smoking sessions. One Indian drew a map of the James River for them. The friendly mapmaker, Nauruans, then served as a guide and ambassador for the English party, running ahead to alert the villages upstream to prepare to greet them. They next arrived at an Indian village about two miles below the falls (near today's Richmond) and about sixty-five miles upriver from Jamestown. The local chief was Parahunt, the son of the paramount chief, Powhatan, who ruled over most of the Virginia tidewater region. In recent years the Powhatans, led by their shrewd and ambitious chieftain, had subdued the other native groups one by one. Some fifteen thousand people under thirty local tribal chiefs lived in his domain in dozens of small villages that were linked by the natives' trails or river travel by canoe. Powhatan collected tributes from them and summoned their warriors to fight the enemies of the Powhatans. Algonquian was their common language, spoken in various dialects.

Captain Newport established friendly relations with Parahunt, who welcomed them at his village. They saw that the falls were impassable for ships; the James would not be the long-sought-after passage to the Southern Sea. Before turning back the English planted a cross with King James's name on it, claiming the land for his majesty. Heading downriver, still guided by Nauruans, the party was greeted and feted by Indian communities, including one led by a woman they called the "Queen of Apamatuck," whom Smith described as "a comely young savage." Beauty is in the eye of the beholder: Gabriel Archer described her as a "fatt lustie manly woman." On May 27 Nauruans suddenly declared he had to leave them. Newport, immediately suspecting that there might be trouble at Jamestown, rushed back there with his men.

He soon discovered that he had reason to fear the worst. Two hundred Paspahegh Indians had attacked the compound the day before with a shower of arrows that pierced the tents, killing a boy and wounding fifteen others, one fatally. The encampment was close to being overrun when an explosive shot from the ship's cannon shattered a tree, frightening the Indians off. Council president Wingfield now agreed that the colonists must swiftly build a fort with palisaded walls to protect the settlement against further attacks. The triangular-shaped fort, covering about an acre, would have a platform mounted with cannons at each corner. Furthermore, the settlers should be "armed and exercised" to defend themselves from Indian assaults.

The Indians, sometimes hiding in the long grass outside the fort, continued to conduct ambushes and small attacks against the colonists as the construction proceeded. A few settlers were wounded, and one man who strayed too far from the fort was killed. Smith's initiative and hard work during this dangerous period clearly impressed the members of the colony's council. His military career had given him a good knowledge of sound fortifications and military training. According to Smith, never one to be modest about his achievements, "So well he demeaned himselfe in this businesse, as all the company did see his innocency, and his adversaries malice, and those suborned to accuse him, accused his accusers of subordination." With the backing of the Reverend Robert Hunt, the chaplain of the company, and Captain Newport, on June 10 John Smith was sworn in as a member of the colony's council.

The palisades protecting the fort were completed by June 15. Within the walls the settlers still slept in tents. A week later Captain Newport sailed for England on the *Susan Constant* and the *Godspeed*, leaving the pinnace in Jamestown. His ships carried a cargo of oak clapboard, used for barrel making, and sassafras. A letter from the colony's council in Virginia to the Virginia Council in London reported that "the land would flow with milk and honey if seconded [supported] by your careful wisdoms and bountiful hands." A hunt for gold had produced some samples of ore, which Newport brought back. The council's letter declared, "We entreat your succours with all expedition lest the all devouring Spaniard lay his ravenous hands upon these gold showing mountains," and Captain Newport reported to the Earl of Salisbury, a leading member of the royal Virginia Council, that the region was "rich in gold." The nuggets turned out to be worthless. The 104 settlers left behind in Jamestown had provisions that might sustain them for a few months if allotted sparingly.

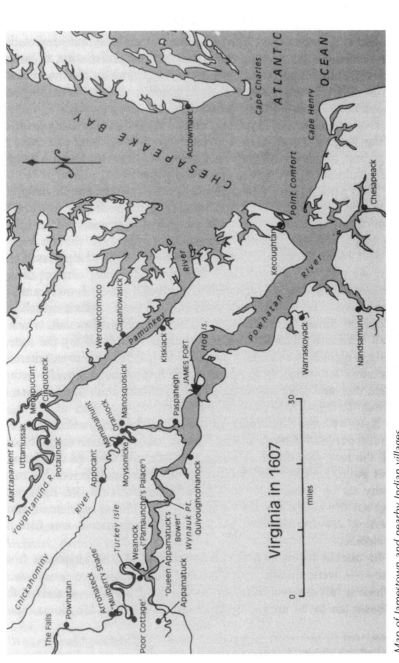

Map of Jamestown and nearby Indian villages.
© 1998 Jamestown Narratives, Edward Wright Haile.

Captain Newport promised to return with more supplies in about five months, but many of them doubted that he could return that soon.

Three days later a messenger from the great chief Powhatan visited the fort. According to Edward Wingfield, he said that the chief desired peaceful relations between the English and two local tribes who were not part of his domain. He would come to the defense of the English if those Indians attacked them, welcome news indeed to the embattled colonists. Another Indian peace delegation arrived with the gift of a deer. They asked about the whereabouts of the English ships, and Wingfield wisely advised them that they were not far away and would be returning.

Then disaster struck the little colony—an outbreak of dysentery, scurvy, and probably typhoid fever. Some men also suffered from wounds that they had received in the attack by the Indians on the fort or in later assaults on those working outside the fort. Almost half the company of 104 men died between June and September, and by the end of the year there were only thirty-eight survivors. "Within ten dayes, scarce ten amongst us could either go or well stand, such extreme weaknes and sicknes oppressed us," wrote John Smith, who also became ill. He recalled that "the living were scarce able to bury the dead." Captain Bartholomew Gosnold, the first English explorer to set foot in New England and a prime mover in soliciting support for the new colony, was among the victims. He was buried with military honors marked by the firing of vollys of shot. He was the most respected member of the colony's council, and his loss was a serious blow to its leadership.

Because of the colony's limited food supplies, council president Wingfield felt compelled to allot very meager daily rations to avoid facing starvation in Jamestown later on, which added to the colonists' weakness and misery. Each man received just half a pint of wheat and the same amount of boiled barley, much of which had become infested with worms in the ship's hold and spoiled. Some sturgeon and crabs caught in the river were a healthy addition to their deficient diet. Several conditions at the crowded little compound could have brought on the disastrous outbreak. The water from the tidal river that the colonists drank was brackish and dirty, "full of slime and filth, which was the destruction of many of our men," reported George Percy. The unsanitary conditions in the cramped fort were conducive to the spread of disease. So was the summer heat, combined with a long drought, and the practice of burying the decaying corpses of the dead inside the fort. The council did not want to reveal the colony's extremely vulnerable state of weakness to the Indians. George Percy wrote, "Our men were destroyed with cruell diseases as Swellings, Flixes, Burning Fevers, and by warres, and some departed suddenly, but for the most part they died of mere famine. There were never Englishmen left in a forreigne countrye in such miserie as we were in this newly discovered Virginia." He described "the pitifull murmer-ings and out-cries of our sick men without relief every day and night for the space of six weekes." Often three or four men a night would die, and "in the morning their bodies trailed out of their Cabines like Dogges to be buried." The sickness ran its course and then subsided during September, when the little colony received a surprising and most welcome manna that surely saved lives: some local Indians came to the fort with a gift of corn, fish, and venison. Shooting wild fowl returning to the river also helped restore the strength of the hungry settlers.

There was other trouble brewing in the little colony. The bitter feud between the fiery John Smith and haughty Edward Wingfield continued. They hated each other. Smith accused Wingfield of hoarding food for him-self and his servants, which Wingfield indignantly denied. Wingfield, in so many words, called Smith a liar and not a fit person to be his companion. Wingfield's conduct had made him increasingly unpopular with the colonists. They were angry at the strict and unbending way in which he had handed out food rations during the time when so many were sick and dying. Some thought that he and an accomplice, George Kendall, had stolen food from the common store, which he controlled. They no longer had any confidence in his incompetent leadership. On September 10 council members John Rat-cliffe, John Martin, and John Smith went to his tent and informed him that the council was removing him from the office of president and the council itself. Captain Ratcliffe was chosen to be the new president, and on the next day he informed the Jamestown colonists at an official meeting of the court as to why they had deposed Wingfield. Wingfield mounted an angry defense, citing the pettiness of some of the charges. It did not impress the court. In regard to Wingfield's false accusation that John Smith had planned a mutiny, the court found that Smith was innocent and awarded him two hundred pounds in damages. The comments in court made clear that many colonists now scorned their former leader, and he was consigned to the pinnace in the custody of a soldier. At the same time Kendall was discharged from the council for disloyalty.

The dismissal of Wingfield marked the beginning of John Smith's evolving role as the dominating leader of the community. His two fellow councilmen, Ratcliffe and Martin, lacked the energy or initiative to take command. By Smith's account, they had shown poor judgment in the face of danger and were not respected by the men. Accordingly, they decided to delegate to Smith the management of the work that needed to be done. The first task was to build cottages in the fort to replace the rotten tents sheltering the men. Smith wrote that most of the men were "in such despaire that they would rather starve and rot with idleness, than be persuaded to do anything for their own relief without constraint." Smith persuaded them with "good words and faire promises," firmness, and by the example he set by his own hard labor. He instructed "some to mowe, others to binde thatch; some to build houses, others to thatch them." It must have taken considerable prodding by Smith, for he reported that the men "notwithstanding our misery, little ceased their malice, grudging, and muttering."

The original company was basically made up of two classes—upper-class gentlemen and workers, including carpenters, bricklayers, and other laborers. About half were listed as gentlemen, and Smith was one of them, but he was unlike most of the others, who felt that manual labor was beneath them. They were eager to find gold, as the Spaniards had done, and live a life of luxury ever after. They did not know that the nuggets of ore that Captain Newport had brought back to England would prove to be worthless. Furthermore, like the first Roanoke settlers, they lacked the basic skills needed to live off the land. Nevertheless, responding to Smith's leadership and example, the colonists got the job done and would live under decent shelter in the coming fall and winter.

Smith recognized that the settlement could not rely on the dwindling provision of food from the local tribes to sustain them over the coming months. He led half a dozen men rowing downriver in the shallop to find other native villages with whom he could trade for a fresh supply of corn. Their first encounter with a new group of Indians started off badly. The Indians, observing the emaciated appearance of Smith's men after their debilitating illness, thought that they had the bargaining advantage and refused to deal reasonably. In the skirmish that followed, the colonists' musket fire, wounding a few braves, quickly changed their minds, and they heaped ample supplies of corn into the shallop. Smith in turn gave the Indians some beads, copper sheets, and hatchets, and they were so pleased that they loaded even more food—turkey, venison, and bread—in the boat. Both sides pledged their mutual friendship, undoubtedly with questionable sincerity, and Smith's party headed back to the settlement with some thirty bushels of corn and other food for the colony. During the fall Smith made several short excursions up the James River and its tributary, the Chickahominy, bartering for corn with the Indians and mapping the region. He visited a half-dozen native villages and generally received a warm welcome from the inhabitants who were eager to trade corn for the metal tools and trinkets offered by the Englishmen.

In Smith's absence gathering supplies of corn, discipline had completely broken down at the little settlement of Jamestown. In *A True Relation* Smith simply reports that George Kendall was executed by a firing squad for mutiny.

THE PORTRAICTUER OF CAPTAYNE JOHN SMITH ADMIRALL OF NEW ENGLAND.

Ætat: 37.
A° 1616

These are the Lines that shew thy Face; but those
That shew thy Grace and Glory, brighter bee :
Thy Faire-Discoueries and Fowle-Overthrowes
Of Salvages, much Civilliz'd by thee
Best shew thy Spirit; and to it Glory Wyn;
So, thou art Brasse without, but Golde within .

Portrait of Captain John Smith, 1580–1631.
Yale Collection of American Literature, Beinecke Rare Book and Manuscript Library.

His *Generalle Historie* version gave a fuller account: Edward Wingfield and George Kendall had plotted with some other disgruntled troublemakers to steal the pinnace and sail back to England, and Smith came back to the fort just in time to stop the pinnace from leaving by firing at it with cannon and musket shot, killing Kendall. Wingfield's account made no mention of his role in the scheme and confirmed Kendall's execution for mutiny. Kendall had earlier been discharged from the council, and Wingfield wrote, "He did practize to sow discord betweene the President and the Council." There is some evidence indicating that the colonists suspected that he was a spy for the Spanish.

While food supplies were plentiful at the time, winter was coming, and nobody knew when Captain Newport might reappear with more provisions. On Smith's next expedition in December to obtain more corn, he planned to go all the way up to the head of the Chickahominy River, which flows from the northwest into the James a few miles upstream from the fort. The royal council had instructed the expedition to explore rivers to their headwaters that might lead to the Southern Sea and Asia, and his fellow local council members now pressed him to pursue this objective.

Smith and his party sailed a barge up the Chickahominy until it became too overgrown and shallow to proceed further. Leaving the barge with seven men, Smith with two comrades and two native guides proceeded further upstream by canoe. In the marshland at the head of the river, Smith went ashore with one of the Indians to hunt for wild fowl to feed his party. Suddenly Smith heard a loud cry and shouting by Indians. Smith later found out that a large band of Indians had surprised and killed the two men that he had left with the canoe. They had also brutally tortured and killed one of the men who had left the barge downstream and gone ashore. Now they were coming after him.

Expecting to be attacked any moment, Smith seized his Indian guide and bound him to his own wrist with a garter, making him a useful shield or negotiator with his attackers. Then the arrows came raining down, and one pierced Smith in the thigh, though not seriously. The Indians surrounded Smith, some two hundred armed with bows and arrows, according to his account. Firing his pistol at them, Smith killed two Indians. He was able to keep them at a safe distance with his pistol, while his guide pleaded for his safe passage, informing his attackers that he was the leader of the English settlers. Retreating toward the canoe with the guide as his shield, Smith slipped and fell into a muddy bog. It was an unusually bitter winter, and the cold water started freezing Smith's limbs. Unable to extricate himself, he threw away his pistol and gave himself up. The Indians seized him. His guide, by identifying Smith as the leader of the English, probably saved his life.

The Indians took their captive to their chief, Opechancanough, the brother of Powhatan, the paramount chief of the region. John Smith had faced life-threatening challenges before, and he appeared calm and resourceful as he faced his captor. He took out his pocket compass enclosed in an ivory case and gave it to the chief. The movement of the compass needle that they could see but not touch under its glass covering fascinated the Indians. Smith then artfully lectured his captors about the roundness of the earth, the universe with its sun, moon, and stars, and how the "Sunne did chase the night about the world continually." He even discussed the diversity of nations in the world and the "varietie of complexions." The Indians could not have understood much, but they appeared impressed, wrote Smith. But not for long. To test his courage they bound him to a tree and prepared to shoot him with their bows and arrows. Then at the chief's signal they untied him and led him off to their village.

The natives celebrated their victory and Smith's capture by marching and dancing in a ring around their English prisoner. They then escorted him to a lodging, which was well guarded by eight braves, and provided him with a large meal of bread and venison. Three women brought more sumptuous meals each day, making Smith wonder if "they would fat him to eat him." However, his captors treated him kindly and gave him back his coat and compass. The guards also protected him from being attacked by the father of a young Indian whom Smith had shot in the marshland fight and who was dying from his wounds. Smith asked the Indians to let him go back to Jamestown to obtain some medicine for the dying brave. They refused, but they agreed to send three men to Jamestown with a message from Smith requesting certain items that he needed. Smith wrote out his message on a piece of paper from a notebook that he carried. He reported that he was safe and gave instructions to his colleagues about meeting the Indians and delivering the articles to them. The Indians then told Smith that they intended to attack Jamestown and he would be extremely well rewarded for advice about the fort's defenses. Smith replied that the fort was well protected with cannons and mines in the field outside. He advised them to call off their plan, which he also reported in his note to the fort. The natives' visit to Jamestown went as intended, and the Indians marveled at the power of communication contained in Smith's little piece of paper.

Smith's captors next took him to visit Indian villages in the region to show off their prize captive, the English commander. Their tour crisscrossed the Virginia tidewater country and its rivers from the Chickahominy to the Rappahannock covering the realm of Powhatan, whom the local chiefs recognized as their supreme ruler. Smith was generally greeted warmly and feted in their travels. When they returned to the village of Opechancanough, Smith was taken to a large house with a blazing fire in the center of the room where his captors proceeded to perform an unusual mystical ceremony. A large medicine man with a strange headpiece of feathers and weasel and snake skins, later joined by half a dozen Indians with black-and-red painted bodies, danced and chanted wildly around the fire, shaking their rattles; sometimes they stopped for a short and loud invocation by the leader. Building a circle of corn grains and little sticks was another part of the ceremony. The natives performed this ritual for three days, telling Smith that their magical practice would tell them whether his intentions were peaceful. Apparently Smith passed the test, because Opechancanough served him a hearty meal and then escorted him to meet his brother, the great chief Powhatan, at his village of Werowocomoco on the northern bank of the Pamunkey, today's York River.

· 7 ·

The King and His Princess

*S*ome two hundred stony-faced members of Powhatan's court gave a great shout when the captive foreign commander was brought into the chieftain's longhouse. They lined both sides of the large room, and behind them stood their Indian women. Their shoulders and faces were painted red, and they wore chains of white beads and ornaments in their hair. The great chief was lying before a fire on a pile of mats on a platform about a foot off the ground, wearing a large robe of raccoon skins with strings of pearls about his neck. A young woman sat on each side of the somber-looking Indian ruler. He had chosen them to bear his children, and after they gave birth to a child they were free to leave him to marry another. Powhatan, with a "grave and Majesticall countenance," welcomed Smith warmly and offered him a sumptuous meal. Powhatan was a tall man with a commanding bearing, probably in his early sixties, with long, gray hair hanging down to his broad shoulders. He was politically shrewd—and ruthless when he needed to be, as Smith would learn soon enough.

The two leaders then conversed, telling each other tall tales that suited their purposes, which certainly included self-preservation on Smith's part. His creative fabrications were stunning. In answer to Powhatan's question as to why the English had come, Smith said that they had retreated from a battle at sea with some Spanish ships and then were forced by foul weather to find a safe harbor in Chesapeake Bay. They had sailed up a river to find fresh water and a good place to build their temporary base until Captain Newport, a renowned warrior and, Smith added, "my father," returned with his ships to take the English home. Why had they gone on to explore the upper reaches of the river? Smith continued to spin his yarn: The English wanted to find a great body of salt water that they had heard was not far to the west. His

81

brother had been slain by an inland tribe that he believed were the Monacans, an enemy of the Powhatans, and they intended to seek revenge. Smith also described the power of the English nation in Europe and its formidable navy, ruled by its "great king whose subject I was."

Powhatan replied that there was indeed a great body of water beyond an inland mountain range, and he went on to describe at some length the fierce and warring tribes, even cannibals, that lived west of the bay. Powhatan then turned away from Smith, consulted for some time with his advisors, and then abruptly ordered two big stones to be placed before him. At his command several braves seized Smith and forced him to the ground with his head on the stones. Two braves stood ready with their clubs "to beate out his braines," Smith wrote later. He had cheated death before, but this time he appeared doomed. Escape was hopeless.

Most Americans know what happened next; it is a legendary event in American history. Pocahontas, Powhatan's pretty daughter, about twelve years old, came forward and pleaded with her father to spare Smith's life, to no avail. She then threw herself down by Smith, took his head in her arms, and placed her own head over his to stop his execution. Apparently her act to save Smith moved her father. Powhatan relented and waved off the executioners. He explained to his followers that he had decided that Smith would be more useful to them alive than dead. He would make metal hatchets for him, like those the English used, and provide bells, beads, and copper for his daughter from the English stores of these articles.

Powhatan had other plans for his English captive. Two days later Smith was placed in a house in the woods and left alone sitting before a fire. Soon he heard a horrible noise. Then Powhatan and two hundred braves, all painted black, suddenly appeared, apparently acting out the final rite of a ceremony adopting Smith into the tribe. Powhatan declared that he and Smith were now friends. In fact, he now regarded Smith as his son, naming him Nantaquoud. He wanted him to return to Jamestown and provide his Indian escorts with two English cannons and a large grindstone, which they would bring back to Powhatan. In return Powhatan would give Smith a piece of land on the York River. Naturally, Smith was happy to agree to any plan enabling him to return to the fort safely.

Smith's account of how Pocahontas saved his life is contained in his *Generalle Historie* published in 1624. He makes no mention of this surprising event in his *A True Relation*, published in 1608, or his *The Proceedings of the English Colonie in Virginia* in 1612, written in collaboration with nine other members of the colony. This omission caused a few critics, most notably Henry Adams, the acclaimed writer from Massachusetts and direct descendant of two presidents, to suggest that the event involving Pocahontas never happened—that it was fabricated by Smith. However, there were good reasons that may have persuaded Smith to leave the story out of earlier versions. He may have simply felt that the episode was not relevant in his report about founding the English settlement in Virginia, or he may have believed it was not politic to mention the incident during the earlier period when he was actively engaged in promoting colonization in Virginia. Furthermore, the story would detract from his self-described role as a brave and skillful diplomat, who had won Powhatan's friendship and saved Jamestown from attack.

Powhatan's way of treating his captive was not uncommon among Indian tribes. Smith himself had been bound to a tree facing a group of braves menacingly aiming their bows and arrows at him before he was released. History even records the rescue of a Spanish captive, Juan Ortiz, from execution by the last-minute intervention of the native chief's daughter, which occurred in Florida in the sixteenth century. Smith did not emphasize or try to dramatize the story about Pocahontas saving his life; he told it in less than fifty words when he wrote his lengthy *Generalle Historie*. The most plausible explanation of the incident is that it was part of an elaborate traditional ceremony leading to Smith's adoption into the tribe by Powhatan—a symbolic killing and rebirth. In this case the chieftain never intended to execute Smith and instructed his daughter to play the role of his savior. There are sound reasons to believe Smith's account, and no evidence has ever been put forward to disprove it.

At the end of December, Smith, accompanied by a dozen Indians, crossed the York by canoe and then walked the rest of the way back to Jamestown. Smith showed his escorts two of the larger cannons and the big grindstone that Powhatan wanted, and, not surprisingly, "they found them somewhat heavie," too heavy to carry back to their village. To demonstrate the firepower of the English, Smith loaded the cannons with stones and fired them at a tree. It was early in January 1608, and the tree was loaded with icicles. The tree's branches and icicles crashed to the ground, so frightening the natives that they ran off. Smith enticed them back and plied them with gifts for themselves and Powhatan, sending them home "in generall full content."

There were malcontents, however, among Smith's fellow colonists stirring up trouble during his absence that Smith now confronted on his return. Captain Newport, before his departure the previous June, had warned Edward Wingfield that Gabriel Archer was the sort of fellow that could be a troublemaker. He had a good résumé—educated at Cambridge, studied law at Gray's Inn in London, and had accompanied Bartholomew Gosnold on his voyage to New England in 1602. He was also extremely ambitious and quite willing to resort to devious schemes to gain authority in the colony. When Smith was away, Archer had talked colony council president Ratcliffe into appointing him a member of the council, an action that completely ignored the London Company's rules for council membership. Earlier, Smith had thwarted a second plot, this time hatched by Archer, to abandon the colony and return to England in the pinnace with some cohorts. Now Archer intended to carry out the scheme. Only this time he had a plan to keep Smith from preventing his departure, as he had before. According to Wingfield's account, Archer charged Smith with being responsible for the deaths of the two men killed by Indians that he had left with the canoe up the Chickahominy River. He was found guilty and sentenced to hang the next day, "so speedie is our law thear," said Wingfield.

Once again Smith escaped execution at the last moment. His savior this time was Captain Newport, whose ship, the *Francis and John*, arrived on January 2, the evening before the hanging was to occur. Another supply ship, the *Phoenix*, which had set sail with Newport, had disappeared in a storm and dense fog. The colonists respected and welcomed the leadership of Captain Newport, who quickly took command of the little colony. The charges against Smith were dropped. Archer was dismissed from the council, and Wingfield was permitted to leave the pinnace, where he had been confined, and live in the fort.

The vessels had carried a mix of gentlemen adventurers and workers. The London Company had selected people with the skills that they believed the little colony needed, and Smith must have been astonished to see some of their choices. The contingent of new arrivals included six tailors, a perfumer, two apothecaries, and a pipe maker for smokers.

Then a new disaster struck the little settlement. A few days after Newport's arrival a fire broke out in the fort, destroying much of their store of food and most of the houses. Lacking shelter, some of the newcomers died from exposure to the bitterly cold weather. Captain Newport supplied the colony with provisions from his ship, and under his command the settlers began rebuilding their housing. Every few days Powhatan's braves delivered food to the fort—cornbread, fish, turkeys, and venison—sometimes accompanied by Pocahontas. Some was sent as a gift for Smith; he and Newport's sailors traded for the rest to supply the colony and ship's crew. Powhatan had been impressed by the courage and knowledge of his worldly new son and his description of the power and authority of Captain Newport, who, Smith had told him, was his real father. Smith had informed Powhatan that Newport would return to Jamestown soon, and he had. According to Smith, the Indians "esteemed him an oracle." Powhatan was also pleased with the gifts that Captain Newport sent him. Newport and the others recognized that Smith had developed a good rapport with Powhatan, who trusted him. When Powhatan invited Newport to visit his village, Newport readily agreed and chose Smith and Matthew Scrivener, a new arrival who had been appointed a member of the council by the London Company, along with a company of thirty guardsmen, to accompany him. Heading down the James and up the York in the pinnace and barge, Newport's party reached the shore near Werowocomoco, Powhatan's village.

Newport and Smith decided to take a cautious approach to Powhatan, fearing the possibility of treachery, and Smith went ashore first with twenty armed men to test the waters. A large crowd of Indians on shore warmly welcomed Smith and led him to meet Powhatan in his longhouse. The great chief, surrounded by his women and lieutenants, greeted Smith enthusiastically, and they feasted, talked, and exchanged gifts. Powhatan was delighted with Captain Newport's gifts for him, some articles of English clothing, including a stylish hat, which Smith presented. Powhatan gave each of Smith's men four or five pounds of bread, and Powhatan's counselors proclaimed "a perpetuall league of friendship" with the English. Smith told Powhatan that Captain Newport, his father, would come ashore to meet him the next day.

Smith then asked Powhatan for the corn and land that Powhatan had promised him. The chieftain replied that first Smith and his men must lay down their arms at his feet, which was the custom of his subjects. Smith, ever the canny diplomat, replied, "That was a ceremonie our enemies desired, but never our friends." Powhatan should not doubt the friendship of the English, and the next day "my father," as Smith referred to Newport, would give him an English child "in full assurance of our loves." They would also help him fight his enemies. Powhatan was so pleased with Smith's response that he declared to his followers that Smith was now a "werowance," a chief of the tribe. All his people should now regard the English not as strangers but as Powhatans, and "the corne, weomen, and country should be to us as to his owne people."

The next day Captain Newport and his men came ashore and, preceded by a trumpet player to impress the Indians, were led to Powhatan's house. Powhatan greeted Newport warmly, and to demonstrate their mutual trust the two leaders exchanged human gifts: Newport gave Powhatan a thirteen-year-old boy named Thomas Savage, whom he called his son, and in return Powhatan gave Newport "his trusty servant" Namontack. The colonists and Indians spent the next several days with feasting, dancing, and trading. John Smith was not impressed with the bargaining skills of his commander, who was set upon cementing good relations with Powhatan. The wily chieftain told Newport that great leaders should not act in a "peddling manner to trade for trifles"; the English should lay down all their articles for trade and Powhatan would choose what he wanted and pay what he felt was a fair value. Smith warned Newport that Powhatan was planning to cheat him, but

Newport agreed to the chieftain's proposal. Smith's warning proved accurate. The English obtained far less corn for their trading goods than they expected and needed. When relations between the two leaders became strained over the outcome of the exchange, John Smith saved the day. He produced some decorative blue glass beads, which Powhatan prized, especially when Smith told him that they were made from a rare substance the color of the sky and should only be worn by "the greatest kings in the world." The trading began again, and this time the English ended up with over two hundred bushels of corn, which was loaded into their barge.

After a couple of days of talking and feasting, the colonists took their leave. Throughout their stay at Werowocomoco Smith had been wary of the possibility of a sudden act of treachery by Powhatan. The chieftain had again asked the English to leave their arms behind when they came to his village. Smith advised Newport to turn down his request, and he did. However, Powhatan treated his guests hospitably, and they departed on good terms with him. A messenger had arrived inviting Captain Newport's party to visit Opechancanough, Powhatan's brother and the chief who had taken Smith prisoner earlier. Boarding their boats, they made their way to his village. This time Opechancanough greeted Smith warmly and entertained Newport's party with feasting, dancing, and "delight." Historians have noted that it was the practice of Indians to offer the services of young maidens to their guests. Smith bargained successfully again with his stock of blue beads for an additional supply of corn. The company returned to Jamestown in early March.

Captain Newport and his crew stayed on in Jamestown for another month, and Smith became increasingly irritated with their presence. First, Newport's men were consuming food supplies that should have been turned over to the colonists, whose regular plain diet consisted of oatmeal and corn. They longed for the sailors' provisions of beef, pork, olive oil, fish, butter, and cheese. Newport's men finally did provide the settlers with food that they would not need on their return voyage, but only by selling it to them at exorbitant prices, in Smith's opinion.

Smith also questioned Newport's single-minded intent to sail home with a cargo of gold ore. The list of passengers on the *Francis and John* and the *Phoenix* included two refiners, a jeweler, and a goldsmith. The gold-hungry gentlemen-colonists seeking quick riches were easily persuaded to back the plan, and Newport set the men to work to "dig gold, wash gold, refine gold, load gold." Smith believed that they should have been doing the urgent and necessary work to strengthen the little settlement instead. He expressed his skepticism about the whole exercise to Captain Martin, the son of the Lord Mayor of London and Master of the Mint, who was in charge of the operation. Smith was right: Newport was loading his ship with "fools gold," probably rocks imbedded with mica. Referring to Smith, one colonist observed, "Never anything did more torment him then to see all necessary business neglected, to fraught such a drunken ship with so much guilded dirt."

On April 10, Captain Newport sailed for England taking with him the two men who had caused so much trouble for John Smith, Edward Wingfield and Gabriel Archer, whom the colonists no longer trusted. Namontack, Powhatan's agent, was also on board, sent on an intelligence mission to learn about the English and their country; he would return on the next supply ship to report to his chieftain. Smith and Matthew Scrivener accompanied Newport in the shallop with a few men as far as Cape Henry. Smith, always interested in exploring new places and sources of food, next led his men up the Nansemond River to the south, where they met the local natives and traded and dined as guests of their chief.

Scrivener had proven to be an able and trustworthy new member of the governing council. The president, John Ratcliffe, was sickly, so Smith and Scrivener shared the leadership in directing the rebuilding of the fort—the palisades, the church, and storehouse—and preparing the fields for raising corn. Ten days after Newport's departure, the colonists gleefully greeted the unexpected arrival of the *Phoenix*, which the colonists assumed had been lost at sea. The *Phoenix*, under Captain Nelson, had been driven by gales to the West Indies, where they had repaired the storm damage to the ship. His crew had fed itself from local tropical foods, so that Captain Nelson turned over to the colonists, to their great joy, the full amount of provisions intended for them, additional stores that were critically needed. The approximately 120 new colonists from the two supply ships increased the population of the little colony to around 160 men.

Council member Captain John Martin, who would go back to England on the *Phoenix*, still believed that her hold should be loaded with what he thought was gold-bearing ore that the colonists were mining. Smith strongly disagreed, calling it worthless "durt," which it turned out to be. He recommended that they load the *Phoenix* with cedar wood, whose value in England for cabinet making was certain. Smith finally won the argument. In the meantime he was facing new troubles with the Indians.

Powhatan's latest proposal was to trade food for swords from the settlers, a deal that was clearly a bad idea for the colony to accept, and Smith rejected the proposal. Soon the Indians began ambushing, grabbing and stealing swords and tools from colonists working outside the fort, sometimes coming right up to its gates. The colony was under orders from the London Company to maintain peaceful relations with the Indians. However, when the Indians set upon John Smith in the cornfield outside the fort, they picked on the wrong man. Firing his pistol, he chased them about the island, and he took seven of them prisoner into the fort, terrifying them with "whipping, beating, and imprisonment." Then the Indians retaliated, taking two colonists captive who had ventured outside the fort. A large number gathered around the fort, threatening to attack without mercy unless the English released the Indian prisoners. Smith boldly went outside to parley with them. He does not tell us what he told them, but in less than an hour he had persuaded the Indians to release the two colonists and he returned to the fort with them. The English continued to hold the seven Indians captive, who, after intensive grilling, confessed that Powhatan had sent them to capture weapons from the English.

The shrewd Powhatan's next move was to send his daughter Pocahontas, with escorts, to apologize for the rash conduct of some of his men and plead for the release of the Indians held by the English. The chieftain declared "the assurance of his love forever." Smith was clearly charmed by the young Indian maiden: "Not only for feature, countenance, and proportion, much exceedeth any of the rest of his people; but for wit and spirit, the only Nonpariel of his Country," he wrote. Powhatan had chosen his ambassador wisely, and Smith and the other council members turned their prisoners over to Pocahontas "in regard of her father's kindnesse in sending her."

On June 2, 1608, the *Phoenix* with its load of cedar sailed down the James bound for England. Captain Martin, often ill and ready to go home, was on board. The ship also carried a long letter from John Smith to an unknown friend telling the story of the expedition and Smith's role in it from the departure from England until the *Phoenix* left. Since the arrival of the colonists just over a year earlier, the original Jamestown council had lost five members: Gosnold had died the first summer, Kendall was executed, Wingfield had returned to England on the *John and Francis* with Captain Newport, and Martin had departed in the *Phoenix*. President Ratcliffe and John Smith were the only remaining members of the first council that had stayed in Virginia. They had been joined by Matthew Scrivener, who had arrived on Newport's first supply ship. Counting on Scrivener's reliability, Smith felt free to resume his exploration of the region.

· 8 ·

Exploring the Chesapeake

$\mathcal{J}$ohn Smith and a company of thirteen men accompanied the *Phoenix* downriver in the barge as far as Cape Henry and then crossed the wide bay to Cape Charles on the eastern shore. He was embarking on another voyage of discovery to explore the upper bay and the Potomac River to the north that Powhatan had told him about; it might possibly be a route to the great South Sea. The colonists sailed north up the eastern shore of the Chesapeake Bay, noting the islands and harbors that might be suitable for future English settlements. In a violent storm they lost their mast and sails and had to bail out the barge swiftly to keep from sinking. They put in at a small island for two days to repair the damage, making a new sail out of the crews' shirts. At their next anchorage on the eastern shore they were greeted with a shower of arrows from the local natives. A volley of musket fire from the barge scattered their attackers. The following day the English, well armed, went ashore, and this time a large crowd of Indians greeted them warmly. The two sides exchanged gifts and parted company on good terms. Smith next crossed over to the western shore of the bay and continued sailing north, probably approaching present-day Baltimore.

After twelve days some of the crew began pleading with Smith to take them back to Jamestown, complaining that their bread had gotten wet and spoiled and about the other hardships they had suffered. In his account Smith relates the talk he gave to inspire his men to continue the mission. He had always endured the same hardships that they did, and in the future they could assign the worst part of "lodging, diet, or whatsoever" to him. They should have no fear as to their safety; the worst was behind them. He urged them to regain "their old spirits," for he would not go back until he had seen the head of the bay and the Potomac River. After running into more foul weather, however, they turned south and a few days later reached the mouth of the Potomac.

As they sailed up the river, the English had several encounters with the local natives. In one a hoard of painted Indians lined the banks of a stream shouting and crying "as so many spirits from hell" to frighten off the foreigners. Captain Smith ordered his men to fire a volley just grazing the surface of the water, not at the Indians, simply to scare them. Once again the tactic worked: the aggressive braves quickly scattered. The two sides held a parley the next day at which the Indians told Smith that they had been ordered to attack them by Powhatan. Furthermore, Powhatan had told them that he had been encouraged by the colonists at Jamestown to assault Smith's party, apparently just another intrigue hatched by the scheming chieftain.

When the English finally reached the great falls on the Potomac, just above today's Washington, they could go no farther. They returned downstream to the river mouth and headed south to enter the Rappahannock. When the barge accidentally grounded at the mouth of the river, they spotted large numbers of fish swimming in a clump of reeds, and Smith began spearing them with his sword. His companions joined in, and soon they had gathered more than they could eat in a day. As Smith was removing a fish from his sword he felt a painful sting on his wrist. The fish was a stingray, and the poison it injected caused excruciating pain for him and made his entire hand, arm, and shoulder swell up over the next few hours. Indeed Smith, who had had a number of close brushes with death, thought the end was near for him and instructed his men to dig a grave. This time his savior was Dr. Walter Russell, the company's physician, who applied a curative oil to the wound, which apparently started the healing process. The pain subsided, and by suppertime Captain Smith had recovered enough to eat a fish, to the great joy of his colleagues.

It was time to return to Jamestown. Before reaching the settlement, the crew decorated the barge with colored streamers, leading the Jamestown residents at first to fear that a Spanish frigate was approaching to spy on or even attack them. Their party reached the fort on July 21, and the colonists were relieved to see that Smith and his fellow explorers had all returned safely. The colony, however, was in very bad shape. Many of the second wave of settlers were sick and unable to work. They were probably affected by the same unhealthy environmental conditions—the summer heat, swampy surroundings, and drinking brackish water—that had brought down the first group. The colonists complained bitterly that Captain Ratcliffe had consumed too much of their food supplies, far more than his fair share, and had ordered the men to build what Smith termed a "pallace" for himself in the forest. The sickly and failing colony was badly in need of new leadership.

Upon Smith's return, the colonists deposed the vain and incompetent Ratcliffe from the office of council president and asked Smith to take his place in running Jamestown. He agreed. However, he did not accept the official duties as president at the time; Jamestown's new chief had other plans. Smith was hopeful that the Chesapeake Bay would lead to the South Sea, as Powhatan and others had suggested, and his fellow colonists were also encouraged by these reports. Finding the shortest route to the Orient was a major objective of the colony, and Smith was determined to explore the upper reaches of the bay beyond the turning point in his last excursion up the bay. Smith considered council member Matthew Scrivener the most trustworthy and reliable member of the company and would leave him in charge, with several assistants whom he appointed.

After two days in Jamestown, Smith departed for the bay in the barge with twelve men, several of whom had been on his last expedition. Adverse winds forced Smith's party to spend several days with the friendly Kecoughtans at the mouth of the James before heading north. They believed that the English would protect them from the Massawomeks, a fearsome tribe that came down from lands beyond Powhatan's empire to hunt and raid in the tidewater region. It was an assumption that Smith let stand.

In the upper bay the English spotted seven or eight canoes bearing down on them, apparently with aggressive intent. Smith was in a fix: half of his company was deathly sick, felled by the same illness that had struck Jamestown. They were unable to fight, lying in the bottom of the barge. Smith had shown his ingenuity in battle before. He and his five remaining able men covered their sick comrades with a tarpaulin. They then placed their hats on sticks along the sides of the barge and set sail, heading straight at the group of canoes, standing ready with all their muskets. The Indians clearly thought they were being attacked by a good-sized band of men. The ruse worked, and the Indians fled to the shore.

Smith's diplomatic skills in dealing with new groups of Indians that the colonists met went to work again with the next ones that they encountered. After the initial tense and threatening contact, he enticed two of the braves to come to the ship where he presented each with a little bell. This generous act attracted their comrades, who came bearing gifts of venison, fish, bows and arrows, shields, clubs, bear skins, and more for the English. They were none other than a Massawomek hunting party. They spoke a different language from that of Powhatan's people, who generally regarded them as enemies invading their territory. Through sign language they indicated that they had just been fighting with the Tockwogh tribe further up the bay and had the wounds to show for it.

The Smith party's next stop was at the Tockwogh village near the head of the bay. When the natives saw all the Massawomeks' shields and other weapons in the barge, they happily assumed the English had captured them in a battle with their enemy, and John Smith did not try to dissuade them of the notion. They entertained their English guests royally, "stretching their best abilities to expresse their loves."

The largest river flowing from the northwest into the head of the bay was the Susquehanna, but rocks blocked the barge from going up it very far. Smith was especially anxious to visit the Sasquesahanocks, living further up-river, from whom the Tockwoghs had obtained tools made of brass and iron. So he sent a messenger to invite them to come downriver to visit him, and several days later around sixty Sasquesahanocks showed up. The wind was so strong in the upper bay that most of the natives in their canoes remained on the western shore, but five of their chiefs boarded the barge to cross the bay to the Tockwogh village, bringing gifts of venison and yard-long tobacco pipes. After observing the colonists' daily prayer service in wonderment, the Sasquesahanocks consulted and then performed their own ceremony. They sang loudly, prayed to the sun, and then directed the focus of their worship to Captain Smith himself, who was undoubtedly embarrassed and tried, un-successfully, to curb their idolization. They embraced him, stroked his neck, presented him with eighteen fur mantles, covered him with a huge, painted bear skin, and draped a heavy chain of white beads about his neck. They also told Smith about other inland tribes including the Massawomeks, their mortal enemies, who obtained metal hatchets and tools from French trappers and traders from the St. Lawrence River region. Their adulation of Smith naturally had a purpose. They also feared the Massawomeks and pleaded with Smith to remain and be their governor, promising him many rewards if he would stay to "defend and revenge them of the Massawomeks." Smith politely declined, vowing to return the following year.

Having explored the head of the bay as far north as they could go, Smith's party turned and headed south toward the Patuxent River on the western shore, which Smith had not yet visited. While mingling with the na-tives there, they met "our old friend Mosco," a native who had been helpful to the English on their earlier exploration of the Potomac. He was notable in having a thick, black beard, a rarity among the smooth-faced Indians, and Smith suspected that he was probably the son of a French trapper or trader. He was pleased to join Smith's party, serving as an interpreter and guide, as they proceeded down the bay to the Rappahannock River.

Mosco warned Smith that the Rappahannocks were a dangerous lot, but Smith ignored his advice. A dozen or so Indians directed the barge into an inlet where the two sides could engage in trading. "According to our custom," Smith asked that they exchange hostages to guard against foul play. The Indi-ans placed a brave on board the barge, and Anas Todkill, a soldier in Smith's party, went ashore with the Indians. Todkill was a brave fellow. Slipping away a short distance from the water's edge, he spotted over a hundred Indians hiding in the woods, ready to attack the English. Racing to escape back to the barge he was seized by the Indians, but not before he was able to shout out, warning his comrades of the ambush.

In the ensuing fight the Indian hostage jumped overboard and was shot by the soldier guarding him. The Indians let fly hundreds of arrows at the barge, but following Mosco's advice the English had used the Massawomek shields to erect a protective covering over the bow of the boat. As the English blazed away with their muskets, the Indian arrows thumped harmlessly off the strong canopy. The natives used up their supply of arrows and, driven off by the English firepower, fled into the woods. Todkill, who had fallen flat on the ground during the crossfire when his two guards were wounded, emerged unharmed.

The remaining days of Smith's bay and river explorations vacillated back and forth between violent or peaceful encounters with the different tribes that the English met. Smith now arranged the shields on both sides of the barge to provide armored protection for his men. As they proceeded upstream to the navigable head of the Rappahannock, probably near present-day Fredericksburg, the natives on the bank, camouflaging themselves with branches, shot their arrows ineffectively at the barge. When they went ashore to find fresh water and dig for precious stones or ore, a hundred or so Indians attacked them, firing off arrows as they ran from tree to tree. The English, responding with their muskets, were joined by their loyal new comrade, Mosco. He shot his arrows so rapidly at the enemy while quickly moving about that they may have believed that the English had other Indian allies fighting alongside them. After a half hour or so the attackers had had enough and vanished suddenly into the forest.

Mosco was about to finish off a wounded Indian lying on the ground when Smith stopped him, recognizing that the native could be very useful. The company's doctor, Walter Russell, treated his wounds and fed him; soon he recovered well enough to provide information through Mosco about the various tribes and chiefs in the region. They had attacked the English because they had heard that they were "a people come from another world, to take their world from them." The captive's name was Amoroleck, the brother of a chief, and he was very grateful for the kind treatment and gifts that he received from Smith. He would urge his chiefs to have friendly relations with the English. As the armored barge headed down the narrow river at night, the Indians on shore yelled and shot arrows in their direction, but they did no harm. As daylight approached, Smith anchored the barge in a wide place in the river beyond arrow range and prepared to initiate peace negotiations.

The English took apart the boat armor, and they revealed themselves, well armed, with their captive, Amoroleck. Mosco then told the Indians on shore how the English had spared the life of Amoroleck when he was about to kill him and how well they had treated their captive. They would free him if the Indians would agree to be their friends. The message was persuasive—the Indians laid down their arms, and the English went ashore to greet Amoroleck's chiefs and released him. Both sides exchanged gifts amicably, and the colonists set sail again, leaving several hundred natives "singing, dancing, and making merry."

The news of the English armed strength spread quickly through the tidewater region. The formerly aggressive Rappahannocks were the next to sue for peace with Smith. He agreed, after first threatening them with destruction if he was not satisfied with their conduct. The Smith party next made its way up the small river on the south shore of the James inhabited by the Chesapeakes and the Nansemonds. Smith thought it "as fit to know our neighbours neare home as so many nations abroad." Unfortunately, the neighbors were not very neighborly, attacking the barge from both sides of the river with a shower of arrows. Once again English musket fire won the day. When the colonists began destroying the natives' canoes, they pleaded for peace and accepted Smith's demands, which included four hundred baskets of corn. According to Smith, they departed "good friends." On September 7, 1608, Smith's party returned to Jamestown.

Smith's expedition had not found a Northwest Passage to the South Sea and Asia, nor had it found a gold mine, for, as we know, neither existed. Smith had explored the Chesapeake Bay, almost two hundred miles in length, and the main rivers flowing into it, and he produced a map of the region that would be useful for years. In his numerous confrontations with the Bay Indians, Smith and his men defended themselves vigorously. Not a single man in his company was killed; one died from natural causes. With threats of destruction, the force of musket fire, smart moves like the taking of hostages, shrewd diplomacy, giving gifts and other kind acts, Smith tried hard to gain the friendship of the Indians. It was not easy to win their hearts and minds. Understandably, the natives deeply resented being invaded and occupied by armed forces from another land.

· 9 ·

Captain Newport Returns

Three days after returning to Jamestown, Smith was elected the president of the council, replacing John Ratcliffe, whose term had expired and whom the men no longer trusted or respected. Smith stopped the work on Ratcliffe's private house, the "pallace," and had the men repair the church and rebuild and enlarge the storehouse. He strengthened the fortifications, organized the watches, and drilled the men on a field outside the fort. Indian spectators were astonished by the force of the musket volleys of the men engaged in target practice. Smith had just dispatched George Percy to trade with the natives in early October when Captain Newport's ship reappeared from England, carrying almost 100 new colonists, including some Polish and German workers to make soap ashes, pitch, tar, and glass. The first two women to join the colony, Mistress West, the wife of colonist Thomas West, and her maid, Anne Burras, were also on board. Newport added two of the new arrivals, veteran soldiers Peter Winne and Richard Waldo, to the local council, which also included John Ratcliffe, Matthew Scrivener, and Smith.

John Smith thought that Captain Newport's agenda, ordered by the London Company, was a foolish waste of time and resources. Newport's orders were not to return home until he had either found gold, or a passage to the South Sea, or survivors of the Roanoke colony, who had not been heard from for twenty-one years. Furthermore, he was instructed to hold a coronation ceremony to crown Powhatan a king and present royal gifts to him, including a bedstead and mattress. He proposed to take 120 men with their supplies and gifts for Powhatan some eighty miles by water to Werowocomoco, Powhatan's village, for the coronation.

Smith was concerned that taking away that many men would severely reduce the necessary work on the fort. He also argued that the most urgent task for the colonists was to acquire newly harvested corn from the natives in preparation for the coming winter. Captain Newport, backed by the council, turned down his objections. Newport said he would bring back ample supplies of corn from Werowocomoco; he would also bring ashore more provisions from his ship. He claimed that Smith was only putting forward "devices to hinder his journey." Smith then suggested that he would go with just four men to Powhatan's village and invite him to come to Jamestown to receive the honors and gifts awaiting him; by land it was only a twelve-mile journey. Namontak, Powhatan's aide who had returned from England with Newport, would return to his village with them. Captain Newport agreed.

Powhatan was away visiting another village when they arrived at Werowocomoco, and a messenger was sent to get him. While awaiting his return, Pocahontas and thirty young women entertained their guests. Their bodies, naked except for scanty loin clothes, were painted in different colors, and they wore horned headdresses. They provided food and drink and sang and danced with abandon for the men. One can surmise from Smith's account that the Indian maidens offered more intimate relations, as was often the custom in Indian hospitality.

When Powhatan arrived the next day, he declined Newport's invitation to come to Jamestown, saying to Smith, "I am also a king and this is my land. . . . Your Father is to come to me, not I to him." When Newport received Powhatan's message from Smith, he decided to send the bulky presents to the chieftain by water; Newport and Smith with fifty armed men would go to Werowocomoco by land.

Powhatan, naturally, had no knowledge of the meaning of a coronation and its royal protocol, which required that he kneel to be officially crowned. The proud chieftain firmly refused to bend a knee, and no one could persuade him to do so. Finally, three men leaning on his shoulders forced him to stoop a little, and they were able to place the crown on his head. Then a prearranged pistol shot signaled the soldiers at the boat to fire a volley to honor the newly crowned king. It badly frightened the chieftain, who feared that the ceremony was simply a trick and the English were about to kill him and his people. However, explanations were given, calm was restored, gifts and polite words were exchanged, and, after purchasing a supply of corn, the English returned to Jamestown.

Captain Newport now had a new project—to explore beyond the falls at the head of the James, hoping to find a route to the South Sea and gold or silver deposits. He took 120 men with him, leaving John Smith with the remaining 100 or so colonists with orders to load his ship for the return voyage to England. Newport's company marched inland forty miles beyond the falls before turning back. The Monacan tribe living in that area gave the

English a cool reception, and they were undoubtedly angry when Newport took a minor chief captive for a short time to serve as a guide. On the advice of a miner in the company, they dug for precious metals and came up with next to nothing—a few bits that he thought might contain silver. Newport wished to acquire a supply of corn for the colony, but the Indians they met refused to trade and had carefully hidden their corn. Some said that they feared that the men from the ships at Jamestown were coming to kill them. The Newport expedition, returning to the fort discontented and hungry, had accomplished nothing.

Smith had dispatched the Polish and German craftsmen, skilled in making glass, pitch, tar, and soap ashes, to go about their work in producing products for Newport's return voyage. Next he took thirty men five miles downriver to cut down trees and make clapboard for the ship's cargo. Many were gentlemen, who had not signed on to do manual labor and were quite unused to rough living in the woods and hard physical work. Again Smith set the example, living and working under the same conditions as his men. He was pleased to note that after a week some gentlemen actually seemed to enjoy their work and hearing "the trees thunder as they fell." They also swore loudly from the pain of the blisters on their tender hands after every few blows of the ax. Smith would not permit blasphemous cursing. He counted the oaths and each evening poured a can of water for each oath down the sleeve of the guilty party. This unique discipline worked, and the swearing ended.

Returning to the fort, Smith was frustrated to see that no effort had been made to obtain more food, which was desperately needed to sustain the colonists with winter approaching. Accordingly, he led two barges with eighteen men up the Chickahominy River to trade with the local tribe for corn. The Chickahominies refused to trade, and Smith changed his approach: he told them that he had come to take revenge on the village for killing his men and taking him captive on his previous excursion up the river. The Indians knew the power of English muskets. They fled into the woods and soon came back with one hundred bushels of corn, plus some fish and foul. They amply supplied George Percy with provisions when his barge arrived a little later. At the same time they complained bitterly that because of a poor harvest they barely had enough for themselves. Shortly afterward Matthew Scrivener was dispatched to Werowocomoco, where he found the natives "more readie to fight than trade." Fortunately, Namontack, who had returned from England with Newport, intervened and obtained several hogsheads of corn for the colonists. By now John Smith strongly suspected that "it was Powhatan's policy to starve us."

During Smith's absences discipline often broke down at the fort, and this was especially true after the arrival of Newport's supply ship. Smith had a poor opinion of many of his fellow colonists, particularly the gentlemen who let others do the work and obtain food, even though everyone was famished, existing on very short daily rations of a pint of cornmeal and water. The settlers lacked the skills to hunt for game or fish; they would not tend gardens or raise enough crops to feed themselves. The ship's crew, on the other hand, had plenty of food on board, such as butter, cheese, beef, pork, aqua vitae, and beer, which the settlers longed for to augment their bare-bones diet. After six or seven weeks it became apparent that a large number of metal tools, axes, hoes, and the like, and even ammunition, had been stolen from the storehouse, and a corrupt, three-party trading scheme within the colony was exposed. Colonists were stealing the tools to trade for furs with the Indians, and then exchanging the furs with the sailors for food. There was a good demand for fine furs in Europe, and the crew had enough food to sell, often at exorbitant prices, to the hungry settlers. Some crewmembers traded directly and illicitly with the Indians at night, spoiling the market for the colonists.

Captain Newport sailed for England in early December 1608, with a cargo of the products produced by the German and Polish craftsmen and clapboard supplied by Smith's team of woodcutters. It was a shipment of low value, nowhere near what the London Company hoped for. John Smith was glad to see Captain Newport and his crew depart. The ship was carrying a sealed envelope containing a letter from him to the London Company bluntly criticizing Newport's leadership and other decisions by the company.

The letter was contained in Smith's *The Generall Historie* of 1624, but not in his two earlier accounts about the founding of Jamestown, and we do not know if it was actually sent and delivered to the company. By 1624 Captain Newport had been dead for seven years, and it's possible that after the passage of so many years since the events he described, Smith felt free to introduce his criticism about the colony's mission and management in this manner. The letter was self-serving and harsh in its criticism. While it seemed sensible and truthful in describing what had transpired, it was certainly not likely to please the company directors. Smith's elite superiors in London would not appreciate the blunt opinions of a soldier of fortune and son of a tenant farmer disparaging their decisions. Smith hoped that the company would view his suggestions favorably, but writing such an offensive letter to the directors was indeed a strange way to win their support.

Smith was replying to a letter from the London Company delivered to him, as the colony president, by Captain Newport when he had arrived from England. It had apparently been reported to the company that divisive factions had sprung up in the colony. Furthermore, they had received only vague reports regarding Jamestown's progress and suspected that the colony's officers may have been concealing information about its accomplishments. The investors in the company were very upset that the return on their large investment had been minimal at best. Smith gave the company fair warning regarding the tone of his reply at the beginning of the letter: "To these particulars I humbly intreat your pardons if I offend you with my rude Answer."

Despite what others had falsely reported, he had not hidden information from the company. As ordered by them, he had followed Newport's instructions in dealing with Powhatan and crowning him, even though he believed that the plan was unwise and dangerous. Newport had stated that he would acquire two bargeloads of corn from Powhatan, which the colony urgently needed to double its supply to feed its increased numbers. Instead, Newport returned from Werowocomoco with a measly fourteen bushels. Newport had then taken 120 of the best men on an excursion beyond the falls on the James to search for gold, the South Sea, or survivors of the Roanoke colony, and to trade for corn. This wasteful effort had accomplished nothing. Indeed, one man could have made the exploration with the same result. On the other hand, Smith had sent the company a map that he had prepared of the Chesapeake Bay and its rivers, based on his explorations, with a description of the region and its inhabitants. "I have made you as great a discovery as he, for lesse charge then he spendeth you for every meale."

Smith complained that they had received very few provisions from Newport's ship. The more than two hundred colonists, half of them sick, were "neare famished," while the sailors were enjoying "good cheare." In fact, Newport's soldiers reported that their officers supported their families from selling goods that the company had intended for the colonists. Unfortunately, the colonists that had been selected lacked the skills to hunt and fish, though wild game, fish, and fowl were abundant. Smith strongly suspected that Newport was falsely portraying to the company the real state of the colony, which could scarcely survive from one supply ship to the next. Despite Newport's hollow pledge that he would leave the colonists with provisions for a year, they had to supply him with three hogsheads from their slender stores for his return voyage. Smith humbly begged the company to tell the colonists what they would receive in the future, so that they were not left relying on "the saylers courtesie to leave us what they please." Smith was sending Captain Ratcliffe home with Newport "least the company should cut his throat." He had been exposed as "a poore counterfeited Impostor," whose real name was Sicklemore.

Smith also advised his superiors on the financial aspects of the enterprise and their investment, noting that Newport's voyage had cost two thousand pounds. Captain Newport was paid one hundred pounds a year for simply "carrying newes," and in Smith's opinion he wasn't worth it. Furthermore, there was no reason for Newport's ships to stay so long at Jamestown, unnecessarily adding to the cost of the crew's wages. Smith had started his men working to produce pitch, tar, soap ashes, and clapboard, and had shipped back a small quantity to the company. However, large quantities of these products could certainly be obtained more efficiently and cheaply in Sweden or Russia instead of burdening the Virginia colony struggling to survive while defending itself against "the inconstant Salvages." There was no point in sending glassmakers and other craftsmen to Jamestown, at least until the colony was in a self-sustaining condition; their products could be purchased in bulk in Europe. Smith hoped the company would send "thirty carpenters, husbandmen, gardeners, fishermen, blacksmiths, masons, and diggers up of trees, roots" instead of "a thousand of such as we have." Smith wanted workers, not indolent gentlemen who simply consumed the colony's provisions "before they can be made good for anything." Having summed up the causes that kept the colony in a weakened state, with his characteristic frankness Smith signed off by saying, "as yet you must not look for any profitable returnes; so I humbly rest."

· 10 ·

Troubles for the President

*A*nne Burras married John Leydon, a worker, in December; it was the first English marriage in Virginia and presumably an occasion for merriment in the little colony. As the freezing winter weather enveloped the region, obtaining enough food to feed some two hundred colonists until spring was the critical challenge facing the colony president, Captain John Smith. The Nansemonds, who lived near the mouth of the James, had promised to supply corn to the colony earlier. Now they refused to trade, saying that Powhatan had ordered them to keep what little corn they had for themselves and not even allow the English to come up their river. Smith resorted to a tactic he had used before: he ordered his men to discharge a volley of musket fire, and the natives fled. Then he set fire to one of the houses in their village up the small river. The natives quickly returned and agreed to provide the English with half of all the corn they had if Smith would spare their village. Smith returned to Jamestown with three boatloads of corn, but the colony needed much more to last through the winter. Smith led one group and sent several other parties to Indian villages to trade for more corn. However, the natives had fled from almost all of the villages before they arrived, obeying Powhatan's orders not to supply any more food to the English.

As Smith was pondering what to do about Powhatan, a message was received from the great chief inviting Smith to visit him. He also requested a team of men to build a house for him, plus fifty swords, some muskets, a cock and a hen, and some copper and beads. In return Powhatan would load Smith's boat with corn. Smith recognized the risk that the scheming chieftain might be luring him into a trap. However, although he had no intention of turning over arms to Powhatan, the colony badly needed food. He would lead a party to visit Powhatan, and he sent ahead a half-dozen men overland

101

to start building the chieftain's house. On December 29 Smith embarked in two barges and the pinnace with about forty men and headed down the James bound for Werowocomoco. All the men were volunteers; others, aware of the danger, found excuses to stay behind. Smith reported that at their first anchorage a friendly local chief warned, "Captain Smith, you shall find Powhatan to use you kindly, but trust him not, and be sure he shall have no opportunitie to seize on your Armes, for he has sent for you onely to cut your throats."

Before leaving the village Smith dispatched colonist Michael Sicklemore (unrelated to the disgraced Ratcliffe), accompanied by two Indian guides, on a mission south of the Chesapeake Bay to see if he could find any trace of the missing Roanoke settlers. George Percy, on Captain Newport's trip up the James in 1607, had reported seeing a light-skinned boy with blonde hair living with the Indians. Sicklemore would report later that he had not found any survivors from the lost colony.

Extremely fierce winter weather—strong winds, frost, and snow—delayed the travelers at several native villages en route, where they obtained food and shelter. On January 12, 1609, they reached Werowocomoco and occupied some vacant houses. When Powhatan learned of their arrival, he promptly sent them some food, and on the following day the chieftain and the colony president started to negotiate.

The wily chieftain first asked why the English had come—he had not invited them, nor did he have any corn to spare. On the other hand, he would exchange forty baskets of corn for forty English swords. Captain Smith asked how he could be so forgetful, pointing to the two messengers standing by who had delivered Powhatan's invitation to him. The chieftain laughed heartily, but still insisted that he would only trade if swords and guns were part of the bargain.

John Smith recorded his ensuing conversation with Powhatan in considerable detail. He had believed in Powhatan's promises to supply the colony with corn and, accordingly, had sent men to build a house for Powhatan as he had requested. He noted, however, that Powhatan had ordered his people in other villages not to trade with the English for food. He had told Powhatan before that he didn't have any swords or guns to spare; the colonists needed them to survive. "Yet steale or wrong you I will not, nor dissolve that friendship we have mutually promised," unless he was forced by Powhatan to defend himself.

Powhatan then agreed to provide what corn he could spare to Smith; it would take two days to gather it all together. Yet he was uneasy. He had been told that Smith had not come to trade for food "but to invade my people and possesse my Country." Again he asked that Smith and his men leave their weapons on their boat, "for here they are needlesse, we being all friends," and again Smith refused. After a tough negotiating session, Powhatan turned over a supply of corn to Smith in exchange for a copper kettle.

Powhatan had reasons to be apprehensive. Smith later found out that three German workers he had sent to build Powhatan's house had betrayed him and joined forces with the Indians, apparently fearing that the colonists would either be slaughtered in a surprise attack by Powhatan or wiped out by famine. Smith had even trusted one of them to serve as a spy on Powhatan for him. Instead the Germans had informed Powhatan about the state of the colony and its "projects," which presumably included its plans for expansion.

Powhatan and Smith then engaged in a lengthy discussion of the prospects of war or peace between the two sides. The chieftain said that he had seen three generations of his people decimated by warfare and knew better than any the difference between war and peace. He was old and would die soon, and he wanted to ensure that his successors—his brothers, sisters, and their two daughters—enjoyed peaceful relations with the English as he had. However, the report that Smith had threatened to destroy the Nansemond village had greatly frightened his people. "What will it availe you to take that by force you may quickly have by love, or to destroy them that provide you food. What can you get by warre, when we can hide our provisions and fly to the woods?" He knew it was far better to eat good meat, sleep quietly with his women and children, and enjoy happy relations with the English than be forced to flee and endure the hardship of lying in the cold of the woods, feeding on acorns and roots, "and be so hunted by you that I can neither rest, eate, or sleepe." If even a twig broke, his tired men on guard would cry that Captain Smith was coming. "Then I must fly I know not whether: and thus with miserable feare, end my miserable life." He added for good measure that Smith might also come to a miserable end when he was unable to find enough food to survive. Powhatan ended with a mixed message. He assured Smith of the Indians' friendship. They would supply the English with corn every year if they would come to trade without their "guns and swords as to invade their foes."

Smith was not particularly moved by Powhatan's emotional appeal, and he felt that the iron fist in a velvet glove was the best tactic called for in response. He reiterated the colonists' "love" for Powhatan, even though some of the chieftain's subjects daily violated his pledge of friendship for the English. For Powhatan's sake the colonists had refrained from seeking revenge; otherwise the Indians might have suffered "the crueltie we use to our enemies." Powhatan surely recognized the power of English arms. "Had we intended you any hurt, long ere this we could have effected it." The colonists had welcomed Powhatan's people to Jamestown carrying their bows and arrows, and the same custom should apply to the English visitors to Powhatan's village, who were carrying their arms as part of their apparel. As for enemies, Smith said, "in such warres consist our chiefest pleasure." They did not need to take Powhatan's goods from him. However, even if he hid his provisions, the English would not starve, for they had a way of finding things "beyond your knowledge."

Powhatan tried again and failed to persuade Smith to disarm his men and send away his guard. Sighing, he complained bitterly that Smith and Captain Newport could take whatever they wanted, and Powhatan's people had to try to satisfy their wishes. No one in his realm refused his orders except Captain Smith. Smith reported that they discussed other matters that he did not record, but he now strongly suspected that Powhatan was preparing "to cut his throat." Some Indians were sent to break the river ice in order for his boat to come in to get him and the corn for the colony. Feeling threatened, he also ordered more of his men to come ashore "to surprise the King," as he referred to Powhatan, while he continued talking to buy some time until his men had landed. He told Powhatan that he had but one God and one king, and he came to him not as a subject but as a friend. He invited him to come to Jamestown with as many men as he liked as a guard, and furthermore, to please him, he would not bring his arms when he visited Powhatan on the following day. However, Powhatan and Smith would never see each other again.

Smith had no intention of disarming his men, and Powhatan in turn distrusted Smith's intentions. Quietly leaving Smith talking with a few of his women, he fled with others into the woods. He also ordered some men to surround Smith's house and, Smith assumed, capture or kill him. Smith was enraged when he discovered the Indians' plot, and, armed with his pistol and sword, he rushed his assailants. "He made such a passage among these naked Divils; that at his first shoot, they next him tumbled one over another, and the rest quickly fled some one way some another." However, no one was hurt, and soon the Indians returned, professing their peaceful intentions. They were led by one of their elders, "an ancient Oratour," who said it was all a misunderstanding. Their chieftain had fled, fearing the English guns, but he had sent his men to Smith's house simply to guard the corn to keep it from being stolen. Powhatan vowed his friendship forever and would meet Smith again, with the usual caveat: Smith and his men must come without their arms, for their weapons badly frightened his people.

As Smith's men stood close by with their muskets at the ready, the English captain forced the natives to put down their bows and arrows and load the corn onto his barges. However, the low tide had left the barges high and dry, so Smith and his men would have to spend another night in the house until high tide the next morning. In his 1624 account Smith reports that Powhatan then devised another plot to kill the English—the Indians would bring them food for their supper and then slaughter them when they put down their arms to eat, or later on. This alarming intelligence was brought by none other than Pocahontas, Powhatan's beloved daughter, who had sneaked through the dark forest to warn Smith of her father's plan. It was the second time that she would save Smith's life. Smith offered her some gifts in thanks for her brave act. "With teares running down her cheekes, shee said shee durst not be seen to have any: for if Powhatan should know it she were but dead," and then slipped out into the night. As she had forewarned, a little later "eight or ten lusty fellows" arrived at the house with platters of venison and other food. Smith refused their request that his men extinguish the matches that discharged their muskets and forced the natives to taste each of the dishes they had brought. Smith told them that he knew that they had come "to betray him at his supper," and they left. The English remained vigilant through the rest of the night, as Powhatan's Indians kept watch outside the house. In the morning Smith and his men, well armed, departed in their loaded barges at high tide. Both sides feigned friendship for the other as the English boarded their barges to leave. Smith, to please Powhatan, left a marksman to shoot foul for the chieftain, and the German workers would continue building his house. He still did not know that they had already betrayed the English and joined Powhatan's campaign to wipe them out.

When Smith's company next headed up the York River to trade for more corn at Pamunkey, the village of Powhatan's brother, Opechancanough, the crafty Powhatan dispatched the two German renegades and a few natives to Jamestown to carry out another scheme to obtain English arms. They told Captain Winne, the officer in charge, that, while everything was going well, Smith needed more weapons, which they were to bring back to him. The Germans, Smith reported, also persuaded six or seven colonists to join their "confederacie," but says no more about this. The colonists, quite recklessly, turned over to them eight muskets, shot and powder, hatchets, eight pikes, and fifty swords, which the Indians brought back to Werowocomoco.

At Pamunkey Smith with fifteen men met Opechancanough, who was accompanied by about forty guards, in the chief's house to negotiate the purchase of corn, only to find that they had walked into an ambush. Hundreds of armed Indians appeared and surrounded the house. Smith records the pep talk (which had the distinct tone of later embellishment for his readers in 1624) that he gave to his shocked and nervous men. "As for their fury, it is the least danger; for well you know, being assaulted with two or three hundred of them, I made them by the helpe of God compound to save my life." If his men but stood and fired their muskets even the smoke would drive off the Indians. "Let us fight like men, and not die like sheep: for by that meanes you know that God hath oft delivered mee, and so I trust will now. . . . promise me you will be valiant." His men agreed to follow his lead.

Smith then told Opechancanough that he knew of his plot to murder him. As neither side had yet harmed the other, he challenged the chief to single combat, unarmed, on an island in the river. The victor would be "Lord and Master over all our men," and his prize would be the Indians' corn or the copper the English had brought for trading. Instead Opechancanough attempted to entice Smith to go outside to receive a gift, where Smith knew that his warriors were waiting to let fly their arrows at him. Smith, enraged at this trickery, seized the chief's long locks of hair, pressed his pistol against his chest, and marched him, terrified and trembling, outside among his men. Fearful for the life of their chief, his warriors dropped their bows and listened to the English commander's talk of friendship and vengeful threats. He had promised to be their friend. "But if you shoot one arrow to shed one drop of blood of any of my men . . . you shall see I will not cease revenge." Wherever one of their tribe might be, Smith would hunt him down. They had promised to load his ship with corn before he left "and so you shall, or I mean to load her with your dead carcasses." However, if they came to trade as friends, he would free their king and not trouble them, for he had not come to hurt any of them.

Over the next few hours a crowd of natives gathered, bringing food to trade with the English. Smith, wearied by receiving them and the tense events of the day, retired to Opechancanough's house to rest, leaving two of his men to conduct the trading. However, the Indians were still intent on capturing or killing Smith. Thinking him asleep, about forty of them, armed with clubs and swords, started to enter the house. They made enough noise to awaken Smith, who quickly grabbed his sword and shield and, joined by some of his men, drove them from the house. Opechancanough and some of his elders then made a long talk apologizing for the intrusion, and the two sides spent the rest of the day exchanging goods peacefully. We can assume that the English kept their guns and swords handy.

While Smith was at Pamunkey one of the colonists, Richard Wiffin, arrived from Jamestown to deliver an important message to him as the colony's president. Wiffin had spent one night in Werowocomoco en route; he had sensed danger there, and with the aid of Pocahontas had got away safely to find Smith. He brought bad news: Matthew Scrivener and ten men, including council member Richard Waldo, while crossing the James to Hog Island, had been lost when their skiff sank in a violent wind. Smith did not disclose this sad news to his men. It was critical that they continue their efforts to trade for more corn to feed their fellow colonists through the winter.

Within the engraving:

C: S

Their   triumph about him

C: Smith bound to a tree to be shott to death
1607

Three engravings portraying John Smith's confrontations with hostile Indians ruled by Powhatan, the powerful chieftain of the tribes in the Virginia tidewater region.
Yale Collection of American Literature, Beinecke Rare Book and Manuscript Library.

King Powhatan comands C. Smith to be slayne, his
daughter Pokahontas beggs his life his thankfullnes
and how he subiected 39 of their kings. reade ye histor

printed by James Reeve

C. Smith taketh the King of Pamavnkee prisoner 1608

Boarding their barge, they headed downstream toward Powhatan's village. Their encounters with the Indians were tense as Smith attempted to trade for corn on the way back to Jamestown; indeed, the English now feared that Powhatan intended to kill them all. After several threatening confrontations in other villages, the natives, always fearful of English musket fire, eventually agreed to turn over corn to Smith. In two villages the women and children wept to give up what little they had. Smith wanted to return to Werowocomoco, surprise Powhatan, and seize his food. However, warned by "those damned Dutchmen," as Smith referred to the Germans, Powhatan had fled, taking his provisions with him. Around the end of January, Smith's party reached Jamestown. They had exchanged copper, iron, and beads for two hundred pounds of deer suet and 479 bushels of corn. Each of the men on the mission was rewarded with a month's provisions.

Upon his return to the fort, Smith observed that the settlers had done nothing to improve their lot—many arms and tools had been sold to the Indians, and the store of food had been consumed, although Smith believed that the colony had enough corn to last until the next harvest with the fresh supply that he had brought back. Peter Winne became ill and died during the early months of 1609, leaving Smith, the president, the only remaining member of the council and without the authority to appoint other council members.

In a brief talk to the colonists, Smith told them bluntly what he expected of them. He warned them that neither his efforts nor the investor's money "will ever maintaine you in idlenesse and sloath." Though some deserved both honor and reward, "the greater part must be more industrious, or starve. . . . You see now that power resteth wholey in myself. You must obey this now for a Law, that he that will not work shall not eate (except by sicknesse he be disabled) for the labours of thirtie or fortie industrious men shall not be consumed to maintaine an hundred and fiftie idle loyterers." No one should doubt his authority under the "Letters patents." There were no longer any other council members to protect them or curb his endeavors, and anyone that disobeyed should "assuredly expect his due punishment." Smith then established a six-hour workday and erected a bulletin board recording each man's accomplishments at work. Many colonists responded to Smith's warning and instructions by carrying out their work assignments, but other troubles for the president were brewing.

The German defectors, apparently with the help of unknown collaborators within the fort, were continuing to steal ammunition, swords, and tools for Powhatan and were even teaching the natives how to shoot the muskets they had acquired. Smith learned that one of them, disguised as an Indian, had gone to the colonists' small glass-making house in the woods about a mile from the fort. Smith went out to the house to confront him, unaware that he was walking into an ambush set up by the German renegade and his Indian cohorts. The account simply tells us that he avoided the trap and sent the traitor fleeing back to Powhatan. On the way back to the fort, Smith was attacked by the chief of the neighboring Paspahegh tribe, "a most strong stout Salvage." The two men grappled, and the Indian forced Smith into the river where he hoped to drown him, but John Smith was no novice at one-on-one mortal combat. After a long struggle he seized the Indian by the throat and, after almost strangling him, drew out his sword to cut off his head. The chief pleaded for mercy, and Smith relented. He took his captive back to the fort and put him in chains.

Smith hoped to persuade Powhatan to exchange the German deserters for the Paspahegh chief, but Powhatan replied that they would not leave and he could not force them to go. The English treated the captive chief well, until, "finding his guard negligent," he made his escape. Smith sent out fifty men to retake the chief, but they only succeeded in burning his house and taking two canoes. Still enraged at their plot to kill him, Smith was determined to punish his enemies and teach them a lesson. With a force of men he killed half a dozen Indians and took as many prisoners back to the fort. He also burned the natives' houses and took their canoes and fishing weirs to use at the fort.

When Smith's party encountered another group of Paspaheghs, the natives threw down their weapons as soon as they recognized him and begged Smith not to harm them. Their spokesman, "a lustie young fellow," wanted Smith to understand why their chief had escaped from the fort and forgive him: "The fishes swim, the foules fly, and the very beasts try to escape the snare and live. Then blame not him being a man." Smith had already exacted his revenge, causing them great loss. The brave pleaded with Smith to let them "enjoy our houses and plant our fields, of whose fruit you shall participate." If the Indians were driven away, they would survive, but the colonists would suffer because "you cannot live if you want our harvest. If you promise us peace, we will beleeve you; if you proceed in revenge we will abandon the Countrye." Smith promised them peace, but peaceful relations between the Indians and English never lasted very long.

When Smith returned to the fort, he found that an Indian who had come to trade had stolen a pistol. Smith immediately imprisoned two Indians who were brothers and companions of the thief. He released one, warning him that if he did not return with the pistol within twelve hours, the English would hang his brother. The other native was placed in a cell, where Smith, taking pity on him, gave him some food and charcoal to build a fire to ward off the cold. Left alone, the poor fellow became badly burned and overcome by smoke from the fire. When his brother returned with the pistol and saw him, he appeared to be dead. The brother was overcome with grief, and Smith promised to restore the victim to life if the brothers swore that they would never steal again. Smith then gave him some vinegar and brandy and was able to revive him, only now he was dead drunk, and his crazy antics upset his brother all over again. Smith let him sleep it off, and the next day he was fine except for his burns, which were dressed at the fort. Smith then gave each brother a copper piece and sent them on their way. The word spread quickly among the Powhatan tribes that Smith had performed a miracle: "Captain Smith could make a man alive that was dead."

These events so impressed and frightened Powhatan and his allies that they sent gifts and articles that had been stolen back to the fort. They also sent some of the native thieves to Jamestown to be punished as the English saw fit. For the time being the colonists and Powhatan's people lived together peacefully.

With the coming of spring in 1609 the colonists were producing glass, tar, pitch, and soap ashes—the products that the London investors expected to receive. They also dug a badly needed well "of excellent sweet water" in the fort, restored the church, and built twenty new houses and a guardhouse on the neck of land joining the fort to the mainland; no one, colonist or Indian, would go in or out without President Smith's permission. They planted about forty acres of land to raise corn and other crops for the next harvest, following the instructions of two Indians who had been imprisoned at the fort. They moved the sixty pigs that three sows had produced downriver to Hog Island, where they built and manned a blockhouse to alert the fort to any approaching ships. There was always the threat of an attack by the Spanish. Those men would also cut timber to produce clapboard and wainscot to be shipped back to England.

Then disaster struck: the settlers discovered the ruinous condition of the colony's food supply in the storehouse. About half the corn, stored in casks, which Smith and his men had so laboriously gathered, was rotten, and the rest was being consumed by a growing number of rats, which had come ashore from the ships from England. This was the food they were counting on to feed them, more than two hundred mouths, until the harvest. Now they would have to live off the land, and Smith well knew the colonists lacked the energy and necessary skills. Some local Indians brought them venison, turkeys, and other small game, but the lack of corn still threatened the colony with starvation. Smith decided to send out three parties from the fort to seek food. One group of about seventy men went downriver to live off the oyster beds on the shore of the bay. A second party of twenty went to Point Comfort at the northern mouth of the James to live off the fish they caught in the bay waters; however, they failed to catch any. Another group of twenty went up the James to the falls looking for food, but they found nothing but acorns. Fortunately, there were plenty of sturgeon in the river and edible roots in the woods that could be made into bread to bolster their meager diet.

Still most of the colonists at the fort, unless forced, were too lazy to go out and find food. Without the discipline Smith imposed, "they would have all starved or eaten one another." These "Gluttonous Loyterers," as Smith referred to them, would have sold everything in the fort—tools, kettles, swords, guns, ammunition, even houses—to obtain food from the Indians. When Powhatan offered to exchange a basket of corn for some articles, Smith bought half a basket, which did not appease his angry critics. They insisted that he buy the other half, even though it would not last more than a week. Some even demanded that Smith abandon the colony and take them back to England. Once again Smith addressed the sullen and discontented colonists and laid down the law.

No one should imagine that he would not force them from their idleness and punish them if they disobeyed, he told them. If he found anyone attempting to flee the colony in the pinnace, "let him assuredly looke to the Gallows." He reminded them that he had risked his life many times to save them and that otherwise they would have starved, and he "never had more from the store than the worst of you." Furthermore, they would gather food for the sick as well as for themselves. "The sick shall not starve, but equally share of all our labours, and he that gathereth not every day as much as I doe, the next day shall be set beyond the river, and be banished from the Fort as a drone, till he amend his conditions or starve." Many of the colonists grumbled that his order was very cruel; nevertheless, it spurred them to work.

The German deserters to Powhatan continued to be troublemakers, so Smith dispatched a Swiss settler to persuade them to return to the fort, promising to pardon them and other benefits. However, Smith's agent, in whom he had placed great trust, treacherously betrayed him and provided the Germans with intelligence about the fort and its outposts to inform their plot to destroy the colony. They planned to persuade Powhatan to command his warriors to attack Jamestown. Some of the disgruntled colonists, opposed to Smith's strict discipline, also were in on the plot. Two of them, "whose christian hearts relented at such an unchristian act," reported the scheme to Smith. Realizing that the traitorous Germans were a dangerous threat to the colony, Smith sent two soldiers to kill them, but they failed to get the job done. As Smith and his officers were considering their next move, on July 10, 1609, a ship sailed into view on the river.

Captain Samuel Argall had been sent to Jamestown by the London Company to test sailing a direct westerly route across the Atlantic, instead of the usual longer and more costly passage through the Azores and the West

Indies. His mission was to return with a shipload of sturgeon, which were plentiful in the river and bay waters. The company's message that he brought to Council President Smith severely criticized Smith's harsh treatment of the natives and his failure to send back ships laden with profitable cargoes. No mention was made of the letter that Smith later claimed he had sent to the company. One can easily imagine Smith's angry reaction. Argall had other important news. A large fleet carrying supplies under Sir Thomas Gates, deputy to the new governor of the colony appointed by the London Company, was getting ready to sail to Jamestown.

· *11* ·

Under New Management

$\mathcal{A}$ report had recently reached the London Company directors that the surviving Roanoke settlers of "The Lost Colony" had been slaughtered by Powhatan's warriors. Maybe they had left Roanoke by boat and ventured north into the Chesapeake Bay area. Powhatan had certainly shown his determination to wipe out the English colonists occupying his domain. Perhaps Powhatan had revealed this startling information to Smith at their last meeting, and Smith had passed it on to Captain Newport, or maybe one of the two Indians that Newport brought back to England in 1608 was the source. Smith does not mention it in his books, but in that he was energetically promoting English colonization in Virginia, this is understandable. There was not any evidence to substantiate the report. Nevertheless, the London Company now focused on a new objective—to depose Powhatan and convert his people to Christianity.

In England the company had been aggressively promoting its plans to strengthen and expand its Virginia colony, which would require raising a substantial amount of capital through a new stock issue. With the king's approval the royal Council of Virginia had turned over control of Jamestown's administration to the Virginia Company of London, led by Sir Thomas Smythe, a successful merchant and founding member of the company. The company would now have the power to appoint the colony's governor and other officers. After the collapse of the Popham colony, the Plymouth Company investors were absorbed into the newly organized Virginia Company. Jamestown was the only English enterprise in America, and the company attracted a little over a thousand investors—nobles and merchants, gentlemen and clerics, common folk and trade guilds—who pledged about eighteen thousand pounds to finance the large expedition that was planned to support the colony. They believed that commercial products from the colony would yield a handsome return on their investment. The company's instructions to the governor called for "tight censorship over letters and shipments to and from England." Bad news about conditions in the colony could lower the investors' confidence and the government's support for the project and discourage the men that the company wished to recruit to settle in Virginia.

John Smith had saved the colony from disaster. Nevertheless, the colony's record of squabbling, near mutiny, and negligible returns had led the company's directors to appoint a new governing team. We can also assume that captains Newport, Ratcliffe, Martin, and Archer had little good to say about Smith's conduct after their return to England earlier. Thomas West, Lord De La Warr, a veteran soldier, who had fought in Ireland and the Netherlands, would be the new governor. He was a privy councilor to James I and came from a distinguished family; his mother had been a first cousin of Queen Elizabeth. Sir Thomas Gates, who had sailed with Sir Francis Drake

Sir Thomas Smythe, the Virginia Company treasurer in London, directed the governance of Jamestown for the first twelve years.
Courtesy of the Library of Virginia.

and signed the petition to the king for the royal charter to colonize Virginia, would be his deputy. He would be in charge of the colony until De La Warr's arrival. In June 1609 Gates's fleet of seven ships and two pinnaces set forth on the southern route to Jamestown. One of the pinnaces had already made the trans-Atlantic passage. The Maine-built *Virginia*, which had brought some settlers back to England from the failed Popham settlement, was ferrying sixteen soldiers to Jamestown. The fleet was carrying about five hundred men, women, and children. Some had been enticed to sign up by the company's vigorous campaign to recruit colonists, promising a house, garden, orchard, compensation, and other benefits. The company still ended up hiring a number of unruly vagabonds in order to fill the ranks of the venture.

On July 24 a violent West Indies hurricane struck the fleet, causing great damage to the ships. Four vessels limped into Jamestown in August 1609. However, the flagship of the fleet, the *Sea Venture*, was missing. Sir Thomas Gates, the deputy governor; Sir George Somers, an admiral who was a veteran naval commander and former member of Parliament; and Christopher Newport, now holding the rank of vice admiral, were on board. They were the newly appointed commissioners with the authority to govern the colony. The lost *Sea Venture* also carried 150 colonists, men and women, and substantial provisions for the colony.

Smith was hardly pleased to see the men who had caused him so much trouble disembark with the new arrivals at Jamestown—Gabriel Archer and John Martin, and one of the other ships reaching Jamestown later brought John Ratcliffe. The pinnace *Virginia* arrived in September, but the *Sea Venture* remained missing. Before he had returned to England the ambitious and scheming Archer had tried Smith on trumped-up charges and sentenced him to hang. Smith detested Archer and Ratcliffe. The feeling was mutual, and they had poisoned the minds of their shipboard passengers against Smith on the long voyage to Virginia. In his letter to the London Company, Smith had stated about the vain and incompetent Ratcliffe, "I have sent you him home, least the company should cut his throat. . . . If he and Archer returne again, they are sufficient to keepe us all in factions," which is exactly what happened next.

The three captains, Archer, Martin, and Ratcliffe, backed by some of the newly arrived colonists, were determined to undermine Smith's leadership of the colony and take control themselves, arguing that this was their right as former members of the colony council. Smith knew that the newly appointed chief officers with the charter setting forth the rules for governing the colony were aboard the missing *Sea Venture*. In their absence he had no legal authority to turn over his command and grant council membership to the new arrivals; he refused to take this step. The insurgent faction led by Archer and

Ratcliffe continued their scheming to thwart his authority. The account by Richard Potts and William Phettiplace in Smith's book stated, "Happie had we beene had they never arrived . . . for on earth for the number was never more confusion, or misery, then their factions occaisioned." When Smith's one-year term as president expired in September, he appointed Captain Martin to be president. However, within three hours Martin resigned and gave the position back to Smith, recognizing his inadequacy to handle the job and the colonists' lack of confidence in him. To quell the insurrection, Smith took firm measures, temporarily imprisoning Archer, Ratcliffe, and five others.

With 350 new arrivals, including raw recruits and "many unruly Gallants," Smith faced the challenge of feeding a much larger colony and decided to disperse the settlers in groups to build new settlements and forage for food independently. He sent Francis West, the younger brother of the newly appointed governor, De La Warr, with 120 men he had chosen up to the falls on the James. He sent Captain Martin with sixty men to the Nancemond country on the south river bank near the mouth of the James.

Colonist George Percy's account of Jamestown, 1609 to 1612, picks up the story and differs in minor ways from Smith's account. According to Percy, Martin's company, provoked by the Indians' murder of two English messengers sent to the local tribe, seized the chief's island. Smith's book records that they captured the chief, set fire to the houses, and ransacked the tribe's tombs. The natives retaliated forcefully, freed their chief, and killed some of Martin's men. One poor fellow, hit by seventeen arrows, lived on for a week before dying. Martin, too fearful to risk his men's lives, refused to go after the Indians' store of corn that they needed. He fled back to Jamestown, leaving his men to fend for themselves.

Smith's next move was to go upriver to inspect West's settlement near the falls. West, who had returned to Jamestown, had chosen the location for the outpost, which he named West Fort. It was low and exposed to river flooding and Indian attack, so Smith negotiated the purchase of a nearby Indian village from Powhatan to house West's men. A key part of the bargain was that the English would defend Powhatan's people against marauding Monacan warriors, their long-time enemies living beyond the falls. However, the Indians soon learned that the most urgent protection they needed was against the rampaging English settlers in their midst. The Indians complained bitterly to Smith that the English were "stealing their corne, robbing their gardens, beating them, breaking their houses, and keeping some prisoners." There was little that Smith, with just five loyal companions, could do to control West's 120 rebellious and undisciplined men, who refused to submit to his commands as president. He boarded his boat and started downriver to Jamestown, but ran aground a couple of miles from the settlement.

As soon as Smith left, the Indians attacked the settlers in and around West Fort, killing many and freeing their native prisoners. Now West's men had a complete change of heart and pleaded with Smith to return and be their commander. Smith agreed and went about moving the men to the spot that he had chosen and purchased for their new settlement. The Indian village had a rude fort, houses, and 200 cleared acres ready for planting. Smith arrested six of West Fort's chief troublemakers, appointed new officers to govern the outpost, and patched up relations with the local natives. Just as Smith was preparing to leave for Jamestown, Captain West showed up. He and Smith quarreled bitterly over the most suitable site for the settlement at the falls. As soon as Smith departed, West moved his men back to West Fort, the first location he had chosen. Captain West, the brother of the missing governor of the colony, and his men simply refused to accept Smith's authority as president.

Sailing down the James with his five companions, the weary Smith fell fast asleep. Suddenly he was rudely awakened by the roar of exploding gunpowder and the shock of excruciating pain from his trunk to his thighs. Somehow the powder bag strapped to his belt had been ignited, perhaps by a careless pipe smoker or by one of the matches kept burning to discharge a musket in the event of a sudden attack. With his clothes on fire Smith jumped into the river to quench the flames and almost drowned before his men could drag him back on board.

Without medical supplies there was no way to dress his gaping wound, and the remaining journey to Jamestown of about sixty miles was agonizingly painful for Smith. Nor was there a doctor at Jamestown to treat his wound. Back at the fort, Smith, almost completely disabled and tormented by pain, decided to board the ship planning to return to England the next day where he could receive the medical treatment he needed.

His old enemies, Archer and Ratcliffe, seeing that Smith in his severely weakened condition was unable to defend himself, immediately conspired to seize his commission as president of the colony. While he lay suffering in his small house, they held up the departure of his ship for three weeks to draw up a list of charges and complaints against him to be delivered to the Virginia Company. A letter from Ratcliffe to the Earl of Salisbury, the king's Secretary of State (prime minister), stated, "This man is sent home to answer some misdemeanors." Some of his loyal "old souldiers" sought his permission to "take their heads that would resist his command," but Smith would not let them. "So grievous were his wounds and so cruell his torments," Smith knew that he was no longer able to carry out his duties as president of the colony; it was time for him to give up. He refused to surrender his commission to Archer or Ratcliffe, knowing that they were completely unfit to govern the colony, and they persuaded George Percy to be the new president as soon as Smith departed. Percy, age twenty-nine, was a brother of the Earl of Northumberland and one of the original colonists that arrived in 1607. On October 4, 1609, almost two-and-a-half years after Captain John Smith first landed in Virginia, his ship dropped down the James bound for England; he was on his way home.

The fort, then the river and the broad reaches of Chesapeake Bay, faded from Smith's view as his ship headed out to sea bound for London. Surely he was furious at his enemies, who had hounded him up until the very day that he left. Yet he felt great pride in his accomplishments. He had faced incredible obstacles—sickness, starvation, and death; hostile and murderous Indians; lazy, unskilled, and rebellious settlers. "Gentlemen, Tradesmen, Serving men, libertines, and such like," Smith would label them in his book published in 1612, "ten times more fit to spoyle a commonwealth, then either begin one, or but helpe to maintaine one." Smith also noted that because the settlers were not permitted to own and farm their own property, they had little incentive to make the colony a success. They were hired hands and had no stake in the fortunes of the venture. The Virginia Company itself admitted in a broadside later that the settlers they had sent to Virginia were a miserable lot "that will rather starve from hunger than lay their hands to labour." In 1610 the royal Council of Virginia frankly acknowledged major reasons for the chaotic and impoverished state of the colony. Its *True and Sincere Declaration* pointed to "the misgovernment of the commanders, by dissension and ambition among themselves, and upon the idleness and bestial sloth of the common sort, who were active in nothing but adhering to factions and parts even to their own ruin."

Whereas the first two English attempts to start colonies in America had failed miserably, Smith's strong leadership had enabled Jamestown to survive. Smith's initiatives obtained the vital food supplies from the Indians that the hungry colonists needed through clever diplomacy and smart trading or sometimes the firepower of his muskets. Powhatan and his people came to both respect and fear John Smith, and his commanding presence, resourcefulness, and military competence protected the little colony from succumbing to Indian attacks. Smith had the good sense to realize that searching for gold and silver in Virginia was a futile exercise, especially since there were far more urgent challenges facing the settlers. As a result of the firm discipline that he imposed as president, many colonists went to work for the first time—fortifying the settlement, building houses and a church, planting corn, stocking Hog Island with pigs, and making commercial products to send home to their investors.

The soldiers and others among the colonists admired their commander's courage and fair treatment of his men, as the colonists' accounts in the 1612 book affirmed. He demonstrated a cool nerve in threatening confrontations with Indians—learning their language well enough to negotiate skillfully with them, or resorting to the force of his men's muskets when necessary. He never asked his men to undertake risks that he was not prepared to take alongside them; he always shared provisions equally with his men, sometimes providing more than his share; and endured the same hardships and rough living conditions that they did. However, ambitious enemies like Archer and Ratcliffe and well-born gentlemen like George Percy clearly resented taking orders from the son of a yeoman farmer. In his account Percy states that Smith was an "ambitious unworthy vayneglorious fellow" who wished to retain his sole authority to govern without the assistance of other council members. He then acknowledged that in the absence of Sir Thomas Gates there was no other legal governing authority than Smith. Percy had no evidence of misconduct by Smith; he simply didn't like him.

Smith ruled with an iron hand and used harsh measures to get his people to work. Modesty was not one of his attributes. He could be boastful, most certainly angry and frustrated with his slothful fellow colonists, and disdainful of the foolish decisions of his superiors in Virginia and London. They in turn were exasperated by his presumption of authority above his proper station in society and his tendency to question their decisions. Captain John Smith could indeed be a thorn in the side of his superiors. Smith was a forerunner in the democratic society of equal opportunity that would evolve in America, breaking away from the old rigid class divisions in England. What happened next in Jamestown in his absence clearly demonstrated the importance of his strong leadership there.

Powhatan was determined to wipe out the English colony, and when he learned that he no longer had to contend with John Smith's forceful protection of Jamestown, he was quick to act. He ordered his people to refuse to supply the English with provisions and to kill them whenever they had the chance. Two parties of colonists, attempting to trade for food with the Indians, were all killed; when their bodies were found, bread was stuffed in their mouths. The message was clear—no more food for the English invaders. Captain West, under attack in his encampment at James Falls, retreated back to Jamestown, losing eleven more men on the way. With about five hundred mouths to feed, President Percy knew that they would run out of food in two or three months, and he sent Ratcliffe with a company to trade for corn from Powhatan.

In Percy's account, "the Subtell owlde foxe" made a pretense of welcoming them, and, when they had let down their guard, captured and killed thirty-seven colonists. Seventeen men escaped and got back to Jamestown, but not Captain Ratcliffe. Powhatan's braves bound him naked to a tree, lit a fire before him, and Indian women scraped flesh from his bones with mussel shells until mercifully he died. Percy next dispatched Captain West with thirty-six men north to the Potomac River to barter for corn and grain with the local tribe, the Potomacs, who were beyond Powhatan's domain. He was successful, and they filled his pinnace with food. At the same time West created bitter new enemies by brutally torturing and beheading two braves. Perhaps West had his own agenda all along. One of the first moves of the council's president George Percy had been to order the construction of a small fort at Point Comfort to serve as a base for fishing and to spot any ships approaching the bay. Its cannons covered the entrance to the James. When West's pinnace reached the newly built Algernon's Fort, instead of heading upriver to Jamestown where, as he was informed, his colleagues urgently needed food, West and his crew adjusted their sails, altered their coarse, and headed across the ocean bound for England. West's betrayal, perhaps forced by his men, was a heavy blow for the colonists, who had counted on his fresh supply of food. It left them "in extreme misery and want," reported Percy. Everyone felt "the sharpe prick of hunger."

George Percy called the winter of 1609 to 1610 "The Starving Time." The colonists first devoured their horses, hogs, and other farm animals. A few who tried to rob the dwindling common store of food were caught and executed. Soon the settlers were eating dogs and cats and rats and mice. Next to satisfy their desperate hunger, some chewed on leather boots and belts. Others risked their lives to search the woods for snakes or edible roots and nuts, and the Indians murdered many who dared to venture outside the fort. Famine, disease, and death descended on Jamestown during the cold winter months. Starving settlers dug up corpses from their graves to eat the putrid flesh, and archeologists have determined that one was the body of a fourteen-year-old girl. One depraved fellow murdered his pregnant wife and chopped her up into pieces that he salted and ate. He was tortured, hung by his thumbs with weights attached to his feet until he confessed to his heinous crime, and then was executed. Others fled from the fort to seek sustenance from the Indians and were never heard from again. The palisades and gates had fallen down, the church was ruined and unattended, and the colonists tore lumber from the houses of the dead to use as firewood. The sick and starving settlers confined to the fort still had their muskets to protect them from attack, but going beyond its walls was far too dangerous; there were Indians lurking in the woods waiting to ambush and kill them. The colonists died by the hundreds—either killed by the Indians or from starvation, including Gabriel Archer, who starved to death. By May there were only sixty wasted survivors left in the Jamestown fort and a small group at Algernon's Fort who, with easy access to the bay for fish, crabs, and oyster beds, had fared better. There had been about five hundred settlers living in the colony when John Smith returned to England. Colonist chaplain William Simmons wrote, "Now we all found [felt] the losse of Captaine Smith, yea his greatest maligners could now curse his loss. . . . This was that time, which still to this day we call the starving time; it was too vile to say, and scarce to be believed, what we endured: but the occasion was our owne for want of providence, industrie, and government."

Then on May 21 the garrison of Algernon's Fort, the small fort at Point Comfort, spotted two pinnaces sailing into the bay. The hurricane that had struck the fleet in July 1609 had blown the badly leaking and battered *Sea Venture* hard on a reef off the isolated island of Bermuda, almost six hundred miles east of the Chesapeake Bay. Sir Thomas Gates, admirals Somers and Newport, and some 150 passengers and crew were all able to get ashore safely with their supplies and tools. They built cabins, dug wells, and lived off the land for the next ten months, dining well on tropical fruits and vegetables and pork from wild hogs left by the Spanish. They built two pinnaces from Bermuda cedar and planks from the *Sea Venture*, and, circling the island in a small boat, Sir George Somers made a detailed map of Bermuda's coastline. On May 10, 1610, the entire company set sail in their newly built vessels, the *Patience* and the *Deliverance*, for Chesapeake Bay and Jamestown. One passenger was John Rolfe, a young widower, whose wife had given birth in Bermuda to the first baby born there. Sadly, the mother and infant had both died in Bermuda. Another was Captain George Yeardley, a veteran military officer.

William Strachey, a Virginia Company stockholder and *Sea Venture* passenger, wrote a letter with a full account of the shipwreck, the life of the ship's company in Bermuda, and the arrival at Jamestown, which was dispatched on the ship returning to London in September 1610. William Shakespeare may have based his play, *The Tempest*, on Strachey's account. The well-educated Strachey was a stockholder in the Blackfriars Theatre where he may have met Shakespeare. The play was first performed before King James at Whitehall Palace in London on November 1, 1611. The playwright located his tale on a mythical Italian isle. In his account Strachey praised John Smith's earlier leadership of Jamestown, and attributed its disastrous downfall leading to the dreadful conditions that the Gates party encountered to "sloath, riot, and vanity."

Sir Thomas Gates was shocked to see the ruined state of the fort at Jamestown and the emaciated condition of the small number of miserable survivors in tattered clothes, as some rushed to greet him crying, "We are starved!" He had only brought enough provisions to feed his own company of 150 new arrivals, which he promptly shared with the starving Jamestown inhabitants. Now he had some 240 mouths to feed. The natives still refused to barter for their corn, and, with their few nets rotted away, the settlers failed in their attempts at catching sturgeon when they were running in the river. The Indians surrounding the fort still aimed to wipe out the English, or force them to flee, and they killed some settlers venturing outside the fort—"the Indian as fast killing without as the famine and pestilence within," wrote Gates. Strachey believed that probably the main cause of the "pestilence within" was the water that the men drank—foul, brackish river water oozing into the well inside the fort.

Powhatan almost succeeded in accomplishing his objective. Gates calculated that even with everyone on short rations they only had provisions to last another sixteen days. He consulted with his officers, and they agreed that they must abandon Jamestown, a decision welcomed by everyone. Gates now had four pinnaces, the two from Bermuda and two from Jamestown, including the *Virginia*, built in Maine. They would sail up the coast to Newfoundland where they hoped some English fishing vessels would take them back to England. On June 7, 1610, the colonists boarded their boats and headed down the James.

At the river's mouth a long boat approached them from Port Comfort with news that the new governor, Lord De La Warr, had just arrived with three ships, three hundred settlers, and a year's supply of provisions. The Gates party returned to Jamestown followed by the governor and his ships. In a formal ceremony, De La Warr took charge of the colony, and in a stern speech he warned the settlers that their idleness and vanities might force him to "draw the sword of justice," which he would rather draw in their defense. On the brink of abandonment, Jamestown, which John Smith had fought successfully to keep alive, had been saved, but its troubles were far from over.

Governor De La Warr, like his predecessors, was immediately concerned about obtaining provisions to feed his colony of more than 500 people, and especially about the lack of meat. The colonists were not skilled at hunting deer, which Powhatan's braves had driven away far from the fort. The Indians would not provide them with venison or any other food. When the settlers were starving the previous winter, they had devoured all their hogs that the Indians had not already killed, along with their chickens and horses. When De La Warr was informed of the abundance of food, especially the wild hogs, in Bermuda, he dispatched Sir George Somers and Captain Samuel Argall in two pinnaces on June 19 to return to the island and bring back a six-month supply of hogs. The ships became separated in a storm and were driven north by strong winds. Argall took advantage of the bountiful fishing off the coast of Maine and returned to Jamestown with an ample supply of cod. Argall, whom the governor had appointed to the colony council, next went up the Potomac River to trade with the Potomacs, and he reported bringing back a thousand bushels of corn for the colony. In September 1610, Governor De

La Warr sent Sir Thomas Gates back to England. He had a cargo of cedar, clapboard, and other products for the London Company investors and would report to them on the state of the Virginia colony.

Sir George Somers had made his way to Bermuda after the storm at sea, but he soon became ill and died there on November 9, 1610. The fifty-six-year-old Somers had led his *Sea Venture* survivors safely through months of perilous conditions and hardship. Captain Matthew Somers, Sir George's nephew, and his men decided not to return to Jamestown and instead set sail for England in the cedar pinnace, *Patience*. They had greatly admired their admiral's courageous leadership and brought his body home to his family in Dorsetshire, where he was buried with military honors. Bermuda was named the Somers Isles in his memory. Somers's men also reported glowingly about Bermuda's suitability as a site for a new English settlement. The climate was benign and good for farming; there were abundant sources of local foods—figs and other fruits, fish, wild fowl, and hogs. One need not fear attacks by hostile natives—the island was uninhabited. Furthermore, Bermuda could serve as a supply base for Jamestown. A group of Virginia Company investors were impressed and financed an expedition to establish a new colony in Bermuda. In July 1612 Governor Richard Moore and sixty settlers landed and began to construct their fort and settlement on the northern end of the island, building their first houses of cedar wood and palmetto thatch. They named their new town St. George. Thus, the shipwreck of the *Sea Venture* led to the successful founding of another English colony in the New World. Sixty more new settlers arrived some months later, the start of a steady stream that would build St. George and spread throughout the Somers Isles.

Governor De La Warr soon realized that Powhatan would not accept peace overtures from the English. He was determined to contain them in a limited area around Jamestown or drive them away completely. His braves continued to kill or capture settlers outside the fort whenever they could, collecting their muskets and swords for Powhatan's arsenal. The governor ordered George Percy and a contingent of veteran soldiers to retaliate in raids on Indian villages. Their attacks were brutal—killing women and children and burning the natives' houses and cornfields. In one attack they captured a tribal queen and her children. They did not take prisoners. They threw the children from their boat into the river, "shooting out their brains in the water." Two soldiers took the queen into the woods and "put her to the sword."

De La Warr also ordered two small forts to be built—forts Henry and Charles on the north side at the mouth of the James River, placing Captain Yeardley and another officer in command. Their soldiers killed a dozen Indians near the forts, burned their houses, and seized the corn from their fields at harvest time. Governor De La Warr then sent a company of one hundred men up to the head of the James on an expedition searching for deposits of gold and silver under the command of Yeardley and Captain Edward Brewster. The Indians enticed the company's skilled mining experts ashore by offering them food. As the hungry miners were eating, the Indians slew them. The English retaliated by killing more Indians and burning their houses. The undertaking was a complete failure.

The governor sent two officers on a diplomatic mission to discuss peace terms with Powhatan; they especially wanted the chieftain to release the English prisoners that he held. Powhatan would have none of it. Either the English should depart altogether or confine their settlement strictly to Jamestown—no more explorations or new outposts up the river or elsewhere. Otherwise, there would be no peace. He would command his braves to attack and kill them. The English should not send any others to negotiate with him unless they brought him a coach and three horses, because he understood from Indians who had visited England that that was the way high officials and lords rode to visit other great men. The killing and atrocities on both sides continued. The Indians tortured English captives until they died, and the governor ordered his men to cut off the hands of a native that he suspected of being a spy.

Governor De La Warr had a poor opinion of the colony's workforce. He wrote that they were "deboisht [debauched] hands" with "distempered bodies and infected minds whom no example daily before their eyes, either of goodness or punishment, can deter from their habituall impieties or terrify from a shameful death." Many colonists continued to be struck down by disease. Once again dysentery, scurvy, and typhoid fever decimated the ranks of the Jamestown settlers, and medicines and drugs were urgently needed to cure "strange fluxes and agues" reported the governor. De La Warr himself became very ill, and in late March 1611 he was forced to return to England to recover his health. The colony had suffered huge losses to sickness and Indian arrows and tomahawks. Only "upward of two hundred" settlers were left when he departed, wrote the governor to the Virginia Company in London. De La Warr left George Percy in charge as deputy governor until the new chief executive, Sir Thomas Dale, arrived.

De La Warr and Sir Thomas Gates, meeting at Cowes near Portsmouth, discussed plans for the colony and the supply ships that should be dispatched to Jamestown in a few months. They were both strong advocates for continuing to support and expand the Virginia colony, despite all the setbacks—the poor selection of settlers to man the colony, the sickness that had taken so many lives, and the determined and violent hostility of the Indians under Powhatan, who killed and captured settlers and refused to trade for corn to feed the colony. De La Warr was encouraged that the colony had found some new reliable sources

Sir Thomas Gates, shipwrecked with a large group of colonists in Bermuda, finally reached Jamestown and later became governor of the colony.
Courtesy of the Library of Virginia.

of food. Samuel Argall had successfully obtained corn from the Potomac Indians, who appeared willing to continue trading with the colonists. He had also found the bountiful fishing grounds off the coast of New England, which could provide the colony with a plentiful supply of cod for years to come. In his letter to the directors of the Virginia Company, De La Warr explained how his illness had forced him to leave Jamestown, and he earnestly expressed the wish that he be appointed to his post there again when he had recovered his health.

Gates in his report to the company, *A True Declaration of the estate of the Colonie in Virginia*, stressed the abundant and valuable resources in Virginia, such as the timber for which there was a ready demand in England, especially for shipbuilding; the trees could produce masts and planks of great size, and "one Firre tree is able to make the maine Mast of greatest Ship in England." Gates's report must have caught the attention of the Royal Navy admirals. Tall, stout trees were prized in largely deforested England. Gates concluded, "It is one of the goodliest Countries under the Sunne; enterveined with five maine Rivers, and promising as rich entrals as any Kingdome of the earth, to whom the Sunne is no neerer a neighbour." While some Virginia Company investors were reluctant to proceed with Jamestown, given the financial losses they had suffered, the company's leaders were determined to back its expansion.

In 1610 the newly appointed governor, Lord De La Warr, arrived just in time to save Jamestown from abandonment.
Courtesy of the Library of Virginia.

In May 1611 Deputy Governor Sir Thomas Dale, a military veteran who had fought with the Dutch against the Spanish in the Netherlands, landed at Jamestown with three ships bringing about 300 colonists, cattle, swine, and a large store of provisions, much of which was badly spoiled. In August Lieutenant Governor Sir Thomas Gates returned with six vessels carrying another 300 colonists, including just twenty women, supplies, and more live-stock. Dispersing Jamestown's population away from its low lying, unhealthy location was now a key objective, and Gates dispatched Dale with 300 men to build a new fortified settlement on the James River about a dozen miles below the falls of the James at the spot that John Smith had chosen earlier. They named it Henrico in honor of King James's oldest son. It was constructed on the high ground of a peninsula with watchtowers, three streets with framed houses, a storehouse, and a church. The climate was far more salubrious than Jamestown, and there were pure, freshwater springs. Henrico spawned the construction of other small settlements, steadily forcing the Powhatans off their lands.

The continuing shortage of food combined with hard labor in the cold winter weather was almost unbearable for the half-starved men building the new settlement. The two old soldiers enforced a strict and brutal military regime to keep the colonists at work and the colony in good order under a document of regulations titled *Laws Divine, Moral, and Martial*. Gates published a set of thirty-seven strict decrees governing civilian life. In an effort to promote good hygiene and health, one stated, "There shall be no man or woman, Launderer or Launderesse, dare to wash any uncleane Linnen or throw out the water or suds of foule clothes in the open streete, within the Pallizadoes, or within forty foote of the same, nor rench, and make cleane any kettle, pot, or pan or such like vessel within twenty foote of the old well or new pumpe." The decree also dealt with handling "the necessities of nature" outside the fort. Another decree stated, "No man shall ravish or force any woman, maid, or Indian, or other upon pain of death." Fornication was punished by whipping, "and for their third they shall be whipped three times a week for one month, and ask public forgiveness in the assembly of the congregation." Whipping was also the punishment for those who failed to attend church services.

Dale contributed a list of provisions of martial law applying to the officers and soldiers. Civilians were subject to military discipline as well and compelled to work. The penalties for violations were very harsh, in some cases execution, and Dale did not bother with trials to determine the guilt or innocence of those charged with a crime. He was the prosecutor, judge, and jury. The daily food rations were meager—eight ounces of meal and a half pint of peas, often moldy or full of maggots. Some settlers caught stealing food from the common store were bound to trees until they starved to death. Those who became too ill to work were denied food. The governor was, in fact, instituting a form of slavery in the colony. When Dale recaptured some of his men who had deserted, they were hung, burned at the stake, broken on a wheel, or shot.

The Virginia Company took steps to prevent bad news about conditions in the colony and protests by the colonists from circulating outside the company. According to the 1623 report of some senior members of the

House of Burgesses, the company's instructions to the governors were that "all men's letters should be searched at the going away of ships." If any of them described "the true estate of the colony," whoever wrote the letter would be severely punished, "by which means no man durst make any true relation [report] to his friends of his own or the colony's true estate."

Gates returned to England in 1614, leaving Sir Thomas Dale in command. Despite the censorship, reports and complaints about the horrendous conditions under which the colonists lived and labored reached London, and Dale's tyrannical leadership and draconian rules drew questions from the Virginia Company directors. In a letter he defended his actions and declared that the company was at fault by not providing adequate supplies to support the colony. In describing the challenges that he faced, Dale reported that many workers yearned to abandon Virginia and return to England. (By intercepting outgoing letters, Dale must have been fully aware of the colonists' complaints.) The men hoped that the company would grow tired of supplying provisions to the colony with little or no return and bring them home. "Now consider this people well and give me your judgment what would become of them did I not compel them to work. Oh sir, my heart bleeds when I think what men we have here; and did I not carry a severe hand over them they would starve one the other by breaking open houses and chests to steal a pottle of corn from their poor brother, and when they have stolen, that poor man must starve." The company should have sent wheat and other grains, and the seeds that they sent were so dried out they were useless, except for the radishes and turnips. The colonists desperately needed new clothing and bedding. A hundred asses and a few horses "would do us infinite pleasure to bear our burdens, to draw our carriages, and to plant our grounds for us—all which our men are constrained to do like so many beasts. And indeed there is nothing kills them sooner, neither nothing so irksome to them and odious as these labours be." Dale announced that for various personal reasons he hoped to return to England in about a year.

Dale was determined to remove the threat of Indian assaults on the colonists. He continued De La Warr's campaign of launching ferocious attacks on Indian villages—against the Nansemonds near the mouth of the James and in the areas around Jamestown and the upper James where Henrico was being built. He was ruthless, as he had been in fighting the rebels in Ireland, destroying the natives' houses and crops and slaughtering the village's inhabitants, including women and children. The Powhatans fought back. In some twenty violent engagements around five hundred English soldiers, Indian warriors, and noncombatants were killed.

However, the colony continued to suffer from the same old problems. In a letter to the Earl of Salisbury, Governor Dale stated, "Every man al-

most laments himself from being here, and murmers at his present state. [The settlers were] such disordered persons, so profane, so riotous, so full of treasonable Intendments, besides of such desased and erased bodies which render them unable, fainte, and desperate of recoverie, as of three hundred not three score may be called forth or implored upon for any labour or service." With an additional two thousand men the colony could become self-sufficient in occupying and farming the lands stretching from Point Comfort up the James River to the falls. Dale had a novel idea for selecting new immigrants with a strong motivation to succeed in making a new life for themselves: for the next three years the company should send to Virginia all the criminals in England scheduled to be executed. The death toll in the colony continued to mount. Seven vessels brought 650 new settlers to Jamestown in 1611; yet by year's end the population was just 450 people.

Sir Thomas Dale imposed harsh military discipline and draconian rules in the Virginia colony, and launched brutal attacks on hostile Indian villages.
Virginia Museum of Fine Arts, Richmond. Adolph D. and Wilkins C. Williams Fund.

In 1612 a promising new development occurred that in a few years would transform the economy of Virginia. John Rolfe, one of the *Sea Venture* colonists, began planting tobacco seeds from Spanish Trinidad or South America that he had secretly obtained, which produced a leaf that was sweeter and more palatable than the bitter-tasting Virginia variety.

Later on the planters' experiments with crossbreeding led to cultivating a local leaf of acceptable quality. For the first time the Jamestown settlers had a reliable cash crop that was easy to cultivate and for which there was a strong and growing demand in England.

Patriotic pride, along with the lure of a profitable return, motivated the Virginia Company's continuing support for the colony. Investment in the company's enterprise was promoted from the pulpit as well as by London's financial houses. The Reverend Alexander Whitaker was a missionary whose calling was to introduce Christianity to the Indians. He had come to Virginia with Sir Thomas Dale and was forthright in urging his countrymen to support the struggling colony. In a letter to Sir Thomas Smythe, treasurer of the Virginia Company, he wrote, "Shall our nation, hitherto famous for noble attempts and the honourable finish of what they have undertaken, be now taxed for inconstancy, and blamed by the enemies of our Protestation for uncharitableness? Yea, shall we be a scorn among princes and a laughingstock among our neighbour nations for basely leaving what we honourably began; yea, for beginning a discovery whose riches other men shall gather so soon as we have forsaken it?"

When a supply voyage to Jamestown was about to depart in 1613, William Crashaw, a prominent London cleric, gave a rousing sermon to the "Adventurers and Planters of the Virginia Company." The colony was of such "nature and consequence, as not only all nations stand gazing at, but even heaven and hell have taken notice of it, the holy angels hoping and the divills fearing that will be the issue. Therefore let all nations see to their amazement that the English Christians will not undertake a publick action which they will not prosecute to perfection." Crashaw urged the Virginia Company investors "to assist this noble action with countenance and counsell, with men and money, and with continuall supplies, till we have made our colonies and plantation able to subsist of itself, until there be a Church of God established in Virginia, even there where Satan's throne is," referring to the hostile, pagan Indians. He urged the settlers about to sail for Virginia, "you that desire to advance the gospell of Jesus Christ . . . go forward in the name of the God of heaven and earth . . . cast away fears and let nothing daunt your spirits remembering whom you go unto, even to English men your bretheren, who have broke the ice before you."

When John Smith, the foremost "ice breaker," landed in London in December 1609, he presumably learned that before Sir Thomas Gates, the acting governor, set sail to Virginia that year, the Virginia Company had instructed him to appoint Smith to be the military commander of Jamestown: "To this Commande wee desire Captain Smith may be allotted as well for his earnest desire as the great confidence & trust that we have in his care & diligence." Smith also received some other unexpected good news. The letter that he had sent a friend in 1608 from Jamestown, after some editing, was published later that year with the title A *True Relation of such occurrences and*

John Smith's map of Jamestown and the Chesapeake Bay was contained in his book, A Map of Virginia, *published in 1612.*
Yale Collection of American Literature, Beinecke Rare Book and Manuscript Library.

accidents of noate as hath happened in Virginia since the first planting of that Collony, which is now resident in the South part thereof, till the last return from thence; it named Captain John Smith as the author.

Smith still had to answer to the Virginia Company to the charges that Archer and Ratcliffe had made against him. We only know that Smith was never punished, although he still remained under a cloud. The company neither cleared nor found him guilty of the accusations. In its article, "A True Declaration of the estate of the colonie of Virginia," the company recognized the daunting obstacles he had overcome to preserve the colony. Much of the article was based on Sir Thomas Gates's report after he returned from Jamestown; it referred to the colonists as "our mutinous Loyterers." Nevertheless, the investors wanted a scapegoat to blame for their losses and that person was John Smith. We can also safely assume that the lords and wealthy merchants did not forget that Smith's ranking in society was inferior to their own. The company never acknowledged his vital contribution in founding Jamestown. Despite their earlier instruction that Smith be appointed military commander of Jamestown, they never offered him another post.

Smith was proud of his accomplishments in Virginia and was determined to defend his reputation against the false charges and rumors denigrating his conduct. Over the next two years he worked at writing a *Map of Virginia*. The book would contain Smith's map of Virginia, and *A Description of the Countrey*, describing Virginia's physical assets, commodities, flora and fauna, and the Indian inhabitants—their culture, religion, and way of life. The second part of the book was titled *The Proceedings of the English Colonie in Virginia*, covering the history of Jamestown from 1606 to 1612. For this section Smith assembled the reports of nine colonists, who without doubt were loyal to him and supportive of his leadership of the colony. Determined to set the record straight regarding his conduct at Jamestown, it would have been unwise for him to appear as the author of *The Proceedings*. The account, according to the title page, was also based on the reports of other unnamed colonists and "confirmed and perused by diverse now resident in England that were actors in this business." The preface by colonist Thomas Abbay stated that the purpose of the book was to present a true account of what took place at Jamestown in view of the false reports, rumors, and charges that some had made. Richard Pots, who had been the secretary of the council in Virginia in 1608 and 1609, first compiled the history. The final editor was the Reverend William Symonds, the respected minister of a prominent London church, who made his own inquiries regarding the account before giving it his stamp of approval. Joseph Barnes, university printer in Oxford, published Smith's book in 1612. The Reverend Crashaw gave Smith and his book an endorsement in a letter to the Virginia Company: "The goodness, riches, and excellency of the country doth undoubtedly promise us, as may appear (besides others) in the book lately put out by Captain John Smith—who was there diverse years, and whose pains and service there deserves in my judgment high commendations."

Near the conclusion of *A Description of the Countrey*, Smith hit back at his critics among the colonists, those who never ventured far beyond Jamestown and never did anything "but devour the fruits of other mens labours." These fellows, having lived sheltered lives, were upset "because they found not English Cities, nor such faire houses, nor at their owne wishes any of their accustomed dainties, with feather beds and downe pillows, Tavernes and Alehouses in every breathing space, neither such plentie of gold and silver and dissolute libertie, as they expected, had little or no care of any thing, but to pamper their bellies" and scheme to flee back to England. For them Virginia was "a miserie, a ruine, a death, a hell," an attitude reflected in their reports. Smith added, "Thus from the clamours and ignorance of false informers are sprung those disasters that sprung in Virginia: and our ingenious verbalists were no lesse plague to us in Virginia, then the locusts to these Egyptians." Smith's description of the discontented Jamestown colonists is almost a mirror image of Thomas Harriot's characterization of the complaining Roanoke settlers who had fled back to England, but the lessons of Roanoke had been forgotten.

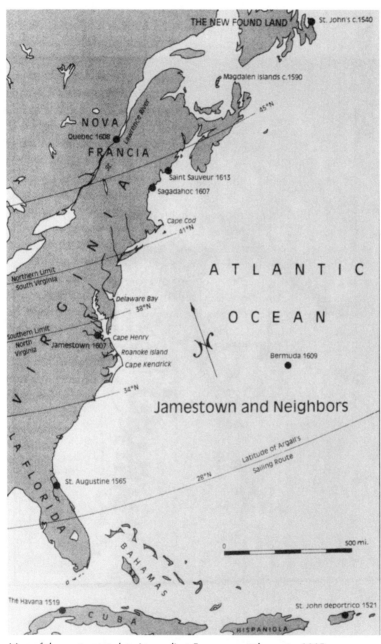

THE NEW FOUND LAND

St. John's c.1540

Magdalen Islands c.1590

45°N

NOVA
Quebec 1608

FRANCIA

Lawrence River

Saint Sauveur 1613
Sagadahoc 1607

Cape Cod
41°N

Northern Limit
South Virginia

Delaware Bay
38°N

Southern Limit
North
Virginia   Jamestown 1607

Cape Henry
Roanoke Island
Cape Kendrick

34°N

A T L A N T I C

O C E A N

Bermuda 1609

Jamestown and Neighbors

LA FLORIDA

Latitude of Argall's
Sailing Route

St. Augustine 1565

28°N

0   500 mi.

BAHAMAS

The Havana 1519

St. John deportrico 1521

CUBA

HISPANIOLA

Map of the east coast showing earliest European settlements, 1615.
© 1998 Jamestown Narratives, Edward Wright Haile.

The 1612 charter to the Virginia Company backed up Smith's charges, referring to "those wicked imps that put themselves a-shipboard, not knowing otherwise how to live in England, or those ungracious sons that daily vexed their fathers' hearts at home, and were therefore thrust upon the voyage, which either writing thence or being returned back, to cover their own lewdness do fill men's ears with false reports of their miserable and perilous life in Virginia."

John Smith believed that Virginia was admirably suited for planting new settlements: "The mildnesse of the ayre, the fertilitie of the soyle, and the situation of the rivers are so propitious to the nature and use of man, as no place is more convenient for pleasure, profit, and mans sustenance under that latitude and climate."

While Smith was working on his book he made a new friend, the Reverend Samuel Purchas, a respected minister and historian whose backing of Smith's book would considerably enhance Smith's reputation. Purchas, like Richard Hakluyt, was intrigued by the prospects of discoveries in new lands and was starting to gather accounts of the voyages and travels of explorers and colonizers. Smith let Purchas review his manuscript, which Purchas acknowledged in a section about Virginia in his own book, *Purchas His Pilgrimage*. It was published in 1612, the same year that John Smith's book on Virginia was produced and offered for public sale.

Northern Virginia
Becomes New England

*T*he collapse of the Popham colony had been a heavy financial blow for the Plymouth Company investors. Ferdinando Gorges and his associates were very discouraged, recognizing that the severe winter weather on the Maine coast presented a huge challenge to building another settlement. However, there was another opportunity for profitable enterprise. The abundance of cod in the Gulf of Maine was now attracting increasing numbers of West Country fishermen, from Devon, Cornwall, Dorset, and Somerset. Some cod could even weigh over one hundred pounds, and a fishing shallop might haul in up to four hundred fish a day. Following the death of Sir John Popham, the backer of the failed colony along with Gorges, his son Francis Popham started sending vessels each year to fish the waters off the Gulf of Maine. Many fishermen chose Damariscove and Monhegan islands to split, dry, and salt their cod on their rocks and beaches, preparing their catches for the fish markets of Catholic Europe and Protestant England, which also had meat-less days. Soon vessels began leaving men year round at Maine fishing bases. They protected and repaired the fishing gear, and fished, weather permitting, during the winter months. In 1608 Humphrey Damarill ran a trading post on Damariscove Island that served the visiting fishermen. Small numbers of English fishermen were living on and off in little Maine fishing stations over a decade before the Pilgrims arrived at Plymouth.

In the spring of 1608 Samuel de Champlain, with the backing of the Sieur de Mons, had sailed up the St. Lawrence River with the goal of starting a new French settlement and trading post in Canada. He chose a place at the base of the cliffs of Quebec, where his men built their houses on the river's shore. A few barely made it through another brutally cold Canadian winter. Without adequate food, most of the company succumbed to scurvy. When a supply ship with more settlers arrived in June 1609, only six of the original twenty-eight colonists were still alive. The struggling little outpost endured to become the town of Quebec, and it became the base for Champlain and other explorers, fur traders, and missionaries following the great river highway into the continent's interior.

The French had abandoned the Port Royal outpost in Nova Scotia in 1607 when the Sieur de Mons was unable to continue supporting it. However, the Sieur de Poutrincourt, the former governor, had retained his rights to the colony, and in 1610 he returned to Port Royal with a group of colonists to reoccupy the settlement. They were pleased to see that the local friendly Indians had not harmed their little hamlet, and they settled in. The following year the captain of a French vessel that had been fishing near the island of Matinicus in Maine's Penobscot Bay reported to the Sieur de Biencourt, de Poutrincourt's son, that his ship had been attacked and robbed by the English. Furthermore, the English claimed that the surrounding coastal territory belonged to England. Some English ships were in the general area where the attack occurred. According to John Smith's account in his *Generall Historie of Virginia, New England, and the Summer Isles* there was a fishing vessel sent out by Francis Popham and another ship dispatched by the Earl of Southampton, commanded by Edward Harlow. Its purpose was to explore and bring back a few Indian captives to London. De Biencourt was deeply disturbed about this English assertion of ownership off the Maine coastal territory. In August 1611 he embarked on an inspection tour of the Maine coast, sailing southwest as far as the Kennebec where he viewed the abandoned fort of the Popham colony. At Matinicus he spotted some English boats fishing, but as they were peaceful fishermen he did not bother them. Instead, he erected a cross with the royal coat of arms of France on the little island.

The Marquise de Guercheville was a beautiful, wealthy, and pious French noblewoman with important friends at the French court, including Queen Marie de Medici, who ruled France as regent for her young son after Henry IV was assassinated in 1610. The marquise was the latest recipient of a royal land grant, which gave her the right to acquire all the territory from Florida to the St. Lawrence, the rights formerly belonging to the Sieur de Mons. Clearly it did not matter to the French that their claim ignored and overlapped existing English and Spanish claims. In 1608 two Jesuit missionaries from Port Royal, Peter Biard and Enemond Masse, started a tiny mission near the entrance of Somes Sound on Mount Desert Island off the coast of Maine. They planned to convert the local Indians to Christianity. In 1613, during the regime of the Marquise de Guercheville, a group of some twenty-five Jesuit monks from Port Royal were sent to join their brothers and establish a permanent Jesuit mission there; its name was Saint-Sauveur. The monks started to build fortified housing, planted a garden, and established friendly relations with the natives.

In July 1612 the Court of the Virginia Company in London had instructed Samuel Argall, now holding the rank of Admiral of Virginia, to drive out any foreign intruders occupying the lands the company owned under its royal charter, which covered the entire coast of Maine. Sailing up the coast from Virginia a year later, he came across the Jesuit settlement on Mount Desert. The monks, who had not finished building their little fort, were taken completely by surprise and offered virtually no resistance to Argall's soldiers. Argall seized the mission, took fifteen prisoners back to Jamestown, and put the others in two small boats to make their way back to Port Royal as best they could.

Soon afterward Admiral Argall returned with three ships to Mount Desert on a voyage of destruction. He burned down the buildings at Saint-Sauveur and went on to the French fort at St. Croix, which he also put to the torch. Next he crossed the bay to Port Royal where the settlers had fled into hiding. He looted the settlement and then burned it to the ground, leaving the colonists without provisions and shelter as winter approached. The French settlers returned and survived to rebuild Port Royal. This cruel act by Argall marked the beginning of the conflict between England and France over the boundaries between French Acadia and the English colonies to the south, and indeed for the control of huge areas of North America. The fighting would eventually result in the expulsion of French rule from North America, although that would not happen for another 150 years. In 1613 Claude de Saint-Etienne de la Tour established a French trading post at today's Castine on Penobscot Bay, a signal by the French that they intended to exercise their rights to occupy the region. Fort Pentagoet was the first permanent European settlement in New England.

Other countries were eager to find a northwest route to Asia and establish trading outposts in the Atlantic coast region. In 1608 John Smith sent a letter and map by a ship leaving Jamestown to Henry Hudson, an experienced ship's captain whom he had probably met in London earlier. He told Hudson about the Chesapeake Bay and the possibility, based on reports from Indians, of a northwest passage to Asia further north up the coast that Smith had not explored. Although Hudson was an Englishman, he was sailing for the Dutch East Indies Company, which, like other European merchant enterprises, was intent on finding a short route to the Orient to bring back the popular spices, silk, and other products. In September 1609 Hudson, with a crew of twenty Dutch and English men, entered New York Harbor on the *Half Moon*. He was probably the first European explorer to view New York Harbor since the Italian captain, Giovanni da Verrazzano, in 1524, who did not venture upriver.

Hudson sailed his eighty-five-foot vessel up the great river named after him to present-day Albany, about as far as he could go. His men in a dory reported that the river upstream became increasingly narrow and shallow. He had not found a northwest passage, and he headed back down the river.

Hudson's encounters with the local Indian tribes were unpredictable, similar to the experience of other explorers. Sometimes his crew was warmly received with gifts by the natives, who were eager to trade, and a local chief was Hudson's host at a sumptuous meal at his lodge. Other times Hudson's men were greeted with a shower of arrows, and in a surprise attack Englishman John Coleman was killed by an arrow stuck deep in his throat. After that, European muskets drove off any Indians attempting to assault the ship. On one of the last days on the river an Indian attempted to steal some articles from the first mate's cabin, climbing in through an open window in the ship's stern. The first mate shot him, which triggered a running battle between the Indian war canoes and the ship, until the Indians, with several dead and wounded, retired.

Hudson continued to explore the New England coast at least as far as the Penobscot River in Maine before returning to the Netherlands. He had been impressed by the fertile lands and imposing forests that he had observed in the Hudson River Valley, the excellent fishing, and the profitable prospects for fur trading with the Indians. The Dutch based their territorial claim to the midcoast region on Hudson's voyage, a claim that conflicted directly with the previous English claims and sowed the seeds of confrontation later on. In 1612 two Dutch ships arrived in New York Harbor and established a small outpost to trade for furs at the lower end of Manhattan Island. It was a move that did not go unnoticed by the Virginia Company in England, whose royal patent included Manhattan. The following year Samuel Argall, returning to Jamestown after destroying the French settlements in Maine and Acadia, anchored off Manhattan in his well-armed ship and forced the Dutch to raise the English flag. This time he did not harm the inhabitants or demolish their base. These English raids against European settlements on the east coast sent a clear signal of their strengthening will to enforce their imperial claims to the region.

Adriaen Block, one of the leaders in the Manhattan settlement, explored Long Island Sound, the Connecticut River, and up the coast to present-day Salem, Massachusetts, before returning to Amsterdam. Block Island is named after him. His favorable report on the region persuaded the Dutch government to grant a charter to the New Netherlands Company, composed of Dutch merchants and ship owners, giving them a three-year monopoly of the fur trade with the Indians. In 1614 the New Netherlands Company dispatched an expedition that established a trading post with a stockade fort near today's Albany to engage in the lucrative fur trade. Another Dutch navigator, Cornelius May, after whom Cape May is named, explored the coast from Delaware Bay to Long Island. The company planned to send over more settlers to increase their presence and trading activity in the region centering on Manhattan Island and the Hudson River Valley.

English and French vessels continued to cruise the New England coast, exploring, fishing, and trading for furs with the natives. The ship commanded by Edward Harlow had returned to London with five Indian captives. One of them was a tall, imposing brave named Epinow, who was "shewed up and downe London for money as a wonder." Epinow was a shrewd fellow and had observed how eager his English masters were to find gold in America; he in turn was seeking a way to return home. He persuaded his captors that he knew of a gold mine on Martha's Vineyard and could lead an expedition to it. When the English ship got close enough to the island, Epinow jumped overboard, swam ashore, and escaped. The vessel returned to England empty handed and with a captain and crew that were presumably quite embarrassed.

John Smith continued to be an impassioned and vocal advocate for developing English colonies in America. He was possessed by the idea and desperately wanted to lead another expedition with this objective. As the Virginia Company no longer desired his service in the Chesapeake Bay area, he would look elsewhere, namely, Northern Virginia (or New England as he would later name the region). Before Smith's friend Bartholomew Gosnold died in Jamestown, he had probably told Smith about his voyage to the coast of Maine and Cape Cod, and Smith knew about the expeditions of the other English explorers to the region after Gosnold. Smith's first step was to find some backers for his voyage, and he was successful in persuading four London investors to outfit two ships for the expedition. One of them, Marmaduke Royden, had invested in other expeditions to America. This was to be a commercial enterprise—the backers expected Smith to catch whales for their valuable oil and look for gold and copper deposits. As for searching for gold, Smith admits in his book published later, *A Description of New-England*, it was really "a device to get a voyage that projected it." He knew how the lure of gold incited his investors. He also knew that no one had discovered any signs of gold in the region. Recalling the fruitless search for gold in Jamestown undoubtedly made him a skeptic on the subject, and he was right.

The two ships with a crew of a forty-five men and boys set sail from England on March 3, 1614; Captain Thomas Hunt commanded the second ship. They made their first landfall in mid-April at Monhegan Island in West Penobscot Bay, the base often used by European fishing vessels. The crews' attempts at whaling were futile. "We saw many and spent much time in chasing them, but could not kill any," wrote Smith. Fish and furs would be the next most profitable cargo for Smith's investors, and Smith's men turned to fishing. Over the next few months they caught, dried, and salted some forty-seven thousand pounds for the return voyage. Leaving most of the crew fishing, Smith with eight men embarked in a small boat to explore the coast and trade for furs with the Indians. They first sailed about Penobscot Bay, noting its many islands and the Penobscot River, which "ranne farre up into the Land." The Indians to the east beyond the bay were little interested in trading with the English. "Our commodities were not esteemed," reported Smith. They had been dealing on good terms with French trappers and traders for some time, perhaps visiting the new French trading outpost at Castine at the northern end of the bay.

As we have seen throughout his life, John Smith was an inveterate explorer and an ardent advocate for building English settlements in America. It was in his blood. Now he seized the chance to explore the northern Virginian coast and search for a good location to start another colony. He also needed to buy more furs from the Indians to build up the value of the goods he would bring home to his investors. Smith headed his little boat southwest down the coast, trading with natives along the way. He gathered 1,100 beaver pelts and many martin and otter skins.

The coastal waters were no longer long, empty stretches without a ship in sight. Smith encountered an English vessel, owned by Sir Francis Popham, trading and fishing near the mouth of the Kennebec and two French ships with the same purpose further down the coast. Smith carried with him six or seven charts of the northern Virginia coast, probably based on English voyages to the area earlier. Smith reported that his maps were "so unlike each to other, and most so differing from any true proportion or resemblance of the countrey, as they did me no more good, then so much waste paper, though they cost me more." Indeed, following these maps could have been misleading and hazardous. Smith decided to draw up his own map for the benefit of future travelers to the area, hopefully future expeditions intending to start new settlements. "I have drawn a Map from Point to Point, Isle to Isle, Harbour to Harbour, with the soundings, Sands, and Land-marks as I passed close aboard the Shore in a little Boat. . . . it will serve to direct any shall go that waies, to safe harbours and Salvages habitations."

From Smith's map one can track his excursion down the coast to Cape Cod, sailing close to shore to plot its harbors, bays, and rivers. Leaving Penobscot Bay and the mountains lining the bay's shore, he went up the Kennebec River thirty miles or so, noting the fertile cornfields by the native villages among the dense forests. The Indians living along today's Maine coast recognized the great Penobscot chief, Basheba, who had met with Champlain, as lord of them all. Smith continued southwest to Casco Bay, observing its many islands and harbors. He named the group of islands off Portsmouth (today's Isles of Shoals) Smith Isles, and today's Cape Ann he named Tragabigzanda after the Turkish mistress to whom he had been given as a slave following his capture by the Turks. Smith considered the Massachusetts coast to be "the paradise of all those parts" as he scouted Boston Bay with its little isles and the Charles River. He admired Hull and the islands planted with fields of corn and native gardens, and the good harbors. Trading with the natives, however, was not fruitful, as they had already established good business relations with the French traders who had visited the area earlier.

The Indians were generally friendly, although one fellow, with whom they had quarreled, and three comrades let fly their arrows at them from a clump of rocks that they had to pass. Cruising down the coast they arrived at Plymouth Harbor, so named later on Smith's map after the notable English port from which many ships embarked for the New World. Relations with the natives remained volatile, similar to Smith's experience at Jamestown, and Smith's party became embroiled in another skirmish, this time quite violent: "Some were hurt and some slaine; yet within an houre after they became friendes," he wrote. They next cruised about Cape Cod Bay, whose sandy topography and sickle shape he described in his book and map. He also reported what he learned from the Indians living on the cape's southern arm about the dangerous shoals and islands to the south. Cape Cod was Smith's last destination; he turned his small boat about and headed northeast to rejoin his two ships at Monhegan Island.

On July 18, 1614, Captain Smith set sail from Monhegan for Plymouth with a cargo of fish and furs, reaching the West Country seaport around the end of August. Captain Hunt commanding the other ship would sail to Spain to sell his cargo of dried fish. Smith disposed of his cargo for £1,500 pounds and quickly went about attempting to secure the command of another expedition to New England, the name he had chosen for the region as far more fitting than "Northern Virginia." This time he planned to establish an outpost and remain there with a small company of men, the start of a new English colony. His excursion down the New England coast had convinced him that the region was an excellent place to build a new settlement.

When Smith reached Plymouth he called upon Sir Ferdinando Gorges, the commander of the fort at Plymouth, who was devoted to the cause of colonizing on the New England coast. He had been a major backer of the ill-fated Popham colony, and after its collapse he had sponsored two more voyages to New England. Gorges was impressed with Smith's report about his findings and was willing to support another expedition led by Smith to New England. After his losses from previous ventures in the region, however, he lacked enough capital to finance the entire enterprise. Smith persuaded some

London investors, who had backed him before, to join Gorges and Dr. Matthew Sutcliffe, a member of the Virginia Company from Exeter, in outfitting a good-sized ship and a smaller one. While the expedition was expected to return with a profitable cargo of fish, Smith and fifteen men would remain in New England to build the new colony Smith envisioned. Among the proposed settlers was Captain Thomas Dermer, who was listed as a gentleman and leading member of the company. In March 1615 the two vessels set sail from Plymouth for America.

The smaller and swifter boat was soon out of sight, leaving the larger ship with Smith far behind. Over two hundred miles from port a gale toppled all her masts. Jury-rigged and leaking badly, with all hands manning the pumps, Smith's ship limped back to Plymouth. Such misfortune would not deter John Smith from his goal. His investors provided him with a smaller bark, and with his fifteen settlers and a crew of fourteen he set out again on June 24. What happened next is reminiscent of his astonishing adventures in those early years before coming to America: he had been caught up in a campaign of piracy at sea on board a French ship before, and in 1615 it happened again.

Smith's bark successfully avoided capture by two pirate ships before running into four French heavily armed men-of-war near the Azores. The French stated that they were only authorized to attack Spanish and Portuguese vessels and requested Smith to come over to their flagship to show them his English credentials. When he went on board the French ship, they took him prisoner, seized his ship, and placed a prize crew on board. For five or six days it joined the French fleet, operating as privateers, in chasing down foreign ships that crossed their path. Then the French apparently thought better of holding an English ship, and, after handing over the supplies that they had taken, they released the bark and Captain Smith to go on their way. Smith instructed the master of his vessel, Edmund Chambers, to send a small boat over to the French ship to bring him back to the bark. Chambers refused, saying the boat was too damaged. (Crewmembers testified later that it was not.) In the dark of night Smith's bark fell astern and disappeared, heading back to Plymouth and leaving its captain a prisoner of the French pirates. The mutineers would claim later that they feared that the French would seize them and their bark. They had run away to save themselves and their ship. All of Smith's clothing, his books, weapons, and other personal possessions were on the bark, which the mutineers divided up among themselves. Smith was only left with the breeches and waistcoat he was wearing. We can imagine how furious Smith was at his crew for abandoning him as he laid his plans for seeking justice and revenge.

Smith was comfortably confined to the "great cabin," or sometimes the gunroom, on the French flagship for almost three months as the French fleet ranged about the waters near the Azores seizing and plundering vessels. Never one to waste time, Smith wrote the manuscript that would later be published as *A Description of New-England*. Smith recorded that they attacked Spanish treasure ships, an English fisherman, a Scottish merchant ship, a Dutch vessel, and a Brazilian carvel. "They kept me in this manner to manage their fights against the Spaniards, and be a prisoner when they tooke any English." In their last sea battle some Spanish ships fired broadsides through the ship's main mast, and in October the French captain set his course for France. He had assured Smith of his freedom and a financial reward for his role in fighting the Spanish when they reached France. However, when they put into port he broke his promise and kept Smith imprisoned on board the caravel. He had no intention of letting Smith claim his share of the bounty from the Spanish ships. When they were at sea again, Smith saw his chance to escape his captors.

During a violent storm at night near La Rochelle in France when all the crew sought shelter below deck, Smith slipped away in the ship's small boat. Bailing constantly to keep his little craft afloat during a terrible night of gale winds and rain, Smith drifted to a small island where some hunters rescued him "neere drowned and halfe dead, with water, cold, and hunger." It was not easy to kill John Smith, and, furthermore, he had kept his precious manuscript with him. He was taken to La Rochelle where he was amazed to learn that the French man-of-war from which he had escaped had sunk in the storm on the same night that he had run away and survived. The French captain and half the crew were drowned, and much of its rich cargo, plundered from Spanish ships, was lost. Some of it was salvaged later, and Smith placed a claim for his share of the bounty with the French admiralty court, backed by the testimony of some of the surviving sailors from the man-of-war. The court appeared to view his claim favorably, but the French wheels of justice turned too slowly for Smith, and he had important business in England. He returned to Plymouth in December 1615 and tracked down his ship's officers who had abandoned him.

He stated in his book that he "laied by the heeles" the leaders of the mutiny. He also presented his charges against them in legal proceedings in order to be recompensed for his losses. Smith wanted justice. They had betrayed him, stolen his possessions, and, worst of all, sullied his reputation in maligning his leadership of the enterprise. On December 8 he arranged for David Baker, his former steward on the voyage, to give a deposition before Sir Lewis Stukeley, vice admiral of Devonshire, and Baker gave a true account of what had occurred. Six gentlemen and crewmembers on Smith's ship confirmed Baker's testimony. It absolved Smith of any misconduct and placed blame for the incident squarely on the shoulders of the ship's master, Edmund Chambers. Smith must have reported to Sir Ferdinando Gorges, the main sponsor of the aborted expedition, and convinced him of the truth of his story, which Gorges later related in his book, *A Brief Relation of the Discovery & Plantation of New England.* Gorges's support was critical for Smith, as he prepared to publish his own new book, *A Description of New-England,* and, in fact, in all matters dealing with English colonization in New England.

Despite the failures of the new settlement projects that he had backed, the Popham colony and two expeditions led by John Smith, Gorges remained obsessed with the idea of starting new colonies on the Maine coast. In 1616, financing a new venture single-handedly, he dispatched a small ship with sixteen of his servants and tenants, led by Richard Vines, to establish an outpost on the Maine coast. They built their snug cabins at Biddeford Pool, just upstream from the mouth of the Saco River, and passed the winter quite comfortably and peacefully. Vines returned to England with the good news: he had demonstrated to Gorges and his associates that with good planning and site selection it was feasible for English settlers to endure the harsh Maine winters successfully, despite the stories of a terribly cold and inhospitable land told by the Popham colonists. He also reported that a terrible plague had struck the native population in the coastal region.

The smaller boat accompanying Smith on his first aborted voyage returned from New England with a full cargo of fish. Word of the fabulous fishing grounds had spread, and some three hundred fishermen from European countries were heading for the Gulf of Maine and the rest of the New England coast each spring. Thirty or so were English vessels from Bristol, Plymouth, and other ports. A few would stay year round to man small fishing camps along the coast, but no group since the Popham disaster had attempted to establish a permanent and complete new colony. In Ireland the development of new English settlements and plantations was proceeding steadily. For John Smith the timing was propitious to put out a new book describing another promising region, New England, and the features that made it admirably suited for colonization.

John Smith's book, *A Description of New-England,* was published in June 1616. It was sixty pages long and included the map Smith had drawn of the coast from Penobscot Bay, Maine, to Cape Cod, Massachusetts. The map was handsomely engraved by Dutch artist Simon Van de Passe, and it had a small portrait of John Smith in the upper left corner, the only likeness of him that exists. A short verse below the portrait praises Smith's discoveries and his success in subduing and civilizing the "Salvages." The final line reads, "Sir, thou art brass without, but gold within." The introduction contained three letters—to Prince Charles, the only remaining son of King James after the death of Prince Henry and heir to the throne, the royal council that dealt with colonization, and investors in the New England expedition.

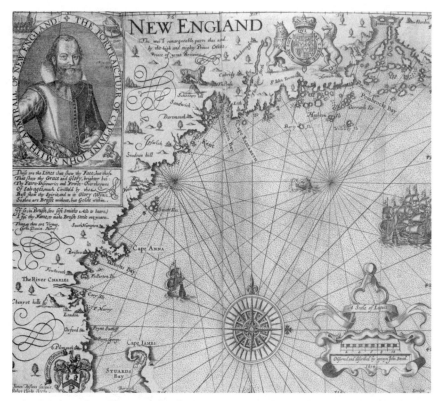

John Smith's map of New England was contained in his book, A Description of New-England, *published in 1616. The map includes the only known portrait of John Smith.*
Yale Collection of American Literature, Beinecke Rare Book and Manuscript Library.

Smith's map identified various geographic locations by their Indian names, and he invited Prince Charles to change the "Barbarous names" to English names of his choosing so "posterity may say Prince Charles was their Godfather." The prince was happy to comply, and, because the book and map had been printed earlier, Smith added a list of the old and new names. In bold letters the map bore Smith's new name for the region, *New England*, and on the map and title page Smith is identified as Admiral of New England, a title that must have met the approval of Prince Charles.

Smith provided his estimate of the value of commodities that businessmen could obtain from the region, ensuring a good profit on their investment. To the investors he said, "I confesse it were more proper for mee to be doing what I say, then writing what I knowe." Although the man of action may have felt unsure of his talent as a writer, his concern never constrained him from writing throughout his life at some length of his exploits and discoveries, nor would it this time. The council members and investors deserved to receive a full account from him of his expeditions and discoveries, he stated, especially in view of the false rumors that had circulated. Although his report emphasized the great fisheries off the New England coast, Smith pointed out that fishing would certainly not hinder the pursuit of other profitable enterprises.

A Description also contained eight poems written by friends, including a cousin and soldiers who had served under Smith in Transylvania and Virginia. The poems praised Smith's valor and accomplishments, which held such promising prospects for England. The expression of admiration for Smith by the soldiers was especially meaningful, for they had observed firsthand his leadership in battle under enemy attack. They also viewed their commanding officer as a true and honorable gentleman: "I never knew a Warryer yet but thee, from wine, Tobacco, debts, dice, oaths so free." The verses of the three Jamestown soldiers confirmed Smith's account of several fights with Powhatan's warriors and ended with these final lines:

> And for this paines of thine wee praise thee rather
> That future Times may know who was the father
> Of this rare Worke which may bring
> Praise to God, and Profit to thy King.

In the opening passages of his book Smith briefly identified the east coast regions of North America and the countries that claimed them, starting in the north with New France and moving south through New England and Virginia to Spanish-held Florida and the West Indies. He complimented all the English explorers who had gone to America before him: "Posterity may be bettered by the fruits of their labours." We can understand why he made no mention of Samuel de Champlain, who had carefully explored the New England coast before him on three voyages and produced a very good map of the region that was published in 1613. Both England and France claimed the territory, and England had taken firm action to enforce her claim. Regarding the English discoveries, Smith acknowledged that "we have touched or scene a little the edges of those large dominions," which extended inland "God doth know how many thousand miles." He declared that Bermuda, Virginia, New England, and New France should have no fear of Spain, which, with limited and thinly stretched forces, claimed control of vast areas in America. (Spain had kept a watchful and wary eye on English activity in America, especially the development of the Jamestown colony, the closest English settlement to Florida. The Spanish ambassador in London gathered intelligence for King Philip III, and three crew members of a Spanish spy ship that arrived at Point Comfort were captured and imprisoned by the colonists at Jamestown for several years.)

Smith then described the topography of the coast, its rivers, some of which extended far inland, and harbors. He had taken soundings in about twenty-five "excellent good Harbours," many of which could accommodate large ships. The many islands and mainland were overgrown with "all sorts of excellent good woodes for building houses, boats, barks, or shippes, with an incredible abundance of most sorts of fish, much fowle, and sundry sorts of good fruites for man's use." Smith told of the forty or so Indian villages that he had spotted along the coast, along with the native gardens and cornfields. He had continued down the coast toward Cape Cod Bay and described Plymouth as "an excellent good harbor, good land, no want of anything but industrious people." Smith wrote with enthusiasm about what he had seen on his tour of the coast: "Who can but approve this a most excellent place, both for health and fertility? And of all the foure parts of the world that I have yet seene not inhabited, could I have but meanes to transport a Colonie, I would rather live here than any where." The climate was "as temperate and fruitful as any other parallel in the world."

Smith, of course, had not spent a winter in New England, and he had his own agenda—he wanted to be the leader of any new colony that might be planned for the region. "But," he declared, "it is not a worke for everyone, to manage such an affaire as makes a discoverie, and plants a Colony; It requires the best parts of Art, Judgement, Courage, Honesty, Constancy, Diligence, and Industrie, to doe but neere well." He observed that "nothing breedes more confusion then misplacing and misemploying men in their undertakings." He did not need to add that he was the best man for the job.

The important message in Smith's book was that the time had come for English entrepreneurs to start building colonies in New England. Smith proposed that a fishing expedition leave him and a company of men on the coast with all the necessary supplies to start a settlement. The vessel would return to England with a cargo of dried fish, and the proceeds would cover all the expenses. Ships would regularly supply the colony, bringing new settlers, and soon depart with a load of fish and other products that the colonists had purchased or produced. It would be a very profitable business for English merchants and investors, giving them a competitive edge over their European rivals. The region was rich in resources. The land was fertile for farming; there were tall evergreens and stately oaks providing ample lumber for building; there was abundant wild game and fowl, and beaver, martin, and other furs could be purchased from the Indians. However, fishing, Smith emphasized, would be the major enterprise that would enable the region to grow and prosper. New England fisheries were the best, excelling those in Newfoundland and other fishing grounds. Smith noted the abundance of cod of good size and other sorts of fish that were plentiful. It was fishing that would provide a stable and profitable economic base for new settlements in New England. Until the settlers' farms were developed, "for a few trifles" Smith could purchase enough corn from the natives to feed three hundred men. The Indians might even go to work for the colonists in preparing fish for export, farming, and in other ways. Thirty or forty good men were all that were needed to keep the Indians under control if the need arose—"if they should be untoward (as it is most certaine they are)." Smith knew more than anyone about the Indians' violent eruptions of hostility toward foreigners settling on their land.

Smith had a grand vision for the colonization of New England. It would offer a wonderful opportunity for thousands of his countrymen—the jobless seeking employment, poor young married couples, carpenters, farmers, and other skilled workers—to start a new life, free from the greedy landlords and crowded conditions that burdened their lives in England. "As here," Smith wrote, "every man may be master and owner of his owne labour and land, or the greatest part in a small time. If hee have nothing but his hands, he may set up this trade; and by industrie quickly grow rich." When Smith had been at Jamestown the settlers did not own their own land; they had worked communally to raise crops or perform other tasks for the colony. It was a system imposed by the London Company and a major factor accounting for the minimum effort that many put forth. Smith now recognized that owning and farming their land or working in their own business gave people the incentive to prosper and build a stable and thriving community.

Smith was a passionate advocate for his cause: "Who can desire more content, that hath small meanes, or but only his merit to advance his fortune, then to tread, and plant that ground hee hath purchased by the hazard of his life? If he have but the taste of virtue and magnanimitie, what to such a minde can bee more pleasant then planning and building a foundation for his Posteritie, gotte from the rude earth, by God's blessing and his own industrie, without prejudice to any?" Smith then asked what could be more agreeable to God than trying "to convert those poor Salvages to know Christ? . . . What so truly sutes with honour and honestie as the discovering things unknown, erecting Townes, peopling Countries, informing the ignorant, reforming things unjust, teaching virtue; and gaine to our Native mother-countrie a kingdom to attend her, find imployment for those that are idle?" Such noble deeds would "cause Posteritie to remember thee; and remembering thee, ever honour that remembrance with praise?" Smith had first directed his appeal for support to investors seeking profitable new ventures; he had then presented the opportunity to poor folks to have a fresh start and promising new life in New England; he was now appealing to the honorable and patriotic instincts of all his countrymen.

Smith needed to impress potential investors in his project and attract a company of "worthie, honest, industrious spirits" to start the new settlement. He was ready to go with them, "not leave them there, but live with them there," and added, "I am not so simple to thinke that ever any other motive than wealth will ever erect there a Commonweale; or draw companie from their ease and humours at home, to stay in New England to effect my purposes." Through their labor and diligence colonists could acquire wealth and live more happily than in England, "for our pleasure here is still gaines, in England charges and loss." Along with farming, boat building and other pursuits, fishing would be a profitable activity for settlers and their wives and children. "He is a very bad fisher, cannot kill in one day with his hooke and line, one, two, three hundred Cods." Even if one fished for only an hour a day, a fisherman would have plenty of fish beyond the needs of his family to sell to a merchant or barter for whatever he wished. Moreover, for gentlemen what activity could be more pleasurable than fishing and hunting for wild game and fowl in the woods, lakes, and rivers of New England?

As we have seen, John Smith often did not hesitate to express his views bluntly. He was frustrated with the wealthy lords and gentlemen who lived idly "onely to eate, drink, and sleepe, and so die," or worse—who lied, cheated, gambled, or engaged in other unworthy activities. Fathers, instead of maintaining their children in "wanton idleness," should invest a modest sum to back their participation in the new colony where in time they might build a fortune even greater than that of the father. However, there were always those, even in the case of "Noble Colombus," who refused to believe news of the discoveries of new lands rich in valuable resources.

After Columbus's discoveries, the Spaniards, Smith noted, had forged ahead in exploring the new regions, building new towns, and seizing the "mountains of wealth" that they had uncovered; and with "constant resolution," they were continuing their explorations and search for new sources of wealth. Yet the English hung back, through sloth, negligence, or just plain ignorance and irrational fear of the unknown, scoffing at those who reported their new discoveries. Smith was certainly not following conventional marketing tactics with these words and must have hoped that he could shame his countrymen into backing his strategy of colonization. He raised the question: "Be we so far inferior to other nations, or our spirits so far dejected, from our ancient predecessors" . . . as to serve these competitor countries "rather than our God, our King, our Country, and our selves? . . . when heere is choise of all sorts, and for all degrees, in the planting and discovering of these North parts of America."

John Smith tried once again to start a colony in his beloved New England. He had more grandiose ideas, but he settled for three ships outfitted by Sir Ferdinando Gorges. The vessels would return to England loaded with fish, and Smith and fifteen men would stay behind to start building a permanent settlement. Misfortune struck again. For three months in 1617 Smith's little fleet was trapped in Plymouth Harbor, blocked by adverse winds from heading out to sea. Finally, Smith decided that it was too late in the year to make the crossing and build a fort to live in before winter weather set in. He abandoned the project and did not join the ships on a fishing expedition to Newfoundland.

John Smith tried and failed to attract backing for another attempt to start a New England colony. For the rest of his life he remained an ardent advocate and prolific publicist for the cause of English colonization in America. To his great frustration and disappointment he never found a way to return to New England to carry out his vision.

In *A Description of New-England* Smith delivered an important message to his countrymen that would inform and inspire their imagination and spur their ambition to plant new colonies in America. His book and map had a far greater impact on England's colonization efforts than that of any of the accounts of earlier explorers. His portrayal of New England as a fruitful place to live and prosper, with significant benefits for its inhabitants and England, helped put to rest its poor reputation derived from the failure of the Popham settlement. Most importantly, John Smith set forth a vision of America, not heretofore proclaimed. It was a land of opportunity where anyone, no matter how poor or low his rank in society, could own his own property and advance and prosper as far as his merit and labor could take him. John Smith's concept of America, unfamiliar in the old world with its rigid class structure, would attract a flow of English and other immigrants for years to come.

• 13 •

Indian Partners

 $\mathscr{P}$ ocahontas, Powhatan's favorite daughter, was a brave young woman. In saving Smith from execution, she had been instrumental in saving Jamestown, for without Smith it is doubtful that the colony would have survived. When still a girl, she defied her father by daring to warn Smith and his comrades about assaults against them planned by Powhatan's warriors. She had also been a lively, free-spirited youngster, who had visited Jamestown a number of times and befriended the settlers. Sometimes she brought food to the hungry colonists or served as a peace emissary from her father; sometimes in a playful mood she led the boys in doing cartwheels about the fort. In the summer when she was younger she would appear naked; when she became a teenager, she wore a leather apron, perhaps decorated with feathers. After Smith went back to England she had stayed away from the fort.

In April 1613 Captain Samuel Argall sailed up the Potomac to trade for corn to replenish Jamestown's food supply. When he learned that Pocahontas was visiting the local chieftain, he decided to kidnap her and hold her as hostage until her father, Powhatan, agreed to release some English prisoners and hand over weapons and tools his braves had stolen from the English. With the connivance of the local chief and his wife, bribed by the gift of a copper kettle, Argall enticed Pocahontas on board his ship and took her back to Jamestown. The English intended to treat their popular prisoner, the royal princess of the powerful chieftain, with respect and kindness.

Pocahontas was her father's beloved child, his "delight and darling" according to colonist Ralph Hamor. Nevertheless, Powhatan was reluctant to give up the weapons and took three months to reply to Governor Thomas Dale's proposal for the exchange that would send Pocahontas back to her home and family. Finally he released seven English prisoners and some broken muskets and tools. His response did not satisfy the governor, who demanded the return of the rest of the stolen arms, including many of the colonists' swords. Early the next year Governor Dale, accompanied by Pocahontas and 150 men, sailed up the York River, intending to obtain the missing arms and turn over Pocahontas to her father. Negotiations with Powhatan's lieutenants broke down, the two parties skirmished, and the English burned down forty native houses and killed a half dozen Powhatan warriors. The next day the two sides agreed to lay down their arms, and later John Rolfe met with Opechancanough, Powhatan's brother. The meeting went well: Opechancanough would try to persuade his brother to accept the English terms, and he succeeded. Powhatan now felt that his people had suffered enough at the hands of the English, and he turned over more of the stolen weapons and some corn to the colonists. Furthermore, there was a new development—a blossoming love affair that would help significantly in restoring good relations between the colonists and Powhatan. Pocahontas was happy to continue living with the English, and her father was now content that she do so.

Governor Dale had sent Pocahontas to Henrico, the newly built settlement south of James Falls, where she was placed under the tutelage of its minister, Alexander Whitaker. Pocahontas received "extraordinary courteous usage" under Whitaker's care at Henrico, wrote Hamor. She increased her fluency in speaking English and learned to read; she adopted English manners and dress. Now she no longer appeared as a bare-breasted Indian maid but was attired as a proper English lady. She was a willing student and ready to adopt English ways, leave her home, and become a Christian. Pocahontas's true Indian name was Matoaka; Pocahontas was a nickname, reflecting her frolicsome traits and bestowed by her father when she was a little girl. When Reverend Whitaker baptized her into the Christian faith, she took the name of Rebecca. There was a good reason for Pocahontas's eager transformation. She and colonist John Rolfe had fallen in love at Henrico, and now that she had "openly renounced her country idolatry, confessed the faith of Jesus Christ, and was baptized," the two could get married, declared Whitaker.

John Rolfe, the widower who had come to Jamestown from Bermuda with Sir Thomas Gates in 1610, was the very successful entrepreneur who had introduced the cultivation and export of tobacco. Tobacco production increased rapidly to meet the growing demand in England, and new tobacco plantations were being planted up the James River where ships could tie up to wharves along its banks. Virginia colonist Ralph Hamor wrote, "The valuable commoditie of Tobacco of such esteeme in England (if there were nothing else) which every man may plant, and with the least part of his labour, tend and care will return him both cloathes and other necessaries." Raising tobacco was about to become the mainstay of Virginia's economy.

Rolfe was captivated by the charming, young Indian maiden. However, much as John Rolfe loved Pocahontas, as he wrote Governor Dale in seeking his approval to marry her, he was uncertain about the reaction that his peers might have toward his marriage to the young Indian woman. Spanish colonials and French traders took Indian wives, but it was unheard of for an Englishman, especially a prominent citizen like John Rolfe, to wed a native woman in an official ceremony. Rolfe was uneasy in his own mind as to whether he was morally right in marrying an Indian maiden who recently had been a heathen. He wrote that he was motivated not "with the unbridled desire of carnal affection, but for the good of this plantation, for the honour of our countrie, for the glory of God, for my own salvation, and for the converting to the true knowledge of God and Jesus Christ, an unbeleeving creature, namely Pocahontas. To whom my hartie and best thoughts are and have a long time bin so intangled, and inthralled in so delicate a laborinth that I was even aweairied to unwind myself thereout." He thought that it was his moral and patriotic duty to save the soul of Pocahontas by marrying her, or so he told the governor.

Rolfe was about ten years older than his teenaged fiancée. He mused about the feelings that had provoked him "to be in love with one whose education hath bin rude, her manners barbarous, her generation accursed, and so discrepant in all nurtriture from my selfe." Yet his conscience would not let him refuse "to performe the duetie of a good Christian, pulling me about by the eare, and crying why dost not thou indevour to make her a Christian? . . . Likewise, adding hereunto her great appearance of love to me, her desire to be taught and instructed in the knowledge of God, her capablenesse of understanding, her aptnesse and willingnesse to receive anie good impression, and also the spirituall, besides her owne incitements stirring me hereunto." Rolfe would not be deterred from marrying Pocahontas by "the base feare of displeasing the world." He was in love and also believed it was his sacred duty to marry and teach this daughter of nature to become a devout Christian and proper English lady.

Governor Dale was proud of the conversion of Powhatan's daughter to Christianity and her adoption of English customs. He gave his permission for the marriage, which took place in the small wooden church in Jamestown on April 14, 1614. The governor attended, and Powhatan, who had given Rolfe his consent to the marriage, sent Pocahontas's uncle and two of her brothers to represent her family. The marriage ceremony was conducted by the minister at Jamestown, the Reverend Richard Bucke, a passenger on the ill-fated *Sea Venture*, who had come to Jamestown from Bermuda in 1610. His friend, John Rolfe, wrote that he was "a very good preacher."

A month after the marriage Sir Thomas Dale dispatched Ralph Hamor, accompanied by Indian guides carrying a bundle of gifts for Powhatan, on a mission to Werowocomoco to make a surprising proposal to the chieftain. Would Powhatan permit his youngest daughter, who was about twelve years old and known widely for her "exquisite perfection," to return with Hamor to live in Dale's household in Henrico, an act in the spirit of "brotherly friendship" that Powhatan professed? Her sister, Pocahontas, yearned to see her again, and Dale himself desired her. With Powhatan's consent, he foresaw making her "his neerest companion, wife, and bedfellow." Nothing was said about Dale's wife whom he had married in England before leaving for Virginia.

Dale declared that "the naturell union" would give firm assurance of "perpetuall friendship" between them, and he planned to dwell in "your country" as long as he lived. Powhatan's reply to Dales's message was that he had just sold her to another "great weroance," but, more importantly, he did not want to lose another daughter to the English. She was his favorite child, and if she were living with the English, he would not see her, because he had resolved "not to put himself into our hands."

Powhatan declared, Hamor reported, that there was no reason for Sir Thomas Dale to fear the Powhatans. "There have been too many of his men and my killed, and by my occasion there shall never be more. I, which have the power to perform it have said it: No, not though I should have just occasion offered, for I am now old and would gladly end my days in peace. So, as if the English offer me injury, my country is large enough; I will remove myself farther from you."

By chance, as Hamor was leaving Werowocomoco he ran into a colonist who had been captured by the Powhatans three years before. The Powhatans had told the English that he had become sick and died. The English captive pleaded with Hamor to ask Powhatan to set him free. Powhatan was very upset at Hamor's request. "You have one of my daughters with you, and I am therewith well content. But you can no sooner see or know of any Englishman's being with me but you must have him away or else break peace or friendship." He very reluctantly agreed to release the man, at the same time demanding a long list of items, including a large grindstone, a hundred fish hooks, and a dog and a cat, that his "brother" [Sir Thomas Dale] should send him in return. Hamor agreed, wrote down the list of articles in his table-book, and departed on friendly terms with the Powhatan chieftain, who gave the English men two white buckskins, two more for his "son and daughter," John Rolfe and Pocahontas, and food for their journey home.

Powhatan did indeed view his daughter's marriage as symbolizing a bond of friendship between his people and the English, and peaceful relations prevailed between the Powhatans and the colonists until the old chieftain died in 1618. The newly wedded couple lived for two years on Rolfe's plantation across the James from Henrico, and on January 30, 1615, Pocahontas gave birth to a son. They named him Thomas in honor of Sir Thomas Dale, his godfather.

When Dale decided to return to England in the spring of 1616, George Yeardley was appointed deputy governor of the colony. Dale was joined by the Rolfes and their infant son. According to her father's wishes, Pocahontas was accompanied by a retinue of a half dozen or so members of her tribe—a kinsman, one of Powhatan's counselors, and some female attendants. Powhatan had assigned his counselor, Uttamatomakin, to gather intelligence about the English and find out what had happened to John Smith. According to Pocahontas, the colonists in Virginia had told them that Smith was dead, but Powhatan didn't trust the word of the English. The party crossed the Atlantic on the *Treasurer*, commanded by Samuel Argall, the Jamestown captain who had taken Pocahontas captive earlier. It carried a cargo of tobacco, sassafras, pitch, potash, and cured sturgeon. They landed at Plymouth on May 31 and made their way to London, probably by coach, where Rolfe had business to conduct with the merchants handling Virginia's tobacco exports. Virginia tobacco was capturing the tobacco market in England from the Spanish shipments coming from the West Indies; some was also exported to Holland. In 1617 Virginia shipped 20,000 pounds to England.

When John Smith heard that Pocahontas had arrived in England, he wrote Queen Anne, the wife of King James, to inform her about her presence, her royal lineage, her courageous act to save Smith from execution, and other valiant deeds assisting the Virginia colony: "During the time of two or three yeeres, she next under God, was still the instrument to preserve this Colonie from death, famine, and utter confusion." Powhatan was the "chiefe King" of the Virginia Indians and Pocahontas was "the King's most deere and wel-beloved daughter." The main purpose of Smith's letter was to urge the royal court to receive her respectfully and honorably, as she so well deserved. For "if she should not be well received, seeing this Kingdome may rightly have a Kingdome by her meanes; her present love for us and Christianitie, might turne to such scorne and furie, as to divert all this good to the worst of evill." However, if "the Queen should doe her some honour," she would be so pleased that her influence would ensure the outcome the king and his subjects desired, a new colony ruled by England based on a lasting peace between the Indians and the English colonists.

Pocahontas was introduced to London society and feted as an honored guest. The Virginia Company presented her as the daughter of an Indian king, who had been civilized and converted to Christianity, a happening that would incite investor support for the Virginia colony. The company commissioned an engraved portrait of her by Simon Van de Passe, whose inscription, translated from Latin, read, "Matoaka, alias Rebecca, daughter of the most powerful prince of the Powhatan Empire of Virginia." Samuel Purchas, the writer and historian, wrote that she impressed people because "she carried

Pocahontas, daughter of Powhatan, became a Christian and took the name Rebecca. She married John Rolfe, the English colonist who introduced the commercial cultivation of tobacco in Virginia.
Courtesy of John Carter Brown Library at Brown University.

herself as the daughter of a king," and added that John King, the bishop of London, "entertained her with festivall state and pompe beyond what I have seen in his greate hospitalitie afforded to other ladies." She and Uttamato-makkin attended court where Lady Rebecca was presented to the king and queen by Lord De La Warr, the former governor of Virginia, and his lady. The Rolfes and Uttamatomakin also saw their majesties at a Twelfth Night masque performance at Whitehall Palace, written by Ben Jonson. Smith wrote that he had heard that it pleased their majesties "honourably to esteeme her." Uttamatomakin found King James to be so physically unprepossessing that he did not realize that he had seen the king. When he met Smith in London, Smith convinced him that he had indeed seen the king of England.

At some point during her visit to London, Pocahontas and her husband were staying at Brentford, a small town on the Thames about ten miles from London, possibly arranged by the bishop of London who maintained a residence there. John Smith with several friends went out to visit the woman who had saved his life when she was a young Indian teenager in Virginia. According to Smith, their first encounter after seven years got off to a chilly and unexpected start: "After a modest salutation, without any word, she turned about, obscured her face, as not seeming well contented." She may have been moved to see Smith again, for she had been told that he was dead. Smith and the others left her alone, until, after two or three hours passed, she was ready to talk to him.

Pocahontas said that she remembered him well and "the courtesies she had done." She recalled the mutual pledges of friendship between her father Powhatan and Smith. "You called him father, being in his land a stranger, and by the same reason so must I doe you." Smith replied that it would not be fitting for "she was a King's daughter." However, Pocahontas was insistent: "Were you not afraid to come into my fathers countrie, and caused fear in him and all his people (but mee) and feare you here I should call you father; I tell you then I will, and you shall call me childe, and so I will bee for ever and ever your Countrieman." Smith did not write any more about how they parted or seeing Pocahontas again. The meeting at Brentford was probably the last time these two legendary figures, who saved the first English colony in America, met.

In March 1617 Pocahontas and her family boarded a ship, again commanded by Captain Argall, to return to Virginia. Already sick before they departed from London, Pocahontas became gravely ill, probably from pneumonia. She was taken ashore at Gravesend at the mouth of the Thames, where she died and was buried at Saint George's church. According to her grieving husband, before she died Pocahontas declared that everyone must die, and it was enough that her child lived on. However, after leaving Gravesend, little Thomas became so ill that his father decided that it would be too risky for him to make the rough ocean crossing to Virginia. When Argall's ship put in at Plymouth before heading out into the Atlantic, John Rolfe arranged to leave young Thomas in the care of Sir Lewis Stukeley, the same gentleman who had taken the deposition about the incident involving Smith and the French men of war. Thomas later grew up in England in the household of his uncle, Henry Rolfe, a London merchant, and returned to Virginia when he reached manhood. He married and had many descendants who traced their roots back to his famous mother, who had played such a significant role in American history.

When John Rolfe and Samuel Argall, the newly appointed deputy governor of the colony, reached Jamestown in May 1617, Argall was dismayed to see that the palisades, church, and other buildings had fallen into disrepair. The settlers had become tobacco crazy, raising the leaf everywhere—outside the fort, on plantations up both sides of the James, and even in the streets and marketplace of Jamestown. The colony was becoming a one-crop economy. Tobacco farming was gobbling up huge amounts of land, mainly land that had belonged to the Powhatans. The tobacco culture spurred the expansion of the settlement area well beyond Jamestown and attracted growing numbers of immigrants. In 1618 Virginia again substantially increased its exports of tobacco to England and in turn imported large supplies of food.

Captain Argall was an excellent seaman, who had performed ably on expeditions to obtain fish and corn supplies for the colony, but he was a terrible governor. Martial law was still in effect in the colony, and the authoritative Argall forced many men to work on public projects. He enforced the laws with rigid discipline and harsh punishments, not just to keep good order, but to line his own pockets. After confiscating the public property of the colony for his own use, he illegally seized the property of an absent landlord. When the man's overseer objected, Argall had him arrested and sentenced him to death. Yielding to the pleas of other colony officers, Argall finally relented and exiled the fellow instead of executing him. The colony's morale was low, the settlers' spirits were broken, and a regime change was called for. Argall was ordered by the Virginia Company to resign his post and return to England to answer for his misconduct.

In April 1618 a ship carrying 200 colonists and Lord De La Warr sailed for Jamestown. The Virginia Company had granted De La Warr his wish to return to Virginia and resume his post as governor of the colony. Unfortunately, the vessel encountered adverse winds and rough weather, and De La Warr became ill and died. The ship struggled into Jamestown later. The new governor appointed by the company to replace De La Warr was Sir George Yeardley, who had been recently knighted by King James. He left England for Jamestown in January 1619. Yeardley, a veteran soldier of the Low Country wars, had sailed with Sir Thomas Gates for Virginia in 1609, been shipwrecked in Bermuda, and then reached Jamestown with Gates a year later. After Gates and Dale left Jamestown, he had been in charge as deputy governor of the colony for about a year before Argall's return in 1617; he had then returned to England.

The lives of some 400 Virginia colonists were changing in significant ways. In 1618 the Virginia Company, seeking to attract new settlers and keep older ones from leaving, offered fifty free acres of land to newcomers and an additional fifty acres for every person they brought with them, such as servants and workers, which enabled affluent colonists to develop sizable plantations. Those who had come to Virginia before 1616 received one hundred acres. Giving the colonists' ownership of their own property in order to build a stable and lasting community was exactly the idea that John Smith had proposed: "When our people were fed out of the common store, and laboured jointly together, glad was he who could slip from his labour, or slumber over his taske; nay, the most honest among them would hardly take so much true paines in a week, as now for them selves they will do in a day."

The building of a successful economy would be based on private, not collective, enterprise. Many English families yearned to own their own land. To acquire free land in Virginia, which offered the promising opportunity to prosper, was an appealing proposition for ambitious and daring young Englishmen who could pay for their voyage. Ships were now bringing a stream of new immigrants, mainly indentured laborers who needed free passage, to work for the landlords, old and new, on the spreading tobacco plantations. In 1619 a Dutch ship sold twenty Africans from Angola to plantation owners. Although this group was treated as indentured servants, later shipments of Africans to Virginia led to the introduction of slavery in an English colony for the first time. The consequences of this practice would divide the nation bitterly for years to come.

There were only a few English women in Jamestown, and the Virginia Company now recognized that it was important to establish communities occupied by families to ensure the colony's future growth. To remedy this situation, the company sent over fifty "young and uncorrupted maids," in the words of the company, providing testimonials regarding each girl's behavior and background. The girls were in their late teens and twenties, and many were orphans; the company provided them with clothing and bedding for their voyage and life in Virginia. Settlers wanting a wife paid the Virginia Company 150 pounds of fine tobacco, and the girls all found husbands quickly.

Sir Edwin Sandys, a major investor in the Virginia Company, was its new treasurer, replacing Sir Thomas Smythe, who had largely directed the company's policies regarding Virginia for the last twelve years. The more liberal-minded Sandys had quite different plans for its future management. Sir George Yeardley arrived in April 1619 with a package of instructions from the company that reflected its determination to correct the abuses of Argall's tyrannical regime. A number of colonists who had been forced to labor on public projects like Henrico during Argall's and Dale's governorships were released from that involuntary duty. Yeardley abolished the harsh military laws that Sir Thomas Dale had put in place and introduced English common law. With the end of the communal economic system, individual properties were assigned to the colonists to own and farm in accord with the new company policy. In 1618 the Virginia Company had issued a new charter of governance for the Virginia colony, providing for a governor, six councilors of state, and a General Assembly, which consisted of twenty elected burgesses, two from each of ten designated settlements. Jamestown was the capital of the colony. On July 30, 1619, Governor Yeardley convened the first legislative body in America in the Jamestown church—the Virginia General Assembly, which came to be known as the House of Burgesses. The Virginia Company had not intended to form a truly democratic system of governance. The laws passed by the Assembly could be vetoed by the governor or by the company in London. However, months would pass with a new law in effect before a London veto message could be returned to Jamestown, given the time required for communication. The new

Sir Edwin Sandys, succeeded Sir Thomas Smythe as the Virginia Company's treasurer. He instructed the colony's governor, Sir George Yeardley, to establish the Virginia General Assembly, the first elected legislative body in America.
Courtesy of the Library of Virginia.

laws dealt largely with local issues: to provide Indians with any kind of English dog was forbidden; to furnish them with guns, ammunition, or other arms was punishable by hanging; on Sundays everyone was required to "frequent divine service and sermons, both forenoon and afternoon." Popular representative government, although limited, had come to America.

When George Yeardley had served as interim governor of the colony for a year following the departure of Governor Dale in 1616, a group of colonial officers later wrote that it was a time of "peace and the best plenty ever it had until that time." And so it was during his later tour as governor for over two years. The reforms in governance and land ownership were popular, increasing food production and spurring the development of new plantations along the James. Yeardley developed his own plantation on the south side of the James, which was named "Flowerdew Hundred." His wife had arrived in Jamestown on the *Faulcon* in 1609 and was one of the few survivors of the "Starving Time." Her charming maiden name was Temperance Flowerdew. The plantation produced tobacco, corn, and livestock and installed the first windmill in Virginia.

However, relations with the Powhatans, as one colonist put it, were based on "fear without love, for such help as we have had from them have been procured by sword or trade." Many colonists continued to die from disease, and some were slain by Indians. Despite the many hundreds of new arrivals, by April 1620 the population of the colony was only 866 persons.

Thomas Hunt, the captain of the other ship accompanying Smith to Maine in 1614, had cruised down the coast before making the crossing to Spain with his cargo of fish. Near Plymouth, Hunt enticed some two-dozen Indians to come aboard his vessel under the pretense of wishing to trade for beaver skins. His crew then seized them, took them prisoner, and Captain Hunt set sail for Spain, where he sold his captives in the slave market in Malaga. Smith was furious at Hunt for acting "most inhumanely and dishonestly," and Sir Ferdinando Gorges agreed: "One Hunt (a worthless fellow of our nation) set out by certaine Merchants for love of gaine; who (not content with the commoditie he had by fish, and peaceable trade he found among the Savages) . . . and was ready to set saile, (more savage-like than they) seized upon the poore innocent creatures, that in confidence of his honestie had put themselves into his hands." Smith observed that Hunt's vile act banned him from employment in the region afterward. He also forecast that it would "move their hate against our Nation" and make his plans for colonization in New England much more difficult. He was right: The Nauset and Pokanoket tribes in the Cape Cod area were enraged by the kidnapping of their people, and English and French ships wishing to trade for furs were no longer welcomed. In 1617 the Indians seized and burned a shipwrecked French ship and killed most of the crew; a few were spared to become slaves of the Nauset tribe.

One of Hunt's Indian prisoners was Tisquantum, who would later be known as Squanto. He was a member of the Patuxet tribe from the Plymouth area, which belonged to the Pokanoket confederation of tribes in Massachusetts and eastern Rhode Island. When Hunt sold his Indian captives in the Malaga slave market, local monks took some to their monastery, including Squanto, to instruct them in the Christian faith. Squanto was naturally eager to find a way to go home, and in time the friars released him and he made his way to London, where he ended up living in the Corn Hill section with John Slainey, a merchant and treasurer of the Newfoundland Company. Squanto learned to speak English, and later on, recognizing Squanto's potential usefulness to the company, Slainey shipped him off on a Bristol fishing vessel to the company's base in Newfoundland. Cuper's Cove in Newfoundland was an English settlement and fishing base founded in 1610 by John Guy, a Bristol merchant, with a company of thirty-nine men, under a charter from James I. It was the second permanent English colony started in North America. More settlers including women arrived in subsequent supply ships. It was probably in Cuper's Cove that Squanto met Thomas Dermer, a ship captain who had sailed with John Smith on his aborted second expedition in 1615. Smith described him as an "an understanding and industrious gentleman." Dermer, who worked for Sir Ferdinando Gorges, wrote Gorges noting Squanto's value as an interpreter and guide for English expeditions to New England. Gorges agreed and instructed him to bring Squanto back to England to make further plans.

In the spring of 1619 Gorges dispatched Captain Dermer, armed with John Smith's map and accompanied by Squanto, on an exploratory expedition to New England. Making their landfall in Maine, probably at Monhegan Island, they sailed down the coast in a small boat to the Cape Cod area. Dermer and Squanto were shocked at what they saw. The coastal Indians from Maine to Rhode Island were virtually all gone, their villages uninhabited, with just the bleached bones of the dead lying about. In 1616 a terrible epidemic, small pox or the bubonic plague, brought to their shores by European fishermen, had decimated the native population, which lacked immunity from European diseases. Thousands had died over the next three years, leaving only a small number of survivors. After five years Squanto finally made it back to his home at Patuxet near present-day Plymouth, so named by Prince Charles on Smith's map of New England. When Squanto had been taken captive and brought to Spain, Patuxet had been a thriving community with gardens and fields of corn, beans, and tobacco. Now his village was abandoned, a ghost town; virtually all of his Patuxet tribe and relatives had been wiped out by the plague.

Sir Ferdinando Gorges had assigned another task to Thomas Dermer—to foster good relations with the Massachusetts Indians who were still furious and vengeful at the English over the disgraceful Hunt kidnapping incident. Squanto introduced him to Massasoit, the chief of the Pokanoket tribes, and Epinow, who had leapt overboard from an English vessel at Martha's Vineyard to gain his freedom and was now the sachem of the Martha's Vineyard Nauset tribe. The initial contacts apparently went smoothly as Dermer negotiated the release of two of the French sailors that had been captured earlier by the Indians. The appearance of peaceful relations, however, was illusory. Dermer went on to Jamestown for the winter, and in his letter of December 29, 1619, to Sir Ferdinando Gorges he spoke of the Pokanokets' "inveterate malice to the English." They reported that an English captain had enticed some of their people on board his ship and then slaughtered them in cold blood with a ship's gun firing small bullets.

Along with some twenty Pokanokets that Captain Hunt had captured and sold into slavery, he had taken seven Nausets. When Dermer returned the next summer to Cape Cod and Martha's Vineyard, he and his men were frequently attacked. Squanto came to assist his English friend—to no avail. Only Dermer, badly wounded, and one man survived an assault by Epinow's warriors on Martha's Vineyard. They sailed back to Jamestown where Dermer died. Massasoit may have feared that Squanto had become too closely allied with the English and planned to undermine his leadership of the Pokanokets. Not trusting Squanto, he decided to hold him captive in the headquarters village of the Pokanokets on the shore off Narragansett Bay. In the fall of 1620 Squanto was only months away from playing a central role in the founding of the Plymouth Plantation.

Dermer, who had visited the Plymouth area with Squanto before he died, believed that it would be a fine location to establish a colony. In his letter to Gorges, referring to the place "which in Captain Smith's map is called Plymouth," he stated, "I would that the first plantation might hear be seated, if ther come to the number of 50 persons, or upwards." William Bradford, the Pilgrim leader, received a copy of the Dermer letter from Gorges from which he quotes in his book, *Of Plymouth Plantation*. Gorges may well have given the letter to Bradford when the Pilgrims passed through Plymouth in England before their departure for America.

· *14* ·

The Leiden Separatists

$\mathcal{B}$y the time he was a teenager, William Bradford, son of a yeoman farmer in Yorkshire, had acquired a deep knowledge and belief in the teachings of the Bible. In the early 1600s he began attending secret Sunday meetings for worship and discussion with a group of men known as Separatists, which took place in the house of William Brewster in the nearby village of Scrooby in Nottinghamshire. Like their fellow Puritans, the Separatists objected to the policies and practices of the Church of England, which they felt too closely followed traditional and elaborate rituals similar to the "popery" that England had abandoned. They preferred a more simple service in which the Bible was the basis of their worship; the Book of Common Prayer was unnecessary. They believed that the church needed purification from widespread corruption, and they opposed the hierarchical control imposed by the bishops on individual congregations.

William Bradford wrote that the Scrooby Separatists protested against the "base and beggarly ceremonies" retained by the church and enforced on the clergy and congregations by the "lordly and tyrannous power of the prelates." The ecclesiastical "offices and callings, courts and canons were unlawful and unChristian and had no warrant in the Word of God." The Separatists differed from the other Puritans in one important way—their goal was not simply to purify the Church of England. Because they vehemently opposed the authority of the state or Church of England to govern their worship of God, they chose to separate themselves completely from the official church. Accordingly, their members, including the little Scrooby congregation, secretly formed their own churches that were entirely independent of the Church of England.

King James was not pleased with the Puritans and Separatists, declaring that if they did not conform, he would "harry them out of the land, or else do worse." Separatists were harassed, others imprisoned, and in Scrooby some citizens scorned and ridiculed them. Fearing persecution by the church and royal authorities, the Scrooby Separatists decided to flee to Holland, where everyone was free to worship as they chose. However, they lacked the official license to emigrate required by law. In 1607 their first secret attempt to leave failed when their English ship captain betrayed them and turned them over to the local customs officers. When their leaders were released from jail they tried again. In several trips that fall and the following year the band of about 125 Scrooby Separatists made their way to Amsterdam, where they all were happily reunited.

In 1609, upset by the quarrels between two existing Separatist congregations in Amsterdam, the Scrooby members elected to move on to the smaller town of Leiden, noted for its fine university, where they would conduct their own affairs with complete independence. By and large they were devout people of high moral character and strong self-discipline, who were ready to work hard to achieve their goals. Their common love for their church and faith in God united them in mutual loyalty in a strange and foreign land. These traits served them well when the simple English farmers were forced to turn to other means of employment in their new home. They became engaged in various trades, especially in producing fabrics and small articles of clothing.

The Scrooby Separatists were fortunate in having able leaders who inspired their respect and loyalty: John Robinson, a Cambridge graduate, had been a Church of England clergyman before becoming a Separatist and minister of the Scrooby congregation. He was their beloved spiritual leader. William Brewster had been an aide to a senior state official and later the postmaster of Scrooby, before becoming the lay leader and elder of the new church. Fifty-three years old, Brewster was the oldest member of the Separatist group and esteemed as its senior advisor. He had a small business printing Puritan books in Leiden. Edward Winslow was a bright, well-educated young English gentleman. William Bradford was a serious student, competent in handling the practical business of the church, and already showing the mark of a leader at the young age of twenty when the congregation moved to Leiden. He was employed in a cloth-making business in Leiden and married Dorothy May, who later gave birth to their son, John.

After living in Holland for about a decade, many members of the Scrooby group in Leiden became uneasy about staying on. Their future in Holland looked bleak; they felt like exiles living in a foreign country. They would always remain English men and women and were concerned about their children's future if they stayed in Holland. They worried that they would not receive a proper education. They feared that their offspring would be tempted to adopt the more liberal lifestyle of the Dutch, forget their

English heritage, and lose the spiritual faith that guided the lives of their parents. Some older ones had already been "drawn away by evil examples into extravagant and dangerous courses," wrote William Bradford. Indeed, it was quite possible that their congregation would break up and be dispersed in time. Others found it difficult to make a living and avoid poverty; it took long days of hard work at low wages to survive in Leiden. Some felt uncomfortable living in the large and bustling city. Bradford wrote that the Scrooby folk had been "used to a plaine countrie life and the innocent trade of husbandry" before coming to Holland. Finally, Holland did not seem a fertile ground for spreading their Christian faith. Edward Winslow wrote, "How little we do or were like to do to the Dutch in reforming the Sabbath." The Leiden Separatists yearned to spread the gospel message, and America was a promising place to start. They would be free to worship as they pleased and also serve the Lord as missionaries in bringing the church of Christ to the heathen natives of the New World.

The first step of the Leiden leaders was to send two emissaries to London, John Carver, a church deacon, who had formerly prospered in business in London, and Robert Cushman, who had been a grocer in Canterbury before joining the Leiden Separatists in 1609. Their mission was to consult about their plans with Sir Edwin Sandys, the acting treasurer of the Virginia Company. Sandys, a prominent investor in the Virginia Company, knew the Brewster family and was favorably inclined toward the Leiden group. The plan of the Leiden representatives was to obtain a patent from the Virginia Company to establish a plantation in America, solicit the support of investors to back the project, and obtain King James's permission to worship in America according to their beliefs. Sandys persuaded a friend in court to take the matter up with King James, but the king and his bishops were unwilling to officially make this concession. Nevertheless, the king let the petitioners know that he would not stand in the way of their plans as long as they conducted themselves peacefully. He was told that the emigrants would earn a profit for investors through fishing. "So God have my soul," said the king. "'Tis an honest trade; 'twas the apostles' own calling." After some delay the company granted the Leiden group a patent to start a settlement. However, new developments steered the Separatists down a different path.

Thomas Weston, a London merchant, was a member of the Merchant Adventurers of London, an association of some seventy merchants and investors. *Adventurers* was the term commonly used referring to investors at the time. When Weston, a smooth-talking business promoter eager to make large profits, learned of the Separatists' emigration plans, he went over to Leiden to offer his group's cooperation to them. In February 1619 a Weston associate, John Pierce, had obtained a patent from the Virginia Company for a settlement near the mouth of the Hudson River that the Leiden Separatists could use. The Leiden leaders, frustrated by the long delays, accepted the Weston group's proposal to provide the bulk of the capital to fund the necessary supplies and outfit a ship for their voyage. The new colony, unlike Jamestown and Popham, would have two distinct parents—the businessmen seeking a profitable investment and the devout pilgrims seeking a new home for their families where they could worship freely and spread the gospel to others. Unlike the earlier venturers, the Leiden folk were not interested in seeking a short passage to Asia or fortune hunters intent on finding gold and silver. Despite a promising beginning, however, the two parties soon quarreled over the financial terms of the agreement.

A joint stock company would be formed. While most of the capital would come from the Weston group, each emigrant would receive one share for their work contribution and another share if they put up ten pounds. The Merchant Adventurers drove a hard bargain, proposing that all revenues from fishing, fur trading, and other activities plus all the assets of the colony be placed in a common fund that would be distributed to the stockholders, largely the Adventurers, after seven years. The colonists' obligation to the Adventurers would then be extinguished. However, the Leiden leaders refused to accept these terms in that form. They argued that it was not fair or wise for the settlers' houses and gardens to be included in the common fund for later distribution. Furthermore, they insisted that the settlers be required to work for the company just four days a week, not six as proposed by the London investors.

In 1619 the Leiden Separatists received the news of the tragic voyage to Virginia of a Separatist group of emigrants from the Amsterdam Church led by Francis Blackwell, a church elder. The ship was far too small for the 180 passengers packed away on board. Northwest winds blew them far off course. They ran out of fresh food and water, and disease brought on by the unhealthy, overcrowded conditions spread throughout the vessel, killing Blackwell, the captain, and a half-dozen crewmembers. The ship drifted about for days, out of control. When it finally reached Jamestown, only fifty people were left alive. The news was terribly disheartening to the Leiden folk planning their own departure for America.

The perilous voyage to a new unknown land was not for the faint of heart. Some also became discouraged by the frustrating delay in arranging their transport and difficulties in selling their goods and properties in Leiden. The Separatists, with meager resources, were almost completely dependent on Weston's Merchant Adventurers to fund their passage to America. The dominating influence of the Adventurers in the relationship gave rise to friction between the two parties on various matters, especially the terms of employment proposed by the Adventurers and coordinating the purchase of provisions for the expedition. Christopher Martin, the purchasing agent appointed by the Adventurers, was an arrogant and domineering fellow who refused to cooperate with John Carver and Robert Cushman, the Leiden agents in England.

Some Separatists changed their minds about leaving Leiden. Others dropped out from the first contingent planning to depart, preferring to join the next boatload of emigrants that would leave after the new settlement had been built. While most of the Separatists would remain in Leiden, many of them hoped to come over later. As the time of departure approached in the summer of 1620, around fifty Separatists were ready to go, including elder Brewster and a few others who had gone over to London and would meet their fellow voyagers later; Brewster would be the congregation's spiritual guide. Thirty-year-old William Bradford was also in the departing group. He and Dorothy decided to leave their little son, John, in Leiden for the time being. The Leidenites' wise and revered pastor, John Robinson, would stay in Leiden to lead his flock; he hoped to join his brethren in America as soon as he could. Miles Standish also joined the emigrants with his wife Rose. The thirty-six-year-old veteran soldier had fought the Spaniards in the Netherlands during Queen Elizabeth's reign and then settled in Leiden; he would be in charge of the military company that would be formed to defend the colony. In addition to the Leiden Separatists, Weston had recruited his own group of some seventy emigrants, mainly from London, to join the company bound for America. The Leiden folk called them the "Strangers" and worried how they would all get along. Some were rough and profane common laborers; others were sympathetic to the Puritan cause.

Early that summer the Adventurers chartered the *Mayflower* to carry the emigrants to America. It was a square-rigged, 180-ton ship, about a hundred feet long with a twenty-six-foot beam and a twelve-foot draft. Its experienced master, Captain Christopher Jones, had engaged it in the wine trade with France for a number of years. Around the same time the Separatists, using the proceeds from selling their Leiden properties, bought the sixty-ton *Speedwell*, a small vessel less than half the size of the *Mayflower*. The *Speedwell*, carrying the Leiden company, would meet the *Mayflower* with its passengers from London at Southampton on England's southern coast. The plan was for the two ships to make the voyage to America together. The *Speedwell* was fitted out with two tall, new masts to increase her speed under sail. Her crew then docked her at the port of Delft Haven to await the arrival of the Leiden voyagers.

The day before the travelers left Leiden was devoted to a service of worship led by pastor Robinson, who gave a stirring farewell sermon. Despite his hopes, he would never join his comrades in America; they did not know that they were hearing him preach for the last time. The next morning the departing travelers boarded the canal barges that took them to Delft Haven, accompanied by their companions who had come to see them off. William Bradford wrote: "So they left that goodly and pleasant city which had been their resting place for nearly twelve years, but they knew they were pilgrims, and looked not much on those things, but lift up their eyes to the heavens, their dearest country, and quieted their spirits." Bradford said it best—he and his comrades were pilgrims pursuing their quest for religious freedom in a faraway land.

The *Speedwell* sailed from Delft Haven on July 22. On the vessel's deck before it left, pastor Robinson fell to his knees along with the assembled Pilgrims and led them in prayers invoking the Lord's blessings on their brave enterprise. The parting scene at the quayside was sad and mournful, filled with tearful goodbyes. Some husbands were parting from their wives, and some parents were leaving their children behind—to join them later. As the ship sailed away the voyagers fired a volley of musket fire and cannon shots in bidding a final farewell to their friends on shore.

In Southampton the Leiden Pilgrims joined the group that had come from London on the *Mayflower*. Some were old friends—elder William Brewster and his wife and two sons and deacon John Carver and his wife. Some of the newcomers would play important roles in establishing the Pilgrim settlement in America. Stephen Hopkins along with his pregnant wife, Elizabeth, and children were members of the group enlisted by the Adventurers; they were accompanied by two servants. Hopkins had already been to America. He had been with Sir Thomas Gates on the ill-fated voyage that ended in a shipwreck on the reefs of Bermuda. He went on with Gates to Jamestown for two years before returning to England. John Alden, a twenty-one-year-old cooper, was hired by the expedition in Southampton.

The Jamestown veteran and New England explorer, Captain John Smith, was still desperately eager to embark on a new colonization venture and was very annoyed that the Pilgrims had not invited him to join them. Smith believed that his firsthand experience in starting a colony and knowledge of the coastal region would make him the perfect guide for the Pilgrims in avoiding the pitfalls that snared the unwary; he had shown his military and diplomatic skills in dealing successfully with the Indians to protect the Jamestown colonists. In his book published later, he spoke of the Pilgrims' "humorous ignorances . . . saying that my books and maps were much better cheape to teach them, than myself." The Pilgrims may have feared that Smith's strong and self-assured personality would lead him to dominate their enterprise. Smith would want to be in command. He simply would not fit in harmoniously among these modest and peaceful servants of the Lord living in

Pastor John Robinson led the Pilgrims in shipboard prayer when they left Holland in 1620 to start a new home in America, where they would be free to worship as they chose. Library of Congress, Prints and Photographs Division.

a deeply religious community. Furthermore, they liked their choice of Miles Standish to be their military leader.

Thomas Weston had come to Southampton to conclude business arrangements between the Merchant Adventurers and the Pilgrims before their departure. He was extremely displeased to learn that the Pilgrims had rejected the terms of the proposed contract regarding the future ownership of the colonists' houses and the number of days they would work for the company. Weston stomped off angrily, declaring, "They must then looke to stand on their own legs." He meant it and refused to provide one hundred pounds to pay some outstanding bills of the expedition. The voyagers were forced to raise the needed funds by selling some provisions, including part of their ample store of butter. In an effort to placate the Adventurers and sustain good relations with them, the Pilgrim leaders wrote them on August 3, stating, "that if large profits should not arise within seven years, that we will continue together longer with you"—in other words, a pledge by the Pilgrims to continue the profit-sharing arrangement under certain conditions beyond the contract's termination date.

The leaders completed the final plans for the long voyage ahead, appointing a governor and assistants for each ship and dividing the company between the two vessels—ninety persons were assigned to the *Mayflower*, whose governor would be the Adventurers' agent, Christopher Martin, and thirty to the smaller *Speedwell*. When all was ready, the two ships left Southampton, and after clearing the Isle of Wight they entered the English Channel and headed west toward Land's End and the Atlantic Ocean. They did not go far before the master of the *Speedwell* reported that his ship was leaking badly. The vessel was overmasted, and the faster she went under full sail, the more she leaked. The two ships had to put into Dartmouth, where the *Speedwell* was overhauled at the dockyard and repaired. The vessels resumed their voyage.

However, the *Speedwell* was beyond repair for an ocean voyage. About 300 miles west of Land's End the vessel was leaking so much that the leaders concluded that, even with steady pumping, it was too dangerous to continue. Both ships returned to the port of Plymouth, where all agreed that the *Speedwell* was not seaworthy or safe enough to make the ocean crossing. The *Mayflower* would proceed without her, and some of the Pilgrims would have to be left behind. There was not enough room for everyone on the already crowded *Mayflower*. After over a month of uncomfortable living on board their small ship without even leaving England, and the mishaps that they had endured, some were glad to give up their places. One was Robert Cushman, who had become extremely pessimistic about the venture's prospects. Eighteen passengers, including the Cushman family, left the expedition at Plymouth, and the remaining twelve from the *Speedwell* boarded the overcrowded *Mayflower*.

In addition to the ship's crew of thirty, there were now 102 passengers on board—thirty-five Leiden Separatists, including a handful that joined in London, and the larger group of Strangers from London, recruited by Weston. From now on history would know them all as Pilgrims. William Bradford wrote, "These troubles being blown over, and now all being compact together in one ship, they put to sea again with a prosperous wind." On September 6 the *Mayflower* set sail across the North Atlantic, and this time there would be no turning back.

Twenty-nine of the passengers were women, with a half dozen or so small children, and many passengers succumbed to seasickness from the constant pitch and roll of the ship as it bucked the never-ending waves. The "prosperous" winds held up until the *Mayflower* was about halfway across the ocean, and then the voyagers' good luck ran out. Fierce storms and gales buffeted the vessel so severely that one of the main midship beams was dislodged, which so alarmed some that they considered turning back. Fortunately, a passenger had brought a giant iron screw from Holland, which enabled the crew to replace the beam. They also caulked the leaking topside decks as best they could. The winds were so overpowering some days that it became necessary to take down all the sails and let the ship be driven freely by the gales. The *Mayflower* pressed on: Captain Jones knew his ship was sound and had confidence in its ability to weather the storms and reach their destination safely.

The Atlantic crossing of the Mayflower, *sailing through fierce storms and gales, took sixty-five days.*
Library of Congress, Prints and Photographs Division, Detroit Publishing Company Collection.

As the storm raged outside, one can imagine the wretched conditions that the passengers endured, huddled in the oppressive, damp, and crowded cabin, their bedding and clothing wet from sea waves pounding over the ship. Their misery was compounded by their fear of the dangers that they would face in an unknown new land. When John Howland, traveling with the Carver family, ventured on deck, probably to get a breath of fresh air after days of confinement in the stifling atmosphere of the cabin, he was tossed overboard by the lurching ship. Fortunately for him a topsail halyard had fallen overboard and was trailing behind the ship. Howland, a strong young man, grabbed it and hung on for dear life, even as he was dragged under water. The crew hauled him back on board with the aid of a boat hook. Howland survived to become a successful citizen in the community and lived until 1673. One crewmember and one passenger, a servant for Samuel Fuller, died during the ocean crossing, and Elizabeth Hopkins gave birth to a baby girl, appropriately named Oceanus.

Around daybreak on November 9 the Pilgrims to their great joy spotted the sandy highlands on the outer shore of Cape Cod. The Pierce patent obtained from the Virginia Company only gave the Pilgrims the right to establish a colony near the mouth of the Hudson River. The leaders consulted, and then the *Mayflower*, under a favorable north wind, sailed south down the outer shore of the cape heading for the Hudson River, some 220 miles away. Captain Jones was unfamiliar with the waters of the region. After about a thirty-mile run to the southern elbow of the cape, in midafternoon the *Mayflower* ran into the treacherous stretch of water that runs south to the northern tip of Nantucket. At Pollock Rip, as the area is known today, strong tidal currents and winds race between Nantucket Sound and the ocean through shoals and shifting ridges of sand. William Bradford described the perilous situation the Pilgrims faced: "They fell amongst dangerous shoals and roaring breakers, and they were so far entangled therewith as they conceived them selves in great danger." In a while the wind died down, and then, fortunately, it shifted around to the south, enabling the *Mayflower* to break free from the threatening disaster.

Captain Jones and the Pilgrim leaders were greatly relieved to escape the perilous waters. They now decided that undertaking the voyage to the Hudson was too dangerous. It was late in the year with winter weather approaching, and a number of passengers were weak and ill from disease. After sixty-five days at sea in a rough and frightening ocean crossing, they had already suffered enough. The *Mayflower* anchored that night off the cape and the next day retraced its course up the shore, around the northern tip of Cape Cod, and anchored in the protected waters of today's Provincetown Harbor, which the Pilgrims named Cape Cod Harbor. Despite the obstacles they had faced, the 102 Pilgrims, now safely anchored, had survived their harrowing voyage remarkably well. One colonist had died, and a baby had been born, so their number remained the same as when they had left Plymouth. There were now thirty-four men, eighteen wives, twenty-eight young men, women, and children under twenty-one, nineteen male servants and workers, and three female servants. "Being thus arrived in a good harbour, and brought safe to land, they fell upon their knees and blessed the Lord in Heaven," wrote Bradford; however, there were earthly matters that demanded their urgent attention before they went ashore.

The Pilgrim's patent from the Virginia Company for the Hudson River location did not apply to New England, which fell under another patent jurisdiction. When the passengers learned that they would now build their new home in New England, some of the London Strangers argued that because there was no longer any legal authority governing them, they were free to do as they pleased. Bradford wrote of their "discontented and mutinous speeches" boasting that when they went ashore "they would use their own liberty, for none had power to command them." John Robinson, the Pilgrims' pastor and mentor in Holland, had written a farewell letter to the Leiden voyagers in Southampton before their departure in August. Recognizing that they were joining a group of strangers, he admonished the Pilgrims to be careful not to give or easily take offense when dealing with the differences that might arise among them. They must become "a body politic, using amongst yourselves a civil government" that would choose its officials and pay them "all due honour and obedience in their lawful administrations." It was time to carry out Robinson's sound advice.

The Leiden leaders, fearing that the Strangers' threats could lead to disorder and even the breakup of the community, summoned all the men (including several close family servants, but not hired laborers) to the main cabin of the ship. The purpose of the meeting was to obtain everyone's agreement to a compact defining the authority for governing the colony. The malcontents were persuaded to give up their rebellious ideas, and on November 11, 1620, all the assembled company of forty-one persons signed the document, known as the Mayflower Compact. The signatories all pledged to "combine our selves together into a civill body politick" that would have the authority to pass "such just and equall lawes, ordinances, acts, constitutions and offices . . . as shall be thought most meete and convenient for the general good of the Colonie, under which we promise all due submission and obedience." Despite their determination to worship God in their own way, the Pilgrims were proud Englishmen and loyal subjects of their king. They were simply responding to the critical need to establish their own governing body in their new home.

The Pilgrims chose John Carver to be their governor for the next year. He was one of the senior and most respected members of the colony. He had been a deacon of the church in Holland, and pastor John Robinson, the leader of the congregation, had relied on him to carry out important tasks. He had served as the Separatists' principal agent in London in raising funds and making arrangements for their migration to America. Carver, probably the wealthiest member of the Pilgrims, had contributed generously to funding the voyage; he was accompanied by his wife, Katherine, who was Robinson's sister, five employees, and a child. Of the forty-one colonists signing the compact, only seventeen were members of the Leiden Separatists. To vote as they did, Christopher Martin and the other emigrants from the London Adventurers group must have been well impressed by the guidance and capability of Carver and the Leiden leaders in the course of the voyage. John Carver, William Bradford, Edward Winslow, and William Brewster were the first four to sign the Mayflower Compact.

In 1619, after years of autocratic rule by appointed governors, the Virginia Assembly had been established, empowering elected representatives of the colonists to enact laws governing the colony. Now the New England Pilgrims had formed their own governing body with a similar purpose. Thus the first English settlers in America, far across the ocean from their mother country, had recognized the need to form institutions to govern themselves under the rule of law and had chosen popular representative government as the means to this end. The introduction of local representative government in the English colonies was a historic first step on the path to winning their independence many years later.

• 15 •

The Plymouth Plantation

The most urgent task facing the Pilgrims was to scout the area to locate the most suitable place to build their settlement. Colony planners usually liked to locate their settlements near large, navigable rivers, such as the James, Kennebec, and Hudson. We are told that William Brewster had a copy of Smith's book, *A Description of New-England*, and his map of the New England coast. If he did, the Pilgrims chose to ignore it. The Charles River, flowing into a fine harbor and Massachusetts Bay some forty miles to the north, was clearly shown on John Smith's map. It was a location that would attract a stream of English colonists a decade later. It was already quite cold, however, time was running out before winter set in, and a number of the Pilgrims were sick and suffering, especially the women and children. The Pilgrims liked their snug harbor. It was a good base from which to explore the inner shore of Cape Cod Bay to find a good place to settle.

The sections of a shallop, a thirty-five-foot sailboat brought over on the *Mayflower*, had been battered by the Atlantic gales, and it would take some time for the carpenters to repair and assemble it. On November 13, after rowing ashore in the long boat, a well-armed party of sixteen men led by Miles Standish and William Bradford set off on foot to explore the local terrain. Other passengers, including women, went ashore to gather firewood, wash, and bathe, "as they had great need." The outing must have boosted everyone's morale after the close conditions that they had endured, although many suffered later from colds and worse from wading in frigid water across the mud flats to reach shore.

The Pilgrims had spotted what appeared to be a small river several miles to the south. After walking down the beach about a mile toward it they saw six Indians and a dog coming toward them. When the Indians saw the white men wearing armor and armed with muskets, they immediately fled. Standish's men followed them, hoping to initiate good relations with their future neighbors and obtain information about the area; they followed their footprints in the sand down the shore, but they could not catch them. The colonists camped out that night, lighting a fire, dining on biscuits and Holland cheese, and posting three sentinels. Nor did they find the Indians the next day. However, they did reach a cleared area where the natives had planted their corn, and further on some Indian graves, the remains of a house, a European kettle, and a man-made heap. They dug open the heap and found baskets full of fresh Indian corn. They loaded as much as they could carry and took it with them. The Pilgrims needed a good supply of seed corn for the planting season. They wanted to compensate the Indians for the corn that they had taken, and they tried to approach them when they saw two canoes some ways away, but the Indians kept their distance.

They continued to survey the terrain and came across the ruins of a small-palisaded fort near today's Truro, built in the European style and probably constructed by Martin Pring in 1603. In walking down a narrow trail, William Bradford triggered a contrivance that suddenly jerked up and caught him by a line pulled tight around his leg. It was a cleverly designed Indian deer trap, and Bradford admired it as a "very pretty device," artfully made of strong rope. After spending another night on the ground, the Pilgrims walked to the bay shore, where they noted the mouth of a small river, the Pamet, before returning to the ship.

When the work on the shallop was completed ten days later, a party of thirty-four, including ten sailors led by Captain Jones, embarked to explore the river that the first party had discovered. Powerful, adverse winds prevented the shallop from progressing far the first day, and it started to snow heavily. Some of the party went ashore, where they spent a bitterly cold and snowy night. The next day the shallop picked them up, and they sailed south to the river's harbor. It was deep enough for boats but not navigable for ships as big as the *Mayflower*. The party trudged four or five miles up and down hills through six inches of snow to explore the main creek flowing into the river, until a weary Captain Jones called a halt. They picked a spot to pass the night, and some went hunting. Their luck changed: they shot three geese and six ducks for their supper, "which we eate with souldiers stomicks, for we had eaten little all that day."

The next day they hiked to the place where they had found the Indians' corn earlier, and they helped themselves to the rest. Digging with their short swords and cutlasses nearby they found more corn, baskets of wheat, and a bag of beans. Jones and a few men who were ill returned to the ship with the food. The bushels of corn they had taken plus what they had obtained before would provide them with a sufficient supply of seed. Eighteen men elected to stay another day, hoping to meet some Indians that they could pay for the corn. In exploring the woods the next day they came across an Indian grave, which they opened, disclosing two corpses, a European man and an Indian boy, and some articles. "We brought sundry of the prettiest things away with us." A little later they discovered two native houses, filled with pots, crab shell baskets, an English bucket, and other household items. Again the Pilgrims seized some articles that they fancied, before returning to Cape Cod Harbor in the shallop. The Pilgrims intended to reimburse the natives for the things they had taken, and they desperately needed the seed corn. Still, it was not a promising way for the foreigners to introduce themselves to their new neighbors.

The Pilgrims debated whether Cold Harbor, the name they had given the Pamet River inlet, would be a suitable spot to build their settlement. One major drawback was that it was too shallow for ships to enter. Secondly, the only sources of fresh water that they had discovered were in small ponds that might dry up in the summer. They still hoped to find a good-sized navigable river flowing into a well-sheltered harbor, and Robert Coppin, a second mate on the *Mayflower* who had visited the area on an earlier voyage, vaguely recalled seeing such a place across the bay. They would keep on looking. There was also good news to celebrate: Susanna White, the wife of William, gave birth to their son, Peregrine, the first English child born in New England.

The bad news was that the winter weather was terrible, bitterly cold and snowy, and many of the passengers on the *Mayflower* were weakening, suffering from severe coughs and worse ailments. One man, a servant to the White family, had already died. On December 6 the third exploratory expedition set sail in the shallop to scout the inner shore of Cape Cod Bay. On board were ten of the principal Pilgrims, including John Carver, Miles Standish, William Bradford, Edward Winslow, and Stephen Hopkins, and seven crewmembers; one was the pilot, Robert Coppin. It was so cold that the salt spray froze to their clothes and "made them many times like coats of iron." Heading down the shore that afternoon they spotted a group of Indians in the distance cutting the blubber off a pilot whale beached on the flats near today's Eastham. The Indians saw them, too, and appeared alarmed as they raced around to and fro. The colonists spent the night ashore behind a small barricade of logs and boughs that they built to protect themselves from the elements and any Indian attack; they also posted sentinels. In the distance they saw the smoke from the Indian campfire.

The next morning the company divided, with eight members staying on shore to survey the area and the rest remaining on the shallop. The land party followed a path into the woods where they came across another group of deserted graves and Indian houses. In the late afternoon they went back down to the beach and signaled the shallop in the distance to come in and join them on shore. Behind another barricade and guarded by their sentinel, they supped and rested peacefully until around midnight, when suddenly they were awakened by "a great and hideous cry," and the sentinel cried, "Arm, Arm!" They shot off a couple of muskets, and the noise ceased. There was no sign of any Indians. The Pilgrims concluded that they had probably only heard the cries of wolves and foxes. Nevertheless, they checked their muskets to make sure that they were all in good working order, a wise move as it turned out.

The next morning some of the men took their muskets down to the shallop from the campsite in preparation for their departure, as the rest got ready for breakfast. Suddenly they heard the sound of Indian war cries. This time it was close by and definitely not wolves, as a colonist came running in, shouting, "They are men, Indians, Indians!" and a shower of arrows fell on the Pilgrim encampment. Four armed Pilgrims behind the barricade, led by Captain Standish, fired back at the attackers. Others raced back to get their muskets at the shallop, which afforded them protection when they began firing at the assailants. After several sharp exchanges of musket fire and arrows, the Indians had had enough and retreated into the woods. A party of Pilgrims followed them a ways, firing off a few shots and shouting to let them know that they were not afraid of them. Surprisingly, not a single Pilgrim was injured in the fusillade of arrows that had been aimed at them. They gave their devout thanks to God for their deliverance and named the beach where the skirmish took place "First Encounter."

The Nauset Indians on the cape had good reasons to fear the arrival of the English vessel. One of their sagamores, Epinow, had been seized by an English ship and taken to London. Seven of their tribe had been kidnapped by another English captain, Thomas Hunt, and sold into slavery in Spain. The Nausets had retaliated by almost killing Thomas Dermer when he was on Martha's Vineyard just several months before, and they were afraid that the English had come to avenge their attack on him.

On board the shallop the Pilgrims continued their exploratory cruise south and then westward along the inner southern shore of the cape. Then it began to snow and rain. In midafternoon the strong winds and rough waves broke the rudder from its hinges; it took two strong men with long oars to steer the craft following the coast and turning to the northwest. The Pilgrims' situation became desperate, as the wild weather continued and the evening grew darker. Then Robert Coppin cried out that he had spotted the harbor he was looking for. However, their troubles were not over. Racing toward the harbor under full sail, the gale shattered their mast. They manned the oars and, helped by the incoming tide, made for the harbor. They almost ran aground at the entrance, but a strong effort by the oarsmen avoided the hazard, and they found a safe anchorage inside near an island. The company went ashore and built a fire to warm themselves through the freezing cold night. In the morning the men worked at repairing the damage to the shallop, dried their gear, and explored the island. The next day was the Sabbath, which they observed with a day of worship and rest.

The island, which they named Clark's Island after the first man to step ashore, was located in a large, protected harbor. On Monday the crew took soundings and found that there was ample depth for ships like the *Mayflower* in the outer portion of the harbor. The Pilgrims went ashore where they found running brooks and abandoned Indian cornfields. There were no signs of any Indians living there recently. William Bradford described it as "a place (as they supposed) fit for situation. At least it was the best that they could find, and the season and their present necessity made them glad to accept it." John Smith's map would have informed them that the place that they had chosen already had been named—Plymouth. He had recommended the area as an ideal site for a settlement in *A Description of New-England*. On December 12 the Pilgrim leaders sailed back to Cape Cod Harbor to bring the good news to their comrades on the *Mayflower*.

Back on board the *Mayflower* the scouting party received the sad news that two more people had died. One was a child, and William Bradford's beloved wife, Dorothy, had fallen from the ship and drowned. Bradford does not mention her death in his account, but it must have been a terrible blow for the Pilgrim leader to lose his wife and mother of their son after seven years of marriage. She had bravely endured the hardships of the life he had chosen. On December 16, the *Mayflower* made the twenty-five-mile bay crossing and anchored in Plymouth Harbor, about a mile and a half from the place where they had chosen to build. The shallop could navigate the inner harbor, but it was too shallow for the *Mayflower*, which drew twelve feet.

The health condition of most of the passengers was deplorable, and the leaders wanted to get them off the sickly *Mayflower* and into shelter on shore as soon as possible. It was the beginning of winter in New England, and they urgently needed sound housing. The colonists would have to stay on board, however, until the men that were fit could build houses. After surveying the area again, the leaders chose the spot to build their settlement—a cleared area near the landing place. It was not far from a huge rock that has gone down in history as Plymouth Rock, the spot where allegedly the Pilgrims first landed. The site had one distinct advantage—a great deal of land had been cleared for Indian cornfields. They had been abandoned several years before when the plague wiped out the vibrant native community of Patuxet at Plymouth that Samuel de Champlain and John Smith had seen. There was "a very sweet brook" and many freshwater springs, a protective inner cove to moor shallops and boats, and a hill suitable for erecting a small fort where a lookout would have a commanding view of Cape Cod and beyond.

Violent storms and downpours prevented the Pilgrims from getting anything done for several days. The *Mayflower* had to put out three anchors to hold her ground, and a party of twenty Pilgrims remaining on shore were left without food for a day and exposed to the cold and drenching rain. Then on December 23 the weather cleared, and for the first time it was possible for a group of able-bodied men to go to work—felling trees, sawing lumber, and carrying it to the building site. Later on they would gather thatch for the roofs of the houses. December 25 was just another working day for the Pilgrims, whose dedicated form of worship rejected celebrating Christmas or other holy days. Captain Jones provided some beer from his crew's stores to the men returning to the ship. Normally the settlers only had water to drink, so it was a special treat for them. For the next few months the arduous labor of building the Pilgrim settlement would be the task facing them each day, weather permitting; often it did not. Most evenings a group of men returned to the *Mayflower*, leaving about twenty others behind a barricade on shore to guard their works and tools. Some days foul weather stranded the workers on the ship; they were forced to wait until the weather turned and the tide was high enough for the shallop to bring them into the landing, a mile and a half away.

The Indians had already attacked them once on Cape Cod, and they had heard the sounds of Indians lurking in the surrounding woods and seen the smoke from their campfires in the distance. The Pilgrims were acutely aware of the danger of another assault. On December 28 they started building a platform to mount their cannons on the small hill at the end of the hamlet. In the afternoon they laid out the sites for the houses. The Pilgrims assigned a house on a small plot to each of the nineteen families in the company, and the single men would be lodged in different households. The families chose the location of their house by lot, and each family would build its own house. About two weeks later the workers completed the first building, a "common house" that would be used for storage and general meetings. As construction went forward, homes would be built below the hill in single rows on each side of a main street alongside the stream known as Town Creek and stretching down to the shore. They would be mainly one-room houses, built of hewn white oak logs and cemented together with mortar; the roofs were thatched with dry swamp grass.

The new buildings were urgently needed to shelter the sick and the dying. Tragically, the Pilgrims were dying at an alarming rate during the winter months of 1621. Scurvy, brought on by their poor and meager diets, exposure to the cold, and diseases that spread during their long shipboard confinement in crowded, unhealthy conditions took a heavy toll. During January and February, the worst time, there were only six or seven persons left in sound health, who, as William Bradford wrote, "willingly and cheerfully" ministered to their desperately ill comrades. "They spared no pains night nor day, but with abundance of toil and hazard of their own health, fetched them wood, made them fires, dressed them meat, made their beds, washed their loathsome clothes, clothed and unclothed them." He especially praised Elder William Brewster and Captain Miles Standish for their unstinting aid to their stricken companions. The Pilgrims chose high ground above the beach as a burial place for the dead. They leveled it and grassed it over so that the Indians would not discover how small and weak the settlement had become.

Bradford himself was one of the patients. On January 11, he was struck down by a severe pain in his hip and carried to the common house where the sick were placed in rows of beds. He recovered. Among the many who did not survive that terrible winter were Katherine Carver, the wife of John Carver, the governor of the plantation; Rose Standish, the wife of Captain Miles Standish; Elizabeth Winslow, the wife of Edward Winslow; Christopher Martin and his wife, Mary; Oceanus Hopkins, the infant daughter born at sea of Stephen and Elizabeth; and the parents and brother of Priscilla Mullins. Some families were entirely wiped out, and a number of children were made orphans. Almost half the crew of the *Mayflower*, sailors and officers, died, too, holding up the ship's departure for England. Of the 102 *Mayflower* passengers who reached Cape Cod in November 1620, fifty-two had died by the start of the following summer. By an odd coincidence in the colonial history of America, when the first English colony of Jamestown was founded, fifty colonists, about half of their company, had also died from disease and malnutrition within a few months after their arrival.

Sometimes, when the settlers left the compound to gather firewood, saw timber, or hunt, they spotted Indians, but the natives kept their distance from the newcomers. One day after Miles Standish and Francis Cooke finished their work in the woods, they left their tools behind them when they returned to the settlement. When they went back to get them, they were gone, stolen by the Indians. The next day two Indians appeared on a nearby hill and beckoned Captain Standish and Stephen Hopkins to approach them. The Pilgrims walked toward them to parley and dropped their musket on the ground as a sign of peace; the Indians ran off again. The Pilgrims had not forgotten the attack at First Encounter beach and remained vigilant. Captain Jones and some sailors brought five cannons from the *Mayflower* and mounted them on the hilltop platform. Captain Standish formed a military company to defend the colony from Indian assault. Standish had much in common with Captain John Smith of Jamestown. They had both been soldiers of fortune and seasoned by the military adventures and rough times that they had experienced; they were both short in stature and physically tough and strong; they were both courageous military commanders who exercised their authority fairly and firmly, recognizing the importance of imposing strict discipline in military training and engagements. Governor Carver and the leaders fully backed Captain Standish, respecting his critical role in defending the little colony.

There were many cold, rainy days during the first two months of the year, and once it rained so hard that it washed out the clay mortar between the logs forming the walls of houses. At the beginning of March 1621, the weather finally turned warm and fair, lifting everyone's spirits, and "the birds sang in the woods most pleasantly," wrote Bradford. House construction went forward, although plans were scaled back in view of the sad circumstances that had reduced the number needed. Initially only seven houses were built, each one housing seven or eight persons. Families with their household goods were transferred from the ship to shore. In early March the last families on the ship moved into their new homes and began planting their garden plots. Then on March 16, as the men were conferring about military matters, the Pilgrims met their first Native American.

There was nothing shy or fearful about the tall, solitary Indian, who marched boldly up the street through the houses toward the common house; he was naked except for a fringed leather apron and carried a bow and two arrows. When the men stopped him and gathered around, to their amazement he saluted them and greeted them warmly, saying, "Welcome, Englishmen." His name was Samoset, and he was not a local native. He said that he had come from Pemaquid in Maine, where he was a sagamore in the regional tribe, and he had been visiting in the Cape Cod area during the last eight months. He was able to speak broken English, which he had learned from the crews of English fishing boats that used Monhegan Island in the bay off Pemaquid as their base, and he astonished the Pilgrims with his memory of the names of vessels and their captains that he had seen. The Pilgrims eagerly plied him with questions.

Samoset identified and described the coastal tribes and their sagamores, their strengths, and numbers of warriors. The Indian name of the place where the Pilgrims had settled was Patuxet. Four years before all the inhabitants had died from "an extraordinary plague," so there was no one left to resist the Pilgrims' occupation of the spot. The nearest tribe to Plymouth was the Pokanokets, whose base was at the head of Narragansett Bay, near today's Warren. The Pokanokets' chieftain was Massasoit, whom Thomas Dermer and Squanto had visited two years before. His domain extended from Massachusetts Bay to Narragansett Bay. The Nausets, who were allied with the Pokanokets and had a hundred warriors, lived on the southern part of Cape Cod and Martha's Vineyard. They had been "much incensed and provoked against the English" ever since Captain Hunt had kidnapped their people and sold them for slaves, after inviting them aboard his vessel to trade. Eight months ago, Samoset reported, the Nausets had killed three English men from one of Sir Ferdinando Gorges's fishing vessels. It was the Nausets who had attacked the Pilgrims on Cape Cod and stolen the Pilgrims' tools that they left in the woods.

Samoset had apparently been treated well by the crews that he had met at Monhegan and felt safe and comfortable among the English newcomers. The English sailors on Monhegan had introduced him to beer, and he asked his hosts for some. The Pilgrims gave him some "strong water," probably aqua vitae, and a meal of biscuit, butter and cheese, a slice of duck, and pudding. "All which he liked well"—so well that when evening approached he was disinclined to leave his new friends, who wished that he would be on his way. Reluctantly the Pilgrims put him up in Stephen Hopkins's house, and kept an eye on him. Before he left the next day the Pilgrims gave him a knife, a bracelet, and a ring and told him to bring back the tools that the Indians had stolen. He told the Pilgrims that he would return with some other natives, their neighbors, and some beaver skins to trade. One of the Indians that he would bring from the Pokanoket village was named Squanto, "a native of this place, who had been in England and could speak better English than himself."

On Sunday, a day later, Samoset returned with four tall, strong natives, bringing back the tools that had been stolen. Following the Pilgrims' orders, they left their bows and arrows a quarter of a mile away from the settlement. The Pilgrims gave them a good meal, and the Indians were so delighted with English hospitality that they sang and danced for their hosts. This was not a proper way for the Pilgrims to pass the Sabbath, their day for worship, and the Pilgrims declined to trade for the few skins the Indians had brought; they should bring more to trade the next time they came. They gave the natives some small gifts and sent them off, except for Samoset, who enjoyed the Pilgrims' company so much that he stayed on for two more days before leaving. Apparently the purpose of the Indians' visit had been to survey the Pilgrim settlement before the upcoming visit of their chieftain, Massasoit, and partake of the English cuisine.

On March 22 Samoset came back to Plymouth with several Indians including Squanto. With his ability to speak English, Squanto would assume the role of translator between the two groups. They reported that the great sagamore Massasoit with his brother Quadequina and their men were nearby, ready to parley with the English. Within an hour Massasoit and sixty braves appeared on nearby Watson's Hill. The two groups eyed each other warily, both holding their ground. Then Squanto went to welcome Massasoit and learn how he wished to proceed. The chieftain asked the Pilgrims to send an emissary to confer with him, and the Pilgrims decided to send Edward Winslow to represent Governor Carver at the initial meeting. Wearing his armor with a sword at his side and carrying a bundle of gifts, Winslow greeted the chieftain. Massasoit and Quadequina were well pleased with the Pilgrims' presents—some knives, a copper chain, ornamental jewels, biscuits, butter, and "strong water." The sagamore also wished to buy Winslow's sword and armor, but it was not for sale.

Winslow told Massasoit that King James "saluted him with words of love and peace and did accept of him as his Friend and Alie." The Plymouth governor wished to meet him, trade with him, and "confirm a Peace with him as his next neighbour." The chief listened attentively to Squanto's translation of Winslow's words and seemed to like what he heard; he also enjoyed sampling the Pilgrims' culinary gifts. It was agreed that Winslow would remain in the custody of Quadequina as a hostage, and Massasoit with twenty warriors walked over to the settlement to meet Governor Carver, leaving their bows and arrows behind. Captain Standish and six of his men armed with muskets saluted Massasoit at the town brook and escorted them to a house to meet Governor Carver. The Pilgrims took six or seven of Massasoit's braves to hold as hostages until Winslow was released, the same practice followed by captains George Waymouth and John Smith in dealing with Indians in Maine and Virginia.

The Pilgrims had put down a green rug and several pillows in a partially constructed house and planned a bit of pomp and ceremony to greet the great chief of the region. Governor Carver, followed by a drummer and bugler and several armed men, entered and welcomed Massasoit. The two leaders kissed each other's hands, exchanged toasts of "strong water," ate some fresh meat, and got down to business. William Bradford described Massasoit as "a very lustie man, in his best yeares, an able body, grave of countenance, and spare of speech." He wore a large chain of white bones and beads, signifying his rank, and a large, long knife hanging on a string; his face was decorated with dark red paint, and he had a small bag of tobacco, which he smoked and offered to his hosts. The parley between the governor and the chief went smoothly, perhaps lubricated by the "strong water" that the chief had consumed, and resulted in the following pact:

1. That neither he nor any of his, should iniure or doe hurt to any of our people.
2. And if any of his did any hurt to any of ours, he should send the offender, that we might punish him.
3. That if any of our tooles were taken away when our people were at worke, he should cause them to be restored; and if any of ours did any harme to any of his, wee would doe the like to them.
4. If any did unjustly warre against him, wee would ayde him; if any did warre against us, he should ayde us.

5. He should send to his neighbour Confederates, to certifie them of this, that they might not wrong us, but might likewise be comprised in the conditions of peace.
6. That when their men came to us, they should leave their Bowes and Arrowes behind them, as wee should doe our Pieces when we came to them.

At Massasoit's leaving, the Indian chieftain and the English governor embraced, and Massasoit went off with his entourage to a place in the woods, about a half-mile from the settlement, where they would spend the night. Quadequina then entered Plymouth with his retinue, "so likewise wee entertained him and convayed him to the place prepared." By signs he indicated that seeing the English armed with muskets made him fearful, and the Pilgrims agreed to put them aside. He appeared to enjoy the Pilgrims' hospitality, and when he left, Winslow and the Indian hostages were released to join their own people.

Concluding a peace treaty with their Indian neighbors, the Pokanokets, so soon after their arrival in New England was a major accomplishment for the Pilgrims. Massasoit and his people would faithfully honor their pledge of alliance with the Pilgrims for the next half-century. The Pilgrims would not suffer from Indian raids like the repeated attacks by Powhatan's hostile warriors on the Virginia settlers. Squanto, as an advisor to Massasoit and an English-speaking interpreter, had played a key role in the successful negotiation of the treaty. Just a few months before the arrival of the Pilgrims at Patuxet the chieftain had been suspicious of Squanto's aims and detained him at his village. However, the Pokanokets had been severely weakened by the epidemic of the plague. They had lost many men, and with only sixty warriors left they were vulnerable to attacks from neighboring tribes, especially the Narragansetts in Rhode Island, who had not been hard hit by the epidemic. Squanto undoubtedly persuaded Massasoit that the Pilgrims, with their muskets and cannons, could be a powerful ally in defending them against their aggressive rivals. The Pilgrims, on their part, were well impressed by Squanto, an Indian who not only spoke their language, but, having lived in London for several years, knew their country and the ways of their countrymen.

Squanto's family and friends at Patuxet had died in the epidemic. He felt at home with the English and made the decision to live with them in Plymouth. They welcomed him, and the day after Massasoit's visit he went fishing for eels and returned with a large number, which he gave to his new friends.

Winter was over. As Bradford wrote, "The spring now approaching, it pleased God the mortalitie begane to cease amongst them, and the sick and lame recovered apace, which put, as it were, new life into them." Almost twenty members of the *Mayflower*'s crew had died during the winter. By April 5 Captain Jones decided that the remaining sailors were now fit to man the ship, and the *Mayflower* sailed for England, bearing the first news of the establishment of the Plymouth plantation. Not a single member of the little colony chose to give up and go home. Driven by strong west winds, the ship made a fast crossing. Samoset returned to his own tribe in Maine where he continued to maintain friendly relations with the English, selling one colonist a large tract of land in 1625. Today a popular hotel and golf resort just up the coast from Pemaquid on the shore of Rockland Harbor bears his name.

It was the planting season, the time to sow the seed corn that the Pilgrims had taken from the Nauset stores on the Cape. The already cleared Indian fields were the perfect place to start. The Pilgrims, who had no knowledge of the local soil and growing conditions, were happy to follow Squanto's expert advice about raising corn on his old home grounds. Corn would be the diet staple, as it had been for the Jamestown and Roanoke colonists. The Pilgrims planned to grow their own corn on some twenty acres, instead of relying on the natives to supply their needs. However, as it turned out, they would face large, unexpected shortages later on, forcing them to buy corn from the Indians. Town Creek was teeming with alewives in mid-April, swimming upstream to spawn, and Squanto taught the settlers how to insert dead fish next to the planted seeds to fertilize the thin soil. The cornfield had to be guarded around the clock for two weeks to prevent wolves from digging up the fish. The Pilgrims also sowed six acres of wheat, barley, and peas, and they raised vegetables in their house garden plots.

Some men continued to fell timber and build more housing; others hunted and fished. It was hard and tiring work for the twenty-seven ablebodied men and boys. On a hot day in mid-April, Governor John Carver left the cornfield where he had been working and retired with a severe headache. Carver, who was one of the oldest members of the company, soon lost consciousness and, after lingering on a few days, died. The Pilgrims grieved at his loss. They greatly respected Governor Carver for his wise leadership and untiring work in their behalf. "He was buried in the best manner they could, with some vollies of shott by all that bore armes." The Pilgrims chose thirty-one-year-old William Bradford to be their new governor.

On May 12 Governor Bradford officiated at the marriage of Edward Winslow and Suzanna White in a civil ceremony, according to the Dutch law that was followed by the Pilgrims. Suzanna White's husband, William, had died in February, and Edward Winslow's wife, Elizabeth, had died in March. Suzanna's baby son, Peregrine, would have a new stepfather. Long periods of mourning after the death of a spouse came much later in New England. At the time of the Pilgrims, widows and widowers recognized the practical necessity of getting on with their lives as soon as possible. Later that spring John Alden married Priscilla Mullins, a romance that was fantasized many years later in the lyric poem by Henry Wadsworth Longfellow, "The Courtship of Miles Standish." Rose Standish had died in January, and Alden at first shared a house with Captain Standish; he was very fond of the old soldier. The poetic story was that Standish asked his young friend to seek Priscilla's hand in marriage on his behalf. He did, and she replied, "Why don't you speak for yourself, John?" The tale is fanciful, but the romance was not. Their sixty-two-year marriage produced eleven children.

John Alden proposing marriage to Priscilla Mullins. Their courtship was the subject of a fanciful poem by Henry Wadsworth Longfellow, but their romance was real. They married and had eleven children.
Photograph by Doug Carr, collection of the Illinois State Museum.

· *16* ·

The Indian Summer

$\mathcal{O}$n July 2, after the planting season, Governor Bradford dispatched a diplomatic mission to meet with Massasoit at the chieftain's village in the Pokanoket territory on the eastern shore of Narragansett Bay, a journey of about forty miles. He chose Edward Winslow, who had already established a good rapport with Massasoit when he visited Plymouth, and Stephen Hopkins to be his ambassadors. Squanto would be their guide and interpreter. Bradford wanted them to survey the lay of the land beyond Plymouth and the strength and organization of their neighbors, the Pokanokets. The English had special gifts for the chieftain—a red cotton horseman's jacket, trimmed with lace, and a copper chain. Bradford instructed his ambassadors to confirm to Massasoit that the English wished "to continue the league of Peace and Friendship between them and us." The Pokanokets often came to Plymouth, and they in turn were visiting him to demonstrate the love and goodwill that the English bore for him. The Pilgrim representatives should also ask the sagamore to pass the word to the Nausets that the Pilgrims very much wanted to compensate them for their corn that the Pilgrims had taken on Cape Cod.

Bradford had another message for Massasoit. The Pilgrims, newcomers and inexperienced with farming in the area, were uncertain how much corn they would harvest later, and corn was the basic food on which they must rely until the next harvest. They regretted that in the future they would not be able to feed the many Indians that visited Plymouth, who often came with their wives and children, as they had before. Nevertheless, they wished to "entertain" [feed] Massasoit or any special friend of his when they came to the settlement. When they visited Plymouth, Massasoit's friends or messengers should wear the copper chain, their gift from the English. The Pilgrims would recognize and warmly welcome and entertain those special visitors identified by Massasoit, as well as those bringing a good supply of beaver skins to sell.

Winslow and Hopkins, led by Squanto, reached the Indian village of Nemasket in the afternoon where the friendly natives fed them a meal of cornbread and shad row. They continued on to the Titicut River, known today as the Taunton, where a group of Indians were fishing for bass using a weir built across the river. The Pilgrims and the Indians shared a dinner of fish and the travelers' provisions, and the next morning the Pilgrim ambassadors, accompanied by six new Indian friends, were on their way. Edward Winslow wrote that thousands of Indians, who had died in the great plague, had lived in villages along the river; they had raised their crops in many well-cleared fields, which now lay unattended and abandoned. Their Indian companions guided their way and helped them to ford streams. The few Indians that they met were also friendly and shared food with them, once they were assured that their party did not belong to the much-feared Narragansetts, the tribe across the bay that raided the Pokanokets from time to time. After dining on roasted crab and dried shellfish, the Pilgrims gave each of their two native hostesses a string of beads.

When the Pilgrim emissaries reached Massasoit's village of Sowans, near today's Warren, Rhode Island, the chieftain was not at home. When he arrived a little later, the English, following Squanto's advice, saluted him with a volley of musket fire. He welcomed them into his house and was delighted to receive their presents, donning the red coat and placing the chain about his neck. Winslow wrote, "He was not a little proud to behold himselfe, and his men also to see their King so bravely attired." Massasoit declared that "he would gladly continue that Peace and Friendship which was between him and us" and willingly agreed to the other requests presented by Governor Bradford's ambassadors.

Surrounded by his braves, Massasoit made a speech naming some thirty villages under his rule that would be at peace with the English and bring them furs for trading, a lengthy harangue that Winslow thought quite tedious. Massasoit and his guests then smoked and turned to discussing the English king. This was King James's country, and he was King James's man, said Massasoit. The English must keep the French out of the region. The chieftain, unprepared for the Pilgrims' visit, had no food to offer them, and they went to bed hungry. Moreover, it was a restless night. To their surprise Massasoit had them sleep on the same crowded wooden platform with himself, his wife, and two other Indian guests. The platform was infested with lice and fleas. Adding to their discomfort were the sounds of the Indians singing themselves to sleep.

The next day more Pokanoket sachems arrived to meet the English emissaries. They enjoyed themselves playing games and then challenged the English to shoot their muskets at a target. One of them did, and the Indians "wondred to see the mark so full of holes." At lunchtime Massasoit appeared with two large fish that he had shot with a bow and arrow. There were forty mouths to feed, the portions were small, and Winslow and Hopkins devoured their shares hungrily. The next morning they took their leave to return to Plymouth. In bidding them farewell, Massasoit was "both grieved and ashamed, that he could no better entertain us." Squanto would remain with the Pokanokets with the task of informing other villages that they should obtain furs to trade with the Pilgrims. Massasoit assigned another Indian, Tokamahomon, to join the English, "whom we had found faithfull before and after on all occasions." The two-day journey home was hard, traveling through a violent rainstorm on short rations. Winslow and Hopkins, weary, wet, and hungry, reached Plymouth on the evening of Saturday, July 7, in time to observe the Sabbath with their families and friends the next day. The Pilgrims were undoubtedly pleased by the success of their ambassadors in cementing good relations with Massasoit and his people.

Later on in July, John Billington Jr., the teenage son of one of the London "Strangers," got lost in the woods. He wandered around for five days, subsisting on nuts and berries, until he came upon the native village of Manomet, about twenty miles south of Plymouth. The Manomet sachem, Canacum, instead of sending the boy back to his people in Plymouth, delivered him to the Nausets, on Cape Cod, their allies in the region. When the English received word from Massasoit that young Billington was being held by the Nausets, they had good reason to be anxious for his safety. The Nausets were the tribe whose store of corn the Pilgrims had raided, and who had then attacked them at First Encounter beach.

Bradford promptly dispatched ten armed men in the shallop to bring back the missing boy. They were accompanied by Squanto, who had returned to Plymouth from his trading assignment, and Tokamahomon, who would serve as guides and interpreters. A violent storm forced them to put in at Cummaquid, today's Barnstable Harbor, the first night. The next morning they spotted some Indians gathering oysters, and the two guides went ashore to parley with them. They reported that young Billington was well and safe at Nauset, near today's Eastham, about twenty miles across the bay, and they invited the English to come and eat with them. Leaving four men to guard the shallop, six Pilgrims went ashore, where they met the local sachem, Ianough. The young chief was handsome, personable, and a generous host. However, a disturbing incident injected a jarring note at their rendezvous.

A very old woman was eager to meet the English visitors, but then began "weeping and crying excessively." Her three sons were part of the group of Indians that Captain Hunt had enticed aboard his ship to trade, and then treacherously seized and taken to Spain to be sold as slaves seven years earlier. "She was deprived of the comfort of her children in her old age," wrote Bradford. "We told them we were sorry that any Englishman should give them that offence, that Hunt was a bad man, and that all the English that heard it condemned him for the same." The Pilgrims promised that that they would not hurt any Indians and gave the old mother some small trifles, which pleased her. The Indians taken captive to England by English captains had generally been treated well. The English colonizers recognized their value as guides and interpreters for future expeditions. Squanto, who had gone to England from Spain; Epinow; and almost all of Captain Waymouth's captives and the Roanoke Indians made it back to their homelands. However, no one knew the ultimate fate of the Indian mother's three sons and the other Indians who were sold in the Spanish slave market.

After dining with the Cummaquid natives, the band of Pilgrims, accompanied by Ianough and one of his braves, sailed across the bay to Nauset to pick up the Billington boy. It was low tide, so they stayed off shore within wading distance to the beach. Squanto and Ianough went ashore to inform the Nauset sachem why the English had come to their village. A group of Nausets approached the shallop, but the Pilgrims only let two come aboard. They remembered that it was at this very beach, seven months before, that the Nausets had attacked their scouting party. One of the Indians owned the store of corn that the Pilgrims had taken in December, and he agreed to come to Plymouth where the Pilgrims promised to fully compensate him. In the evening the Nauset chief, Aspinet, with a large company of braves, arrived at the beach with the boy, and one carried him through the shallow water to the shallop. Young Billington was in good condition. The two sides pledged to maintain peaceful relations, and the English thanked Aspinet and the native who had cared for the boy by giving each of them a knife.

However, they also heard some very troubling news, a report that the Narragansetts were on the warpath. It was said that they had attacked and killed some of Massasoit's braves and taken the chieftain prisoner. "This strucke some feare in us, because the Colony was so weakely guarded"; there were only about seven able-bodied men left at Plymouth to defend the settlement against an assault. The English wanted to reach Plymouth as quickly as possible by sailing directly across the bay, but adverse winds and a lack of fresh water forced them to follow the southern shore and put in at Cummaquid again. The sachem Ianough and his people gave them a warm welcome, and while he led some Pilgrims to search for fresh water, "the women joined hand in hand, singing and dancing before the shallop." The Pilgrims arrived safely back in Plymouth the following evening, glad that they had rescued the Billington boy and established good relations with the Cape Cod Nausets, the same Indians that not so long ago had attacked them.

It was true: Massasoit was being held by the Narragansetts. The latest troublemaker for the Pilgrims was Coubatant, a minor sachem of the Pocassets under Massasoit, who may have been acting for the Narragansetts at the time. He disdained the English and their friendly relations with the Pokanokets and the Nausets. He despised Squanto for his friendship with the English and his role in bringing about the peaceful accords. Coubatant was plotting to overthrow Massasoit's authority in the region, and the Pilgrims received word that he had gone to Menaschet, about fifteen miles from Plymouth, "to draw the hearts of Massasoit's subjects from him."

Hobbamock was a trusted lieutenant of Massasoit, who, like Squanto, had elected to live with the Pilgrims in Plymouth. He and Squanto were dispatched to Menaschet to find out what had happened to Massasoit. They were taken by surprise there and seized by Coubatant's men. Squanto was taken prisoner, but Hobbamock, as Coubatant was threatening to stab him, broke free and raced back through the woods to Plymouth. Governor Bradford immediately held a council of war, which concluded that the Pilgrims must take immediate action to honor their treaty pledge to back their ally Massasoit and his people when an enemy attacked them. Other tribes would be unwilling to form peaceful alliances with the Pilgrims if they failed to do so, for the English would appear weak and untrustworthy. Governor Bradford wrote, "For if they should suffer their friends and messengers thus to be wronged, they should have none would cleave unto them, or give them any intelligence or doe them serviss afterwards; but nexte they would fall upon themselves." The Pilgrims feared that Coubatant had already killed Squanto. Coubatant had declared at Menaschet, "If he were dead, the English had already lost their tongue."

The next day, August 14, ten armed Pilgrims, led by their tough commander, Captain Miles Standish, and guided by Hobbamock, headed off for Menaschet. If Squanto had indeed been killed, they would find Coubatant and behead him, the common form of capital punishment for traitors practiced in England. At midnight, the band of Pilgrims surrounded Coubatant's house. It had been pointed out by Hobbamock, who would interpret Standish's orders to the natives. A few troopers entered the lodging where a number of men, women, and children were sleeping in the dark room and demanded loudly that they surrender Coubatant to the English. No one else would be harmed, nor should anyone try to escape until they had searched the building. At first the Indians were too frightened to speak. Several who attempted to flee through a back door were shot and wounded by the English guards outside. Finally, when the natives understood the purpose of the English intrusion, they informed the Pilgrims that Coubatant and his men had fled from the village earlier; furthermore, Squanto was alive and well, living nearby. Hobbamock climbed to the rooftop and called out for Squanto, who, upon hearing his voice, joined the English band along with Tokamahomon, another friendly Indian who had also been taken captive by Coubatant.

The next morning good relations were restored between the two groups as the village inhabitants, bringing gifts of food, gathered around the Pilgrims. Before departing the Pilgrims had a message for the local natives, knowing that they would pass it on to Coubatant and the Narragansetts: "Although Coubatant had now escaped us, yet there was no place should secure him and his from us if he continued his threatening us, and provoking others against us, who had kindly entertained him, and never intended evill towards him till he now so justly deserved it." Moreover, if Massasoit was not returned safely by the Narragansetts to his people, or if Coubatant should rebel against him, or attack Squanto, Hobbamock, or any of Massasoit's subjects, the English would seek revenge and overthrow him and his people. The English then left, bringing a man and woman they had wounded in the fray back to Plymouth with them, where their surgeon treated the natives' wounds.

The news of the Pilgrim's forceful action in coming to the aid of their ally, Massasoit, and rescuing Squanto spread quickly among the neighboring tribes. They were impressed and eager to join the Pokanokets in forming an alliance with the Pilgrims. Seven sachems dispatched their messengers to Plymouth to affirm their desire for peaceful relations. One was sent by Epinow, the sachem of Capawack, today's island of Martha's Vineyard, which surprised the Pilgrims; they had not dealt with him before. Others were sent by Aspinet, the sagamore of the Cape Cod Nausets, and Canacum of Manomet. Even Coubatant sent word through Massasoit, who had rejoined his tribe, that he, too, now wished to make his peace with the Pilgrims. On September 13 the Indian messengers signed a formal document acknowledging that they were loyal subjects of King James.

Encouraged by the success of their expeditions to visit the neighboring tribes, the Pilgrim leaders decided to send an exploratory mission north to the country of the Massachusetts Indians, who, they had been told, were hostile toward the English. The Pilgrims intended to survey the Massachusetts Bay area and establish friendly relations and trade with the natives. On September 18, ten men accompanied by Squanto and two friendly Indians set out in the shallop for the bay, about thirty-five miles to the north. After spending a night anchored at the southern end of today's Boston Harbor, a scouting party, led by Captain Standish, went ashore. An Indian woman gathering lobsters directed them to the local sachem, Obbatinewat, who treated them kindly and declared that he was an ally of Massasoit. He also told them of his fear of the Tarrantines, the tribe living near the Penobscot River in Maine, who had come on raiding parties from time to time, stealing their corn at harvest time and killing their people. The Pilgrims replied that a number of sachems had pledged their loyalty to King James and the English, "and if he also would submit himself, we would be his safeguard from his enemies." Obbatinewat agreed to ally his tribe with the English.

The expedition then sailed north through the many islands dotting the huge harbor, probably anchoring near today's Charlestown across the Charles River from Boston. The colonists were interested in scouting the harbor and surrounding terrain and were very impressed with the place as a port that could accommodate many large ships. They also observed the mouths of two large rivers, today's Mystic and Charles, flowing into the bay. Some of the islands had been cleared for farming but were now abandoned. Their inhabitants had died from the plague or been driven off by it, the same fate that most of the Indians in the region had suffered. The next day the company marched several miles inland, leaving two men to guard the shallop, and came across the deserted home and fort of the former chieftain of the Massachusetts people, who had been killed by the marauding Tarrantines in 1615. Nearby they met some women tending their corn and a man, who were terribly frightened to encounter the English strangers. The colonists calmed their fears, assuring them that they came in peace and wished to trade for beaver skins and furs. That evening, by the light of the moon, they sailed back to Plymouth with a number of beaver skins. They recognized that the area would have been a splendid location for their colony. Eight years later another English settlement would be built and flourish there.

By late September the settlers had harvested their crops and produced a good store of Indian corn. Their planting of barley had fared less well, and their peas, parched by the sun, were not worth picking. Their fishermen had caught cod, bass, and other fish, and lobsters, mussels, and eels were abundant along the shore. Some went hunting for wild fowl and game. Governor Bradford sent four men fowling as flocks of migrating birds overflew the area, and they shot enough ducks and geese to feed the company for a week; others killed wild turkeys and deer. Governor Bradford wrote that the Pilgrims "being all well recovered in health and strength, had all things in good plenty." Even though half the company had died during the devastating winter months, the Pilgrims had built their housing, planted and harvested their crops, hunted and fished, traded for furs, and, with respectful diplomacy, negotiated an enduring peace with their Indian neighbors. It was time to "rejoice together, after we had gathered the fruits of our labours," wrote Edward Winslow.

It was not, in fact, the first Thanksgiving but a fall festival celebrating a successful harvest, which had been a long tradition in England. In 1619 the Berkeley Hundred plantation near Jamestown had officially celebrated the day on which they first went ashore at the site of their new plantation on the James. The roots of the modern Thanksgiving, thanking God for his blessings, stemmed from the religious services of the Massachusetts Puritans some years later. Thanksgiving was proclaimed an annual national holiday by President Abraham Lincoln in 1863 in the midst of the Civil War.

At the Pilgrims' first festival the Pokanoket chief, Massasoit, with ninety members of his tribe, joined the celebration, and a few braves went out and killed five deer, which they presented to Governor Bradford and Captain Standish. The number of Indians at the feast was almost double the number of colonists, and the party lasted for three days. One can assume that everyone was well fed, as they gathered around the outdoor fires where the women were roasting venison and cooking vegetable stews and other dishes. Perhaps they played games—Edward Winslow reported that "we exercised our armes" in target practice.

John Smith had been stuck in Jamestown with a number of indolent, quarrelsome, gold-seeking gentlemen, some of whom were real troublemakers. He would have been pleased to lead a band of colonists like the Pilgrims. They were ready to work hard in building their homes and farming their fields. They were, for the most part, well-disciplined, kind, and decent people, who were strongly motivated by their religious faith. After his history with Powhatan's warriors in Virginia, he would have marveled at the close and friendly relations that the Pilgrims and their Indian neighbors enjoyed. "We have found the Indians very faithfull in their Covenant of peace with us," wrote Edward Winslow, "very loving and ready to pleasure us, we often goe to them and they come to us." Winslow also said that they feared the English settlers. The noise and firepower of the English muskets shocked the Indians, as the Pilgrims' "First Encounter" on Cape Cod had demonstrated. They also had a healthy respect for the tough military commander, Captain Miles Standish. Furthermore, Massasoit's tribes had been decimated by the plague. In their terribly weakened condition they needed a powerful ally on their side to help defend them against the assaults of their aggressive enemies to the north and south.

On November 11 a small ship arrived unexpectedly in Plymouth Harbor. The Pilgrims had received word from the Nausets on the cape that a vessel, which might be French, was headed their way. Bradford ordered a cannon to be fired to signal all the colonists working outside the settlement to return immediately and man their military posts. They were relieved to see the ship flying the English flag as she drew nearer. It was the *Fortune*, which had been dispatched by Thomas Weston of the London Merchant Adventurers and carried thirty-five new colonists. She had left the English port of Plymouth at the end of August. The passengers seemed healthy after the long voyage, and one woman, recently widowed before they had left England, gave birth to a son on the night that they landed. Among the new arrivals were William Brewster's oldest son, Jonathan; Edward Winslow's brother, John; Thomas Prence, who one day would govern the colony; and Robert Cushman, the Pilgrim business agent, who had been discouraged about the project's prospects after the misadventure of the *Speedwell* and elected to remain behind when the *Mayflower* sailed for America. Cushman had brought his son with him. Weston had assigned Cushman to carry out a mission for the Merchant Adventurers, and he would go back to England on the return voyage of the *Fortune.*

The Pilgrims were glad to welcome the newcomers who would strengthen their thin ranks. Governor Bradford reported that "most of them were lusty yonge men," mainly "Strangers," who were bachelors that he would assign to live with the families in the existing houses and public buildings until more houses were built. However, their arrival presented a huge problem. There would be thirty-five new mouths to feed, including eight women and children, during the long winter months that lay ahead. Making an exact count of the corn and other provisions they had stored for consumption during the winter, Bradford concluded that they could barely survive for six months if everyone was restricted to half rations. The Pilgrims would face another New England winter with a severely limited supply of food, and they would not harvest their corn until late the following summer. Bradford wrote, "So they were presently put on half allowance, one as well as an other, which begane to be hard, but they bore it patiently under hope of supply." Furthermore, the new young men were poorly equipped, lacking such household items as bedding, cooking utensils, and sufficient clothing. Bradford stated, "The plantation was glad of the addition of strength, but could have wished that many of them had been of beter condition, and all of them beter furnished with provisions; but that could not now be helpte."

The *Fortune* brought a letter to Governor Carver, who had died in April, from Thomas Weston, representing the London Merchant Adventurers. Because no other ship had come from Plymouth since the departure of the *Mayflower*, Weston had not learned of Carver's death. Weston complained angrily that the *Mayflower*, after a long delay, had returned without a cargo, on which the Adventurers were counting to profit from their investment. He criticized Carver for poor judgment—too much time had been spent in "discoursing, arguing, and consulting." He urged the Pilgrim leaders to sign the business contract that they had rejected earlier and submit a statement of the expenditures from the funds invested by the Adventurers. "And consider that the life of the bisssines depends on the lading of this ship." If the *Fortune* returned with a profitable cargo enabling the Adventurers to recoup their investment, "I promise you I will never quit the bussines, though all the other Adventurers should." Weston also reported that his group had obtained a new patent from the Council for New England, recently formed by Sir Ferdinando Gorges, which granted them rights to the region occupied by the Pilgrims. The patent was issued to John Pierce, who was associated with Weston.

Captain John Smith had received a similar letter in Jamestown from his London Company backers, criticizing his leadership as president of the colony and complaining that they had received a minimal return on their investment. In both cases the investors, seeking quick profits and far away across the ocean, had little idea of the hardships and dangers that the colonists faced. Smith had replied bluntly, as was his style. William Bradford was more circumspect and dignified in his answer to Weston, but his message was clear.

Governor Carver's "care and pains was so great for the common good, both ours and yours, that . . . he oppressed him selfe and shortened his days." He had worked himself to death on behalf of his fellow Pilgrims. Bradford recognized that the Adventurers had sustained financial losses, "but the loss of his and many other industrious men's lives, cannot be vallewed at any price. Of the one there may be hope of recovery, but the other no recompence can make good." He described the terrible winter that they had endured, first on Cape Cod searching for a suitable place to live and then at Plymouth, at a time when people were dying daily. To blame the settlers for not preparing cargo for the *Mayflower* when they were barely able to tend to the sick and bury the dead was unfair and greatly discouraging to them. Those that said that they wasted time in "discoursing and consulting" were liars. "Indeed it is our callamitie," wrote Bradford, "that we are (beyond expectations) yoked with some ill conditioned people, who will never doe good, but corrupt and abuse others." There were a few malcontents among the "Strangers," who had apparently sent letters home on the *Mayflower* complaining about the conduct of the Pilgrim leaders, according to Bradford. Bradford also warned that the new colonists brought by the *Fortune* "would bring famine on them unavoydably" if a new supply ship did not arrive in time.

Robert Cushman gave a persuasive address in the common house urging the Pilgrim leaders to execute the contract with the Merchant Adventurers, which they did. They also gave Cushman a statement of the colony's expenses; he would deliver both documents to Weston on his return. The Pilgrim leaders had complied fully with Thomas Weston's demands, and Cushman was confident that "they should have a speedy supply." He set sail for home the next day leaving his son in the care of Governor Bradford. The *Fortune*, fully loaded with a cargo of clapboard and two hogsheads of beaver and other skins valued at five hundred pounds, departed for Plymouth in England on December 13. As it turned out, the voyage of the *Fortune* was a complete financial loss for the Merchant Adventurers. As she neared England, the *Fortune* was captured by a French cruiser and was taken to the Ile d'Yeu, where her captors stole all her cargo. She was then released and, with Robert Cushman on board, reached England on February 17, 1622.

In addition to the business documents, Cushman brought back with him three important communications that would inform the Adventurers and others about the state of affairs in the first New England colony. Edward Winslow had written a day-by-day account of the colony's first year with an opening chapter by William Bradford. Cushman turned over the manuscript, which later carried the title of *Mourt's Relation*, to George Morton, an active member of the Leiden Pilgrims, to arrange its publication; it was published by John Bellamie in 1622 and sold at his shop in London. Perhaps Morton for his own reasons chose to use a nom de plume, or a printer's error, not uncommon at the time, caused the misspelling of "Morton" in the book's title. Cushman also delivered William Bradford's letter to Thomas Weston and a letter by Winslow to a friend, probably George Morton, whom he expected would come to Plymouth on the next supply ship. The letter was included as an addendum to *Mourt's Relation* when it was published.

While Winslow had presented a detailed account in *Mourt's Relation* of the terrible hardships that the Pilgrims had endured during their first year in New England, he had another purpose in mind in writing this letter. It was the same that Captain John Smith had when he wrote *A Description of New-England*. Both writers were trying to encourage new settlers to emigrate to New England, and in Winslow's case to Plymouth. Accordingly, he presented a very rosy picture of the colonists' current life in the region. After describing the Thanksgiving feast with the Indians, Winslow wrote that although food was not always so plentiful as it was at that time, "yet by the goodnesse of God, we are so farre from want that we often wish you partakers of our plenty." Winslow described the many attributes of the region—the colonists' success in raising Indian corn; the abundance of wild game and fowl, and in the summer cod, lobsters, and other fish; the plentiful strawberries, raspberries, plums, and grapes, both red and white. As for the weather, "I never in my life remember a more seasonable yeare then we have here enjoyed." With horses and livestock "men might live here as contented as in any part of the world." Winslow and Smith could have been hyperbolic travel agents in any century.

Winslow expressed the hope that the Adventurers would be pleased with the *Fortune*'s cargo and furnish them with the supplies that they needed, which would encourage them to put forth their best effort. Expecting that his friend, along with others, would be coming before long, Winslow made a list of items that he should bring with him, including a musket or fowling piece for hunting birds, gunpowder and shot, and paper and linseed oil for window panes; glass was too expensive. Winslow praised the close and friendly relations between the Indians and Pilgrims. The settlers could walk as peacefully and safely in the woods around Plymouth as on the roads of England. They entertained the Indians in their homes, and sometimes the natives brought them gifts of venison. They were "very trustie, quick of apprehension, ripe witted, just." However, Winslow had not reckoned with the scheming Narragansetts of Rhode Island.

The Narragansetts were a large and powerful tribe, perhaps thirty thousand strong with several thousand warriors. They had escaped the plague, which had wiped out thousands of natives from the New England coastal tribes to the east. Canonicus, the aggressive Narragansett chief, who had fought his neighboring tribes in the past, now aimed to subdue the weakened Pokanokets under Massasoit. Shortly after the departure of the *Fortune* a Narragansett messenger delivered an unusual package to the Pilgrims—a bundle of arrows tied about with a rattlesnake skin. Squanto explained the meaning of the symbolic message: it was a challenge and a threat to the English, virtually a declaration of war, from the Narragansett chief. Canonicus wanted to rule over the Pokanokets, and the English stood in his way. Under their alliance with the Pokanokets they had pledged to defend them if they were attacked. After consulting with his colleagues, Governor Bradford sent back the following message: "If they had rather have war than peace, they might begin when they would." The English did not fear them and would be ready for them. He also sent back the snakeskin filled with bullets and powder. Canonicus was so alarmed by the parcel's contents that he quickly got rid of it, and after being passed around among the Indians, it ended up back in Plymouth.

While nothing further came of the incident, the Pilgrims now recognized that in the event of an Indian attack their little settlement was virtually unprotected. During the winter the colonists built a palisaded wall around their settlement with four protruding gun placements called flankers at strategic spots. A watch guard was on duty at night, and the town gates were locked. Captain Standish formed four squadrons from the company who would go to their assigned stations when a warning alarm sounded.

Christmas Day, 1621, presented a challenging disciplinary problem for the governor. Because the Leiden Pilgrims did not celebrate the day, considering it a pagan holiday, Bradford ordered everyone to go to work as usual. Most of the newcomers that had arrived on the *Fortune* objected, however, saying, "It went against their consciences to work on that day." So the governor told them, "If they made it a matter of conscience, he would spare them until they were better informed" and led the rest off to work outside the settlement. When the workers returned for lunch they found the others making merry in the street playing spool-ball and other games. The governor promptly confiscated their balls and bats. "It was against his conscience," he told them, "that they should play and others work." If they intended to observe Christmas Day as "a matter of devotion" they should do it in their homes, but no more "gaming or reveling in the streets." Apparently the Pilgrims did not wish their neighbors a "Merry Christmas" in those days.

Emerging Conflicts

$\mathcal{W}$hen Governor Yeardley of Jamestown asked to be relieved in 1621, the Virginia Company sent over a new governor, Sir Francis Wyatt, with additional instructions for governing the colony. The governing body should see to it that divine service was administered "according to the form and discipline of the church of England." In Jamestown, as in Plymouth, attendance at the Sunday church services, morning and afternoon, was officially mandatory. The government was charged with making the people "apply themselves to an industrious way of life and to suppress all gaming, drunkenness, and excess in apparel." The Virginia Company wanted the colonists to develop a more diversified economy than the current one based solely on tobacco: "And they ordered them, particularly by the king's advice and desire, to draw the people off from their excessive planting of tobacco." (It will be recalled that King James despised smoking.) The colony should become self-sufficient in providing food for its people and produce other commodities like wine and silk. Plans were made to establish an ironworks and to renew the abandoned glass-making operation.

Powhatan, the great chieftain of the Virginia tidewater tribes, had died in April 1618; he was about seventy years old. He was a proud and imposing leader who had successfully united the tribes under his rule. Once he had said to John Smith, "If your king has sent me presents, I too am a king, and I am in my own land." With stubborn determination he had led his people in resisting the invasion of the English on his lands until the marriage of his daughter Pocahontas to John Rolfe. Since that symbolic union of his people and the English colonists, he had kept his word to maintain peaceful relations as long as he lived, and now he was dead. Powhatan was succeeded by his brother

Opechancanough, whom John Smith and the English had confronted several times before.

Governor Wyatt was instructed to make sure that "no injurie or oppression bee wrought by the English against any of the natives of that countrie wherby the present peace may be disturbed." In cultivating "peace and friendship" with the Indians, he was to use "all probable means to bringing over the natives to a love of civilisation, and to the knowledge of God and his true religion." They could "draw the best disposed among the Indians to converse and labour among our people, for a convenient reward"; they might then persuade their own people to turn to a civilized Christian way of life. Another idea was for each town or borough "to procure by just means, a certain number of their children, to be brought up in the first elements of literature." Finally, Wyatt was instructed to build a college "for the training up of the children of those infidels in true religion, moral virtue and civility, and for other godly uses." In 1622 the governor sent a colonist emissary to discuss these matters with Opechancanough, the new chieftain of the Powhatans.

While Opechancanough was courteous and confirmed his wish to maintain peaceful relations with the colonists, inwardly he had long seethed with hatred against the English for their invasion and continuing expansion into Indian lands; he had also suffered personal humiliation at the hands of John Smith. One can imagine the fiery, bloodthirsty speeches that he made to his warriors denouncing the tyranny of the English. No longer were the colonists confined to Jamestown and its environs. They had spread their settlements and plantations widely up and down on both sides of the James River from Chesapeake Bay to Henrico, encroaching steadily on Indian lands. More and more shiploads of settlers were arriving all the time—well over 1,000 settlers landed during the year ending in the spring of 1622. Over seven years of harmonious relations since the marriage of Pocahontas had lulled the colonists to complacency regarding their defenses against an Indian attack. They were too busily focused on their profitable tobacco business to take the time to plan and practice the military exercises needed to defend themselves. For Opechancanough and his warriors the time had come to strike.

On the night before the onslaught, Indians from different tribes in the Powhatan empire moved stealthily to their assigned points of attack, concealing themselves in the forest. Other Indians, on good terms with their English neighbors whom they had often visited, were already inside the settlements targeted for attack. They came unarmed, or with concealed weapons, to avoid any suspicion by the colonists of foul play. Some had brought venison and other food with the avowed purpose of trading with the colonists. When the signal for the attack was given at midday on March 22, they treacherously seized the colonists' own tools, turned on the unsuspecting settlers, and bludgeoned or stabbed them to death. Those hidden in the woods burst out with frightening war whoops and joined the assault on the colonists and their families in outlying farms and fields. In the course of an hour the Indians massacred 347 men, women, and children at thirty-one different places, often mutilating their corpses. Many families were completely wiped out in their scattered homes on the plantations; livestock was killed, and houses were burned to the ground. Martin's Hundred, seven miles from Jamestown, contained a hamlet in the midst of its scattered individual farms; it was probably the largest and best equipped plantation. At Martin's Hundred seventy-three people were slaughtered, more than at any other single location, and fifteen women were taken captive. At Henrico sixty-one were killed and the new ironworks was destroyed; at Edward Bonit's plantation fifty colonists were murdered.

The inhabitants of Jamestown and those living close by were saved from the massacre by the action of an Indian named Chanco, who had converted to become a Christian. Chanco was living with colonist Richard Pace. When his brother informed him of the secret plan the night before the massacre and told him that he must murder his master, he was appalled. After his brother had left, he told Pace of the plot. Pace informed the governor of Jamestown, and there was just enough time for the settlement to mount its defense against the attack. The lives of many families were completely disrupted by the massacre, as settlers retreated from the outlying plantations to move their families closer to the protection of the Jamestown fort.

The immediate shock felt in Virginia and England over the massacre was soon supplanted by fury and the call for merciless destruction of the enemy, to effect "your just revenge and your perpetuall security," declared the Virginia Company. Two months later the Jamestown soldiers went to war against the Powhatans. Retaliation by the colonists was swift and brutal. Many Indians, fleeing from the white man's onslaught, had sought protection by hiding in the dark forests. Later, induced by the colonists' pledges that they would not be harmed, they returned to their villages and cornfields. It was an English ruse to lure the natives into the open, and they attacked them with vengeful wrath. Annihilation was their purpose: nobody was spared, as they killed men, women, and children, destroyed their crops, stole their corn, and set fire to their villages. There is no record of the number that were killed, and many, including Opechancanough, escaped into the forest. For the next several months the killing continued as parties of armed colonists raided tribal villages, before the bloodshed ended in a sullen peace. The fierce battles with the Powhatans were forerunners of the largely one-sided Indian wars over the next two-and-a-half centuries, as the rapidly growing numbers of white settlers spread steadily throughout the country.

The Powhatan Indians, led by Opechancanough, attacked and slaughtered three hundred and forty-seven English colonists in 1622 at their farms and plantation homes. Courtesy of the Library of Virginia.

In New England intrigue involving the nearby tribes continued to threaten the Pilgrims' peaceful existence with the Indians. Captain Standish was planning to lead a party to trade with the Massachusetts natives in late March 1622 when Hobbamock, the other friendly Indian living with Squanto at Plymouth, reported some disturbing news to the Pilgrim leaders. He suspected that the Massachusetts planned to attack the Standish party after it left the settlement and then join the Narragansetts in an assault on Plymouth. Furthermore, he believed that Squanto, who had been secretly meeting with Indians in the forest, was an active member of this conspiracy. Governor Bradford decided to proceed with the plan for sending out a trading party, and ten men, accompanied by Squanto and Hobbamock, left in the shallop. The colony desperately needed the Standish group to replenish its store of food; its provisions were almost all consumed. The colonists were placed on guard duty to defend the settlement against attack.

Soon after the Standish company departed, an Indian, who was a relative of Squanto, came running up to the gate of the settlement, which was now surrounded by a stout wall. He was fleeing for his life, he said, from a war party of Narragansetts, joined by the Pokanokets and led by Massasoit and Coubatant, the aggressive Pocasset sachem. They had gathered in Namaschet, just fifteen miles from Plymouth, and, taking advantage of the absence of Standish and his men, they intended to attack the settlement. His face was bloodied by a wound that he had received when he spoke out against the plot. Governor Bradford ordered the town's cannons to be fired, sounding the alarm, and Standish and his men in the shallop, not yet far away, heard the signal and rushed back to the settlement. When Hobbamock was informed, he said flatly that the Indian's warning was absolutely false. As a high-ranking advisor to Massasoit in the Pokanoket tribe, he would have been consulted if any such plan was being contemplated, and he assured Governor Bradford of Massasoit's faithfulness and loyalty to the English. "There was no cause wherefore he should distrust him, and therefore should do well to continue his affections," wrote Edward Winslow. The Standish party departed again to trade with the Massachusetts, where they successfully bargained for an ample supply of food.

Hobbamock, at Bradford's bidding, then sent his wife on a private mission to Massasoit to see that all was well. Massasoit confirmed that no attack on Plymouth had been contemplated. He was grateful for the governor's trust in him, and, honoring his peace treaty with the Pilgrims, he would warn them if he heard of any plot to harm them. Moreover, he was furious at Squanto, whom he believed had attempted by devious means to turn the English against him and even incite them to launch an assault on his people. The Pilgrim leaders also now recognized that Squanto was scheming to undermine Massasoit's rule and replace him as the leader of the Pokanokets. His ambitious, power-seeking strategy was to demonstrate to his fellow tribesmen that his influence with the English was so great that "he could lead us to peace or war at his pleasure," as Winslow put it. He would demand gifts from the tribes in return for protecting them from attack by the English. He had told them that the English stored the plague in the ground, which they could release against their villages whenever they wanted. For months he had terrified the Indians in secret meetings with such tales. Only he could protect them.

Governor Bradford severely reprimanded Squanto and passed the word to neighboring tribes that they had nothing to fear from their allies, the English. Anyone who said otherwise was a liar and should be punished. However, the governor would not expel Squanto from Plymouth for his bad behavior. He was too valuable as an interpreter and advisor to let go. He relied heavily on Squanto to introduce the Pilgrims and present their peaceful intentions to regional Indian tribes. Furthermore, a personal bond of friendship had developed between the two men. With Squanto's critical help, Bradford had led the colonists in their struggle through the perilous early days.

However, Massasoit was not about to let Squanto off so easily and argued vehemently with Bradford that Squanto must pay with his life for his treacherous plotting against the chieftain. When Bradford demurred, Massasoit sent messengers later with the same demand. One brought Massasoit's own knife; it was to be used to cut off Squanto's head and hands, which they would then bring back to the chieftain. Bradford was in a quandary. Squanto claimed that Hobbamock had spread false reports about him, and there was clearly bad blood between the two Indians, as their rivalry smoldered in vying for influence with the English. Nevertheless, Bradford believed Squanto was guilty. Furthermore, Squanto was a subject of Massasoit, chief of the Pokanokets, and under the Pilgrims' treaty with Massasoit, the English had no right to retain him. Then, as Bradford was arguing with Massasoit's emissaries, the colonists spotted a boat approaching. Not knowing the identity of the vessel or its intentions, Bradford told the messengers that he was not ready to turn Squanto over to them. First he would have to make sure that the boat was not part of some new plot to attack Plymouth, perhaps a combined French and Indian assault. Massasoit's emissaries departed angrily.

The boat was a shallop belonging to a vessel sent by Thomas Weston and another Merchant Adventurer to fish for cod at Damariscove near the mouth of the Damariscotta River in Maine. Seven passengers disembarked carrying letters from Weston, but no food, not even for themselves. The most important message affecting the Pilgrims was that Weston expected the colonists to house and feed the newcomers until they moved on sometime later to build their own settlement. Secondly, Plymouth would not receive a supply ship any time soon, despite Robert Cushman's promise of "a speedy supply." Weston signed his letters, "Your loving friend," as was customary at the time.

Governor Bradford said of the letters, "Sundry other things I will pass over, being impertinent and tedious." He was angry. Weston and the Merchant Adventurers had sent more settlers, but no provisions to feed them or the rest of the colonists, and harvest time for their corn was three months away. At the end of May 1622 the colony's store of food was empty. The colonists had been on short rations throughout the winter. They had had to feed the thirty-five newcomers that had arrived unexpectedly on the *Fortune*, and now they had to feed the latest seven arrivals.

Weston's shallop also brought a letter from John Huddleston, the captain of one of the ships fishing near Damariscove, which contained the shocking news of the Indians' massacre of the English colonists in Virginia in March. Bradford sent Edward Winslow and a crew off in the Pilgrims' shallop to Damariscove to purchase fish and food from the fishing fleet gathered there. He met Captain Huddleston, who generously provided a modest supply of provisions for the colony, whatever he and a few other friendly fishermen could spare. Winslow returned with a small but vital addition to the colony's empty larder. The colonists were not equipped with seines and other fishing gear that would enable them to catch large quantities of bass and cod in the waters around Plymouth, and it was not the season for wild fowl. Instead they gathered shellfish along the shore to help sustain them until the harvest. Just like the first Jamestown settlers, they had to scramble desperately for food in order to survive. The frightening news about the Virginia massacre and rumors regarding the intention of the Narragansetts to go on the warpath incited the Pilgrims to strengthen their town's defenses. During the summer they built a fort on the hill within the settlement, which was already surrounded by a strong stockade. They placed their cannons behind the rooftop ramparts, where their range would cover the fields around the settlement, and they stationed a guard there to be on the lookout for any signs of danger. The Sunday church services, led by elder Brewster, would convene in the meeting room on the ground floor of the fort.

At the end of June two other ships belonging to Thomas Weston, the *Charity* and the smaller *Swan*, sailed into Plymouth Harbor and disembarked sixty men. Bradford received letters from Weston, two Merchant Adventurers, Robert Cushman, and John Pierce, the gentleman who had obtained the patent authorizing the Plymouth Plantation. None contained any good news. Weston had parted company from the Merchant Adventurers and was now planning to set up his own colony in the Boston Bay area. Until he chose a spot he expected the Pilgrims to care for the latest group of colonists that he would drop off with them. The Adventurers were glad to get rid of Weston, whom the Pilgrims should not trust, according to their letter. Thomas Weston's brother, Andrew, was "a heady young man and violent and set against you there and the company here." The two brothers were scheming to steal from the colony. Even Weston admitted that many of his men were "rude fellows," and Robert Cushman wrote, "the people that they carry are no men for us; wherefore I pray that you entertain them not. . . . I pray you therefore signify to Squanto that they are a distinct body from us, and we have nothing to do with them, neither must be blamed for their faults, much less can warrant their fidelity." John Pierce added that Weston's men were "as in all appearance not fit for an honest man's company."

Helping those in need came naturally to the devout Pilgrims, and they also felt obligated to Weston for his initial assistance to them. They accepted the burden of sheltering and caring for the sixty new arrivals, albeit reluctantly. The newcomers turned out to be just as corrupt and undisciplined as the letters to Bradford had warned: they stole and ate the unripened green corn from the Pilgrims' cornfields, which severely depleted the crop that the English were counting on to sustain them through the coming year. By the end of August Weston's scouts had selected a spot to build their settlement, which the Indians called Wessagusset, near today's town of Weymouth northwest of Plymouth on Boston Bay. Leaving their sick in the care of the Pilgrims, the rest of Weston's company left Plymouth in the *Swan* for the new location, where they built a small fort. Disorganized and poorly led, they were soon up to their old tricks. The Massachusetts Indians reported that Weston's men were stealing their corn and "other abuses."

The Pilgrims faced the coming winter and months until the next harvest with a diminished store of corn that was far too small to sustain them. To make matters worse, they no longer had any goods left to trade for corn from the Indians. Then their fortunes changed, "another providence of God," wrote Bradford. At the end of August two new ships arrived in the harbor, the Virginia Company's *Discovery* and Weston's *Sparrow*, both bound for Virginia. The *Discovery* carried an ample supply of beads, knives, and articles for trading with the natives, and Captain Thomas Jones was willing to sell some to Governor Bradford. Now the Pilgrims would be able to replenish their stores of corn and buy beaver pelts from the Indians.

Weston's men in Wessagusset soon realized that they, too, would have to trade for corn from the Indians to survive. They sent a message to Bradford proposing that they and the Pilgrims embark on a joint mission on the *Swan* to obtain corn from the Indians living south of Cape Cod, and the governor agreed. Violent winds aborted the first two outings before Governor Bradford took charge of the expedition in November. Squanto, who believed that he was now back in the good graces of Massasoit, wrote Winslow, thought that he could guide the *Swan* through the dangerous shoals south of the cape, the same treacherous waters that had forced the *Mayflower* to turn back. He said that he had made successful crossings twice before. The *Swan's* captain did not share his confidence when they encountered the breakers and sand bars in the risky passage. Instead he navigated his vessel into the harbor at Manamoyick, today's Pleasant Bay on the ocean side near the cape's elbow. Bradford's party, with Squanto serving as interpreter, went ashore, where the natives, after overcoming their initial fear of the strangers, welcomed and fed them. The next day the Pilgrims traded successfully to acquire eight hogsheads of corn and beans.

Suddenly Squanto was struck down by a deadly illness, which Bradford called the "Indian fever," and, bleeding from the nose, the Indian guide died a few days later. Some historians have speculated that Massasoit had not forgiven Squanto and ordered an ally to poison him, although there is no evidence backing this theory. In his last words to Bradford he desired "the Governor to pray for him that he might go to the Englishmens' God in heaven." He also bequeathed some of his possessions to "his English friends." Bradford had suffered the loss of a helpful Indian ally, who had become his friend. Plymouth had lost a valuable interpreter and guide in reaching out to the Indians of the region. Squanto's scheming to overthrow Massasoit had endangered the Pilgrims. On the other hand, his assistance to them had been critical. In Bradford's view he had been "a special instrument sent of God for their good beyond their expectation."

After a fruitless effort to obtain more corn from the Massachusetts natives near Boston Harbor, Bradford's party returned to Nauset, at today's Eastham on the inner shore of the cape. Aspinet, the Nauset sachem whom the Pilgrims had already met, greeted them warmly and sold them another eight or ten hogsheads of corn and beans. The weather was terrible. In a violent storm they lost their shallop, leaving them no way to transport their corn back to the *Swan*, which was standing well offshore some distance away. They found the shallop later, but it was too damaged to use. It had been driven by the storm high up on the beach and was almost completely covered with sand. They covered their corn for preservation and secure storage, and Aspinet promised to guard it until the English sent a party back to retrieve it. They walked on to Mattachiest, near today's Barnstable, where they purchased and stored more corn from the natives that the friendly local sachem would protect until they returned. Bradford sent word for the *Swan* to return to Plymouth without him. He and his men walked back to Plymouth, about thirty miles of hiking in cold winter weather, stopping at Indian villages en route where they were hospitably received.

In January 1623 Captain Standish and some of Weston's men sailed across Cape Cod Bay to fetch the corn, which they found in good condition; their carpenter also repaired the damaged shallop. While spending the night ashore at Nauset, an Indian sneaked into the English camp and stole some beads, knives, and other trading articles. Miles Standish was not one to ignore an act of Indian thievery. He immediately reported the theft to the sachem, Aspinet, and threatened revenge if the articles were not returned. The next morning the sachem and his men turned over the stolen articles to Standish and saluted the English "in a stately manner." The sachem had beaten the thief for his crime. He presented a gift of some bread freshly baked by his women, apologized profusely, and declared that he "was glad to be reconciled" with the English. The Standish party returned to Plymouth safely, and Weston's men departed for Wessagusset with their share of the corn.

Obtaining enough corn to survive was a constant challenge, and during the winter months Bradford and Standish led excursions to several native villages that were successful in buying additional supplies. While Standish was visiting Manomet, a Massachusetts chief named Wituwamat arrived whom Winslow described as "a notable insulting villain." He bragged about having killed English and French men and boasted about his own courage and their weakness. Standish would not forget his arrogant and threatening manner.

In March Governor Bradford received word that Massasoit was dying. When a prominent Indian was near death, it was the custom for his friends and allies to visit him or send their emissaries to show their friendship and respect for him. Accordingly, Governor Bradford dispatched Edward Winslow to see the dying chieftain, accompanied by John Hamden, a London gentleman, who had arrived on the *Charity* and wanted to see the country, and Hobbamock, their guide and interpreter. When they reached the Pokanoket village, Massasoit's house was filled with people, including several powows or medicine men "making such a hellish noise, as it distempered us that were well, and therefore unlikely to ease him that was sick," wrote Winslow. Massasoit, who had lost his sight, was told that his English friend Winslow had come to see him, and he replied, "O Winslow, I shall never see you again." As Hobbamock translated, Winslow told the chieftain that Governor Bradford was very sorry to hear of his sickness; other important business kept him from coming himself, so he had sent Winslow with some things "most likely to do him good in his extremity."

Little by little Winslow fed him some fruit preserves, the first food he had swallowed in two days. The chieftain's tongue was furred and swollen; Winslow scraped his tongue, washed out his mouth, and gave him some water and more of the preserve. Gradually Massasoit's condition improved, and he regained his sight. The next morning Winslow concocted a broth of sassafras roots, raspberry leaves, and corn, which the sachem drank down heartily. His appetite had so improved that he gorged himself on a duck that Winslow had shot and became ill again, but after a sound sleep he recovered. Winslow complied with Massasoit's request that he treat some of the other sick natives in the village. He gave them the same broth that had helped their chief recover and washed out their mouths, a task that he understandably found most distasteful.

Massasoit slowly regained his strength. A messenger had brought two chickens from Plymouth for the sachem's cooking pot, and he now decided to save them for breeding stock. One of his lieutenants informed the visitors that continued to come as to how, when Massasoit was near death, his English friends had arrived and saved his life with their treatment of his illness. Before the English had arrived one sachem had stated that their absence showed that they were not true friends of Massasoit. The chieftain, on the road to recovery, declared, "Now I see the English are my friends and love me; and whilst I live, I will never forget this kindness they have showed me," and he didn't.

As the English were about to depart, Massasoit pulled Hobbamock aside to report some ominous news for him to pass on to Winslow. The Massachusetts were planning to attack the Weston settlement at Wessagusset and then Plymouth and had persuaded the Indians living south of Plymouth at Nauset, Capawack (Martha's Vineyard), and a few other villages to join them. Massasoit, who would not betray his English friends, had refused their proposal. The Massachusetts were determined to wipe out the troublesome Weston colony, whose people had stolen their corn. They believed that the Plymouth settlers would retaliate to avenge the death of their countrymen, and therefore they planned to attack that settlement as well. Massasoit strongly urged his English friends "to kill the men of Massachuset, who were the authors of this intended mischief" in a preemptive strike before it was too late.

During the winter Weston's men, without firm leadership or discipline, had consumed all their corn and were starving to death. Some stole from the Indians; others even sold their clothes or worked as servants for the Massachusetts to get food. Governor Bradford had sternly advised John Sanders, the overseer at Wessagusset, to stop his men from stealing Indian corn, which was against "the law of God and nature" and the policy of "the King's Majesty and his honourable Council for this place . . . in respect of the peaceable enlarging of his Majesty's dominions." Antagonizing the Indians would surely endanger the lives of the settlers in both plantations, and when his Majesty or the Council of New England learned of the crime, "the principal agents should expect no better than the gallows." He added that the Plymouth colonists had little corn left and were gathering groundnuts, clams, and mussels to eat; Weston's people should do the same.

Back in Plymouth, Winslow reported Massasoit's startling news to Governor Bradford. About the same time another sachem, the brother of Obtakiest, the chieftain of the Massachusetts, disclosed the plot to the English; he had decided his best course was to be on their side in the coming confrontation. Bradford met with his advisors. Edward Winslow wrote, "It much grieved us to shed the blood of those whose good we ever intended and aimed at." Nevertheless, they had to protect the lives of their fellow countrymen and themselves. The news of the Indian massacre in Virginia was still fresh in their minds. Miles Standish would lead a party, ostensibly on a trading mission, to the country of the Massachusetts, where he would first meet with Weston's men to get the lay of the land. If Captain Standish was convinced that the reported threats against the English were certain, he should take action to forestall an Indian attack. His special charge was to kill Wituwamat, "the bloody and bold villain" whom Standish had confronted at Manomet, and bring his head back "that he might be a warning and terror to all of that disposition." Standish had persuaded his peace-loving colleagues that the dangerous sachem, who had already killed English men and insulted Standish at Manomet, must be put to death.

As Standish and the band of eight men that he had chosen were preparing to depart, one of Weston's men, Phineas Pratt, who had hiked overland from Wessagusset, walked into Plymouth. He described the pitiful conditions at the settlement. Many of the starving men had left the base to seek whatever bits of food they could find. Those who had sold their clothes for corn and could not scrounge for food were dying from the cold and starvation. John Sanders, their overseer, had sailed to Monhegan Island to buy bread from the English fishermen. Whether they could survive until his return was questionable. The Massachusetts were becoming increasingly aggressive. They taunted the emaciated settlers and consumed the pots of groundnuts and shellfish that they collected. Some of the settlers had already starved to death, and the Indians had perceived the growing weakness of Weston's men. They were not appeased when the settlers hung one of their company for stealing corn from the Indians. The settlers had little powder and shot left to defend themselves and feared an attack could come any time. Pratt had not dared to remain with Weston's men any longer; he had made the difficult journey to Plymouth "to make known their weak and dangerous estate" and remain there "till things were better settled at the other plantation." Pratt's report confirmed the urgency of the need for Standish's mission, and with a fair wind his band set sail the next day for Wessagusset with Hobbamock as their interpreter.

At Weston's walled settlement at Wessagusset, Standish informed the men in charge of his plan to thwart the Massachusetts plot to attack the two

English settlements. Afterward, if they felt it was too dangerous to remain among the Massachusetts, they could come to Plymouth, or he would try to help them in any other course that they chose. They replied that "it was God's mercy that they were not killed before his coming, desiring therefore that he would neglect no opportunity to proceed." Standish swore them to secrecy about the plan. They should order the members of their company who had left the fort to return immediately to protect it from attack. Standish also provided them with a small stock of corn.

The word soon reached the Massachusetts that a group led by Standish was at the fort. Pecksuot, a Massachusetts brave, told Hobbamock that he knew that Standish had come to kill him and the other Indians. They did not fear him, "let him come when he dare, he shall not take us unawares." The Indians boldly visited the fort from time to time where they made insulting remarks and threatening gestures such as ostentatiously honing and sharpening the points of their knives before Standish. Wituwamat was proud of his knife, which had the picture of a woman's face on the handle. He added, "I have another one at home, wherewith I have killed both French and English." Pecksuot noting that Standish was short in stature, told him that "though he were a great captain, yet he was but a little man; and . . . though I be no sachim, yet I am a man of great strength and courage." Standish bore these affronts patiently, waiting for the opportune moment to strike.

The next day Standish enticed Wituwamat, Pecksuot, another Indian, and Wituwamat's teenage brother into a room at the fort by offering them a meal of corn and pork, a rare delicacy for the Indians. Three or four of Standish's men were with him, all ready to carry out their plan of attack. When the door was closed, Standish grabbed Pecksuot's sharp knife hanging from his neck and started stabbing him. Pecksuot struggled fiercely before dying. Like John Smith, another short man, Miles Standish was powerful and ferocious in one-on-one combat. At the same time, Standish's companions assaulted and killed Wituwamat and the other Indian. Hobbamock, who had watched the killings take place, smiled and told Standish, "Yesterday Pecksuot, bragging of his own strength and stature, said, though you were a great captain, yet you were but a little man; but today I see you are big enough to lay him on the ground."

Standish had not finished carrying out his plan to put an end to the Massachusetts' threat to the English settlements. His men seized the brother of Wituwamat and hung him. Standish and his companions killed three other Indians and then clashed in a skirmish with a group of warriors who finally retreated into a swamp and escaped. Almost all of Weston's men chose to sail to Monhegan Island where they hoped to obtain passage back to England on one of the fishing vessels gathered there. Standish gave them some corn and saw them off in the *Swan* as they cleared Massachusetts Bay. A few Weston settlers joined Standish's company when they headed back to Plymouth in the shallop. They brought their prize trophy, the head of Wituwamat, with them.

Standish and his men were greeted joyously by their colleagues at Plymouth, who were delighted with his success in thwarting the Indian attack on their little settlement. Wituwamat's head was placed on a pole mounted on the roof of the fort as a warning to any Indians conspiring against the colony. The practice of publicly displaying the heads of slain rebels, English, Scottish, or Irish, was common in England. A young Massachusetts Indian, who had come to Plymouth after Standish had left, had been imprisoned by Governor Bradford, who suspected that he was a spy. He was grateful to the Pilgrims for treating him fairly, and when he recognized the head of Wituwamat, he disclosed that the Massachusetts had indeed planned to kill Weston's settlers. Standish and his men had arrived just in time to save them. Five leaders had recommended the plot to the Massachusetts sachem, Obtakiest, and the English had killed the two principals, Wituwamat and Pecksuot. The young Indian said that he had not had a hand in the scheme and pleaded for his life.

Governor Bradford freed the Indian youth so that he could deliver a message to Obtakiest: the English had never contemplated taking action against them "till their own treachery forced us thereunto, and therefore they might thank themselves for their own overthrow." If they again pursued a similar course, the governor "would never suffer him or his to rest in peace, till he had utterly consumed them." Finally, he instructed Obtakiest to send three of Weston's settlers that he held back to Plymouth. Sometime later a Massachusetts woman arrived at Plymouth with a message from Obtakiest. Unfortunately, he had already killed the three English prisoners before he had heard from Governor Bradford; otherwise, he would have complied with Bradford's wishes. He desired peaceful relations with the English, but his men were now so frightened by them that they did not dare come to Plymouth to talk. Fearing that "we would take further vengeance on him," the sachem had left his home and was moving about from place to place.

The Cape Cod tribes that had intended to join the Massachusetts were also "terrified and amazed" by the sudden massacre at Wessagusset carried out by Captain Standish and his men. Many fled their villages to hide out in swamps or the woods, fearful that the English would come after them next. Edward Winslow reported that the consequences of this major disruption in the lives of the Cape Cod Indians were tragic. Many died from disease, including the leading sachems in the area—Canacum of Manomet, Aspinet of Nauset, and Ianough of Mattachiest, who had said before he died that "the God of the English was offended with them, and would destroy them in his anger." In abandoning their homes to hide from the English the natives neglected to plant their corn and other crops, the basic food they needed to survive, and more Indians perished as the year wore on. As a gesture of good-will, one tribe sent a boat filled with presents for Governor Bradford across the bay to Plymouth. It foundered and sank, drowning the three peace emis-saries on board. For the Cape Cod Indians Ianough's prophesy was coming true.

In the eyes of the Plymouth colonists the imminent threat to their lives and those of Weston's men fully justified their swift and deadly assault on the Massachusetts. This view was reflected in Edward Winslow's account of the incident in his book, *Good Newes from New England*, and Governor Bradford in his book, *Of Plymouth Plantation*, played down the brutal episode. Their companions across the ocean in Leiden must have been stunned—their col-leagues' ambush and slaughter of Indians who had not attacked them seemed completely out of character and difficult to comprehend. Once they had put to death the ringleaders, why was it necessary to hang the youth and hunt down and kill more Indians? When John Robinson, their esteemed pastor in Leiden, heard about the killings led by Captain Standish, he wrote Governor Bradford "to consider the disposition of their Captain, who was of a warm temper. He hoped the Lord had sent him among them for good, if they used him right; but he doubted where there was not wanting that tenderness of the life of man, made after God's image which was meet." Robinson added, "O how happy a thing had it been that you had converted some before you killed any."

The English assault at Wessagusset had dramatically changed human relationships in the region. The Plymouth settlers had demonstrated their will to defend themselves with strong and aggressive action. Through their firm alliance with the Pilgrims, Massasoit and the Pokanokets gained consid-erable influence in the Cape Cod region, especially since the Cape Cod tribes had been disrupted and weakened by sickness and the loss of their sachems. Like the Massachusetts, who now called the English "cutthroats," the Cape Cod natives were now so fearful of ruthless English violence that they stayed away from Plymouth and remained in hiding. The colonists suffered as well from this new turn of events. Their ability to acquire beaver pelts and furs from the local tribes, needed to repay their debt to the Merchant Adventur-ers, was now severely limited.

In Virginia, Governor Yeardley had abolished the communal farming system in 1619. Thereafter, every settler received a parcel of land to own and farm for his own benefit, as John Smith had recommended earlier. In April 1623 as the corn-planting season got underway, Governor Bradford, after deliberating with his officers, decided to do away with the communal system in Plymouth. Every farmer had been working for the common store. Some contributed far more than others and still received the same portion of food;

hardworking, single young men resented a system that required them to labor to supply the families of other men with no additional compensation. Tensions arose, crop production suffered, and producing an adequate supply of corn was critical for the colony's survival. Accordingly, Bradford decreed that each family would plant its crops for its own consumption, putting aside a small portion for the common good, such as providing for public officers and fishermen. The number of family members determined the size of the plots that were assigned, and because the condition of the land varied, the plots were drawn by lottery.

Not surprisingly, growing their own food energized the Pilgrim farmers. Even the wives, bringing their youngsters with them, went out to the fields to join their husbands in planting corn, and more was planted than ever before. Unfortunately, Mother Nature refused to cooperate. "But it pleased God for our further chastisement, to send a great drought," wrote Edward Winslow. For six weeks during June and July hardly a drop of rain fell. The corn and beans became stunted and parched, and the prospects for a bountiful harvest at the end of the summer were considerably dimmed.

To feed the colony during the summer, several teams of six or seven men were formed to take turns fishing for bass and other fish in the settlement's only boat; others gathered shellfish along the sandy shore, and occasionally hunters returned with a deer that they had shot. Pilgrim families were on very short rations and became increasingly discouraged, "at night not many times knowing where to have a bit of any thing the next day," wrote Bradford. As the drought continued, the leaders designated a day for fasting and prayer, "hoping that the same God who had stirred us up hereunto would be moved hereby in mercy to look down upon us and grant the request of our dejected souls," wrote Edward Winslow. When the Pilgrims gathered to pray that morning, the sky had been clear and sunny. That evening dark clouds gathered, and the next morning it rained, "such soft sweet and moderate showers of rain" that continued, off and on, for two weeks. "It was hard to say whether our withered corn or drooping affections were most quickened or revived," said Winslow. Hobbamock was greatly impressed with the quick and beneficial effects following the Pilgrims' prayer for rain, admiring the goodness and power of the Pilgrims' God. The Indian rain gods did not always produce such good results. It was only fitting, declared Governor Bradford, to "set apart a day of thanksgiving," and on July 30, 1623, the Pilgrims gave thanks to God for his blessings. The corn and other crops revived and flourished, assuring a fruitful harvest, and just in time.

During the first weeks of August two new ships, sent by the Merchant Adventurers, arrived at Plymouth, the larger *Anne*, followed by the pinnace *Little James*. Sixty new settlers for the Plymouth colony disembarked, including some wives and children of Pilgrims already at Plymouth. Some of the newcomers were "very useful persons"; others were clearly unfit to be responsible members of the colony, wrote Bradford, and he thought that he might have to send them home the following year. One group that arrived was not party to the financial agreement between the Adventurers and the Pilgrims and would live independently beyond the settlement, subject to certain restrictions and obligations, such as participation in the common defense. They were identified as persons who had come over "on their Particular," or on their own account. Robert Cushman in a letter to Bradford said, "It grieveth me to see so weak a company sent you. . . . You must still call upon the company here to see that honest men be sent to you, and threaten to send them back if any other come. . . . Neither is there need we should take any lewd men, for we may have honest men enow." Cushman, who was associated with the Merchant Adventurers, had done his best, he said, to prevent unsuitable persons from joining the departing colonists, but he was not the final authority.

Elder William Brewster's two daughters arrived on the *Anne*. So did the widow Alice Southworth with her two boys. The Southworths and the Bradfords had been friends in Leiden, and about two weeks after the new settlers landed, Governor Bradford, whose wife had drowned at Cape Cod Harbor, and Alice Southworth were married. Massasoit and a large company of Pokanokets attended the wedding in an unusual tribute to their English ally. Captain Standish, whose first wife had died at Plymouth, soon married his second wife, Barbara, another passenger on the *Anne*. Old neighbors from Leiden rejoiced to see each other again, although the newcomers were distressed to see the worn-out physical appearance and ragged clothing of their friends in Plymouth. They soon understood the reason: there was very little food to feed everyone. William Bradford wrote, "The best dish they could present their friends with was a lobster or a piece of fish without bread or anything else but a cup of fair spring water."

A few weeks later a plentiful harvest of corn, beans, and other crops lifted the community's spirits. Bradford wrote, "Instead of famine now God gave them plenty, and the face of things was changed, to the rejoicing of the hearts of many, for which they blessed God." Allowing the colonists to produce their own crops to feed themselves and their families had succeeded in providing enough food for the coming year. Some of the more industrious farmers had produced enough corn to spare some, which they sold to others. The new system was working, and famine would no longer be a constant threat in the future.

The *Anne* set sail for England on September 10, 1623, with a cargo of clapboard, beaver pelts, and other furs. The *Little James* would remain at Plymouth to be used for trading and fishing expeditions; it sunk later in a storm. The colony sent Edward Winslow, their chief ambassador, back on the *Anne* to report to the Adventurers and the Pilgrims' companions in Leiden. Winslow brought back to London the manuscript of his account of events at the colony that took place during 1622 and 1623; *Good Newes from New England, A True Relation of Things Very Remarkable at the Plimoth Plantation in New England* was published in London in 1624.

Winslow had some words of advice to potential investors in Plymouth or other New England colonies. Some of the colony's most serious problems had stemmed from the poor decisions of the London investors that led to constant friction between the Pilgrims and their backers. In *Good Newes from New England* he warned against "the vain expectation of present profit, carelessness of those that send over the supplies of men unto them not caring how they be qualified; so that oftimes they are rather the image of men endued with bestial, yea, diabolical affections, than the image of God endued with reason, understanding, and holiness." Winslow prayed God, "If there be any who are too desirous of gain, to entreat them to moderate their affections and consider that no man should expecteth fruit before the tree be grown." He beseeched the sponsors of colonies "to have the care of transporting men for the supply and furnishing of plantations, to be truly careful in sending such as may further and not hinder so good an action." John Smith would have wholeheartedly agreed with Edward Winslow's advice.

Winslow returned to Plymouth about six months later with some clothing and other necessary supplies including three heifers and a bull, the first cattle brought to New England. He reported that there was a strong faction among the Adventurers that were reluctant to continue supporting the venture. Some would-be colonists, who had come to Plymouth "on their Particular," had quickly become dissatisfied and returned home. They complained bitterly to the Adventurers about conditions at the colony, raising a host of silly objections, such as that the land was barren, the water was impure, there were foxes and wolves, and the people were annoyed by mosquitoes. To the latter charge Bradford replied with unaccustomed wit, "They are too delicate and unfitted to begin new plantations and colonies that cannot enduer the biting of a musketo; we would wish such to keepe at home till at least they be musketo-proofe."

Edward Winslow addressing the complaints about life at Plymouth wrote, "And can any be so simple as to conceive that the fountains should spring forth wine or beer, or the woods or rivers be like butchers' shops or fishmonger's stalls where they might have things taken to their hands? If thou canst not live without such things, and hast no means to procure the one, and wilt not take pains for the other, nor hast ability to employ others for thee, rest where thou art; for as a proud heart, a dainty tooth, a beggar's purse, and an idle hand, be here intolerable, so that person who hath these qualities there is much more abominable." Once again Captain John Smith would have agreed completely.

At the start of 1624 there were about 180 settlers living at Plymouth in thirty-two small houses. Almost all of them had come over on the *Mayflower*, the *Fortune*, the *Anne*, and the *Little James*. On March 25 the Plymouth colonists reelected William Bradford to be their governor, despite his modest demurral that a change in the chief personnel holding public office would be wise and appropriate. His fellow colonists did not accept his argument. In the election the colonists also chose six men to be members of the governor's council, or assistants, as they did each year. Except for two brief interludes Bradford would serve as governor of Plymouth until he died in 1657, a total of thirty-one years in office since the arrival of the *Mayflower*.

The Pilgrims continued to harvest an ample supply of corn, sometimes producing a surplus, which they traded to the Indians for beaver and other furs. In 1624 each colonist was given ownership of an acre of land to farm. Morale was high in the little colony. The Pilgrims had persevered and overcome incredible hardships. A year later William Bradford wrote a friend, "The Pilgrims never felt the sweetness of the country till this year." Some forty years after Sir Walter Raleigh's failed attempt to establish a settlement at Roanoke, the future of the first English colony in New England seemed assured.

The Plymouth colonists pressed for more land for their crops and growing herds of cattle, which were divided among the colonists in 1627. Heads of families received twenty acres for each family member. In 1630 William Bradford and his Plymouth associates received a patent from the royally chartered Council of New England confirming the boundaries and title to their lands and giving the colony the right to enact its own laws as long as they did not conflict with English laws.

The Plymouth colony also established several trading posts up the coast and inland to purchase beaver pelts and furs, with the proceeds from their sale going to reduce the debt owed the Merchant Adventurers. In 1626 Issac Allerton, Bradford's former deputy, negotiated an agreement in London with the Adventurers for Plymouth to pay off the debt that the colony owed them and eliminate their proprietary interest in the colony. Over the coming years angry disputes erupted between the Pilgrims and their London creditors. Bradford believed the Adventurers were cheating them—overcharging them for supplies and, with questionable accounting, paying too little for the furs that the colonists sent them. Finally the parties reached a new agreement, and Bradford and a few Pilgrim leaders satisfied the final claim of an Adventurer in 1645.

Massasoit was true to his word and maintained friendly relations between the Pokanokets and the Pilgrims for the rest of his life, while providing a fruitful fur-trading business for the Pilgrims. The Pokanoket chieftain died in 1660. The Pilgrims, however, faced a different and unexpected problem with their own countrymen—convicting and expelling a few rebellious troublemakers that had been sent to Jamestown by the Merchant Adventurers. They also had to deal with an obstreperous, hard-drinking group at the new English settlement of Mt. Wallaston, near present-day Braintree, who were selling guns to the Indians and cutting into the colonists' fur trade with them. Governor Bradford, the devout Pilgrim leader, was shocked at the shameless conduct of these men. "They also set up a Maypole drinking and dancing aboute it many ways together, inviting the Indian women for their consorts, dancing and frisking together like so many fairies, or furies" and reviving "the beasly practiseses of the madd Bacchinalians." They gave their settlement a new name, Merry Mount. Arming the Indians with guns posed a mortal danger to the colonists of Plymouth and outlying settlements. When Thomas Morton, the ringleader, rejected Bradford's warning to stop providing arms to the Indians, the governor dispatched Captain Standish and a company to handle the matter, and he did, capturing the drunken Morton and shipping him back to England in 1628.

Based on Henry Hudson's earlier exploration of the area, the Dutch still claimed the territory encompassing the Delaware and Hudson River valley region, where they had earlier established two small trading outposts. In 1624 the Dutch West Indies Company transported thirty families to settle in several separate groups—at the southern tip of Manhattan Island, at Fort Orange up the Hudson River (at today's Albany), and at a site on the Delaware River. A year later another company of Dutch colonists, mainly farmers with their livestock, settled on Manhattan, where they built a small fort at the tip of the island. When Peter Minuit, the colony's new director, arrived in 1626, he negotiated the purchase of Manhattan Island from the Indians for a bunch of trinkets worth no more than twenty-four dollars, according to the generally accepted estimate. He also named the colony New Amsterdam. The Dutch built a flour mill in New Amsterdam and established the Dutch Reformed Church. In October 1627 Issac de Rasieres, the Secretary of New Amsterdam, visited Plymouth to initiate trading relations with the colony. He wrote a friend that he was impressed with the well-ordered life of the community, the disciplined military guard, and noted that the colonists' laws were especially strict regarding incidents of sexual immorality.

In New England a number of small new settlements were starting to spring up—a fishing base first at Cape Anne and later at Salem, led by Roger

Conant, who had left Plymouth earlier; a settlement at the mouth of the Piscataqua River near today's Portsmouth; another in Maine at York and trading and fishing stations on Monhegan and Damariscove islands and at Pemaquid; Plymouth trading posts up the Kennebec River in Maine and at Windsor in the Connecticut River valley; and small clusters of colonists settling outside Plymouth and approaching the Boston Harbor area. In 1630 there were about 400 Dutch in New Amsterdam, probably about 900 English settlers in Maine and New Hampshire, and over 2,000 in Virginia.

An estimate 2500 English settlers and several hundred African slaves were living in Bermuda in 1630. The first band of English colonists to settle in the West Indies, eighty settlers and ten slaves, landed in Barbados in 1627. A growing number of English colonists would migrate to a handful of Caribbean islands before long to raise sugar cane with African slave labor.

From time to time a few new settlers were dropped off in Plymouth by passing ships. Plymouth remained the largest and only significant English community in New England for almost a decade after the arrival of the *Mayflower*. In all of Massachusetts, however, there were still probably not more than three hundred English colonists before the Puritans sailed into Massachusetts Bay.

· 18 ·

John Winthrop and the Puritans

*O*n September 6, 1628, forty Puritan immigrants, whose company had received a patent from the New England Council, arrived and settled in Roger Conant's outpost at Salem. They were led by a tough soldier and ardent Puritan, John Endicott. The following year a group of prominent Puritans, after gaining control of the patent, obtained a royal charter for their Massachusetts Bay Company from King Charles I, who had succeeded to the throne after the death of his father, James I, in 1625. It authorized them to "govern and rule all His Majesty's subjects that reside within the limits of our plantation," the coastal area from three miles south of the Charles River, today's greater Boston, up to the Merrimac River, about thirty-five miles to the north, and extending indefinitely inland. The new charter gave the colonists a large measure of independence; their colony was virtually a self-governing state in America. Settlers, who had to be members of the church, would elect their own governor and principal officers. In April 1629 the company dispatched six ships bringing four hundred settlers, supplies, and livestock to Salem. One of their ministers, the Reverend Francis Higginson, and others sent back enthusiastic reports about the attributes of the region; Higginson declared "A sup of New England's air is better than a whole draft of old England's ale."

During 1629 the Puritan leaders in England, led by their elected governor John Winthrop, had been laying their plans to build a new colony in the Massachusetts Bay area. Winthrop was a forceful forty-year-old lawyer, a country gentleman from an old Suffolk family, and a landowner who was in debt and facing mounting financial pressures. The Puritans sought to remove themselves from the dictates of the Anglican Church, with its bishops, vestments, and rituals, to become free to worship God in their own manner, the purer form of the early Christians. Furthermore, many were dismayed by the social and economic system in England that left a large number of people mired in poverty. They were discouraged by the rampant political corruption in their country as King Charles, after dissolving the last session of Parliament for twelve years in 1629, imposed a heavy burden of taxation on his subjects to finance his extravagant expenses. New England, where English immigrants could readily acquire their own properties and prosper, offered far greater economic opportunity than the prevailing conditions in England. John Winthrop in a letter to a friend declared his uneasiness about his country: "I am verily persuaded God will bring some heavy affliction upon this land, and that speedily; but be of good comfort. . . . If the Lord seeth it will be good for us, He will provide a hiding place for us and others. . . . Evil times are coming when the church must fly into the wilderness." Winthrop wrote his wife, "The whole earth is the Lord's garden and He hath given it to the sons of men. . . . Why then shall we stand striving here for places of habitation and in the meantime suffer a whole continent, as fruitful and convenient for the use of man, to lie waste without any improvement." Selling his properties and migrating to New England with his family, servants, and workers, was the answer, as it was for his Puritan colleagues.

In the spring of 1630 Governor Winthrop in the *Arbella* and a huge fleet of ten other ships set sail from Southampton for Salem, carrying about nine hundred immigrants—men, women, and children, plus supplies and livestock. Most of them moved on from Salem to settle in Charlestown, and later across the river to Boston. John Winthrop's goal was to establish "a city upon a hill," a community of Puritans proudly living according to their ideals that would become a shining example for others to follow. Like their colonizing predecessors, the newcomers soon ran low on provisions and faced famine and death; nearly two hundred died during the bitter winter months. Nevertheless, the Great Migration, as it became known, had begun. In 1633 the persecution of Puritans in England was intensified under the new Archbishop of Canterbury, William Laud, who believed that the Puritans' form of worship was blasphemous. The number of emigrants surged. By 1634 some ten thousand Puritan colonists had settled in New England, and by 1640 about two hundred ships had delivered over twenty thousand new settlers to Massachusetts Bay.

There were marked differences between the Pilgrims and the Puritan newcomers arriving in New England a decade after them. The Pilgrims in their little religious community were small farmers, laborers, craftsmen, and fishermen. On the other hand, a number of Puritans were men of substance—landed gentry, merchants, professionals, and many sturdy yeomen farmers; they had not been beholden to London backers to finance their enterprise. Still, the two groups had much in common, and the Pilgrims were quick to welcome the new settlers. They were fellow countrymen, who, like themselves, had come to New England seeking the freedom to worship in their own way and govern themselves. In 1629 and 1630 Massachusetts Bay Colony ships carrying Puritan settlers brought over two groups of Separatists from Leiden, who went on to Plymouth after landing in Salem.

A number of colonists in Endicott's initial expedition in 1628 had become ill from bad food during the ocean voyage. Poorly sheltered after landing in Salem in September, they began dying off as the weather turned colder. Endicott had learned that Samuel Fuller, a church deacon of the Plymouth Colony, was a physician and sent word to Governor Bradford asking for his assistance. Bradford sent Fuller to Salem to attend to the sick patients. His compassionate treatment of the sick and his conversations with Endicott about the Separatists' devout practice of their religious faith greatly impressed Endicott. In a letter of March 29, 1629, he wrote Bradford, "I acknowledge much bound to you for your kind love and care in sending Mr. Fuller among us, and rejoice much that I am by him satisfied touching your judgments of the outward form of God's worship." Endicott prayed that "we may as Christian brethren, be united by a heavenly and unfeigned love." Fuller had been persuasive in explaining that the Plymouth Separatists were not as radical as the Puritans had thought.

The residents of the old colony of Plymouth and the newcomers of the Massachusetts Bay Colony got along well. Governors Bradford and Winthrop liked and respected each other and exchanged visits between Plymouth and Boston from time to time. One time Governor Winthrop and his pastor walked twenty-five miles from Wessagusset to Plymouth where Governor Bradford was his host for a few days. Winthrop spoke at the Sunday church service, and the distinguished guest was invited to dine with several families. Another time Governor Winthrop lent twenty-eight pounds of gunpowder to the Pilgrims, which they urgently needed.

As the new settlers poured into the port of Boston, they needed more and better farmlands and began spreading out beyond the Boston area. A few wished to be free from the Puritans' strict political and religious regime in Boston. Many went westward to settle at Hartford and other new settlements in the fertile Connecticut River Valley. In 1636 the Reverend Thomas Hooker led around one hundred colonists from his church congregation at Cambridge to Hartford, along with their household goods and cattle; they were soon followed by hundreds of others from the bay region. In 1638 three Connecticut River towns, Hartford, Windsor, and Wethersfield, joined together to become the independent self-governing colony of Connecticut with the capital at Hartford. Later, New Haven on the coast was settled, and another new colony was formed adding Stamford, Guilford, Milford, Branford, and on the eastern end of Long Island, Southold.

John Winthrop was the leader of the Puritans and the first governor of the
Massachusetts Bay Colony.
Courtesy, American Antiquarian Society.

Roger Williams was a dissident opposed to the strict Puritan regime
that banned participation in other forms of religion in the Massachusetts
Bay Colony. Those found guilty were exiled and sometimes hung. In the Bay
Colony the church and the state were the same. Williams was a strong be-
liever in religious tolerance and the separation of church and state, ideas that
the Puritan leaders abhorred. He was sympathetic to the plight of the Indians
as English settlers eagerly took over their traditional lands. He also held the
view that perhaps God was willing to accept the Indians' form of worship just
as He accepted Christianity, which was a scandalous idea in the eyes of the

Puritans. He and his family stayed at Plymouth for two years before moving on to Salem when his independent religious views began to disturb his Separatist hosts. In 1636 he founded Providence; Rhode Island then became a separate non-Puritan colony, which attracted dissidents fleeing from the strict authoritarian regime of the Bay Colony.

Families were also leaving Plymouth to start new hamlets further away, often to acquire more pastureland for their growing herds of cattle. Selling grain, livestock, and pigs to the Bay Colony Puritans was a profitable new business for Plymouth farmers. Following their regular practice, the colonists negotiated and purchased their new lands from the Indians. Governor Bradford was dismayed to see so many separate themselves from the parent settlement as the trend continued. "As their stocks increased and the increase vendible," wrote Bradford, "there was no longer any holding them together. . . . And no man now thought he could live except he had cattle and a great deal of ground to keep them, all striving to increase their stocks. By which means they were scattered all over [Plymouth] Bay quickly, and the town in which they lived compactly till now was left very thin and in a short time almost desolate."

Nearby Duxbury was the first offshoot to be incorporated, and the families of his good friends, Miles Standish, John Alden, Jonathan Brewster, and other prominent Pilgrims chose to move and build sturdy new homes there. The new settlement was named after Miles Standish's ancestral home, Duxbury Hall in Lancastershire. For several years, at Bradford's request, the Duxbury residents returned to the protection of the Plymouth settlement each winter, which facilitated their attendance at church and meetings of the General Court. The first church in the colony outside of Plymouth was built in Duxbury. Over the coming years other Plymouth folk would move to the Bay Colony, and a few Puritans, tired of living under the strict religious authority of their government, settled in Plymouth Colony. *Handmaid* and other ships landed new settlers for Plymouth from time to time. As the colony's population grew, the new towns of Marshfield, Scituate, Barnstable, Taunton, Yarmouth, and Sandwich were started within the colony. Each town sent two deputies to Plymouth to represent their residents at the meetings of the General Court, the legislative body, three times a year; the town of Plymouth was awarded four deputies.

In 1633 John Alden was appointed assistant to the governor and later first assistant or deputy governor of the colony, offices that he held for many years, along with various official posts in Duxbury. Alden, the youngest signer of the Mayflower Compact, died in 1686 at the age of eighty-seven. The families of Miles Standish and John Alden were joined when Standish's eldest son, Alexander, married Sarah, the daughter of John and Priscilla Alden, and the young couple built a home in Duxbury.

The exodus from Plymouth diminished the attendance and support for Bradford's beloved church, which was very discouraging for him: "The poor church left, like an ancient mother grown old and forsaken of her children, though not in their affection yet in regard to their bodily presence and personal helpfulness, her ancient members being most of them worn away by death, and these of later time being like children translated into other families, and she like a widow left only to trust in God. Thus, she that had made many rich became herself poor."

William Bradford was also disheartened that so many men whom the Merchant Adventurers had sent to Plymouth had turned out to be "wicked and profane people." They were not committed to the church and lacked the moral values that guided the Pilgrims. Furthermore, they substantially outnumbered the Pilgrims and their families, which did not bode well for the future of the colony. The colony's "General Fundamentals" expressed the basic principles and rights of English law, including representative government, trial by jury, and no punishment except by due process of law. Edward Winslow's warning to English investors to take great care to select well-qualified persons to settle in Plymouth had unfortunately fallen on deaf ears, and by the 1640s the list of crimes being tried in the Plymouth court ranged from murder to theft, blasphemy, drunkenness, slander, bestiality, and adultery. Unlike the Bay Colony, and to Plymouth's credit, there were no charges of witchcraft made in the colony.

Pregnancies out of wedlock were punished. There were a number of cases of unmarried young women becoming pregnant or giving birth before the girl and her fiancée had wed. Depending on the circumstances the lovers were punished by paying a fine, time in the stocks, or a whipping. Peregrine White, born on the *Mayflower*, and his wife, Sarah, were fined for having sexual intercourse before they got married. It was far easier for ministers and sheriffs to detect and punish the couples engaged in illegal romantic liaisons in the small New England villages than it was for the authorities with the same duties in Virginia, where the population was dispersed among the widespread plantations.

The growing number of colonists settling in Connecticut triggered the first major conflict in New England between the English and the Indians, namely, the Pequots living in Connecticut. Escalating violence in a series of raids and counterattacks between the English and the Pequots killed a number of Indians and settlers. The English destroyed a native village on Block Island; the Indians retaliated in attacking Wethersfield, killing eleven men and kidnapping two girls. In June 1637 a troop of ninety soldiers from Connecticut attacked and set fire to a palisaded Pequot village near today's Mystic. Over five hundred men, women, and children were burned to death. Those that tried to escape were shot down by the soldiers outside the fort, and only a handful got away. A Plymouth company of sixty troops were too late to join the attack, but William Bradford witnessed the slaughter and had this to say about the Puritans' horrendous act of brutality, which decimated the tribe: "It was a fearful sight to see them thus frying in the fire, and the streams of blood quenching the same, and horrible was the stinck and sente thereof, but the victory seemed a sweete sacrifice." So the Puritans gave thanks to God for delivering the enemy into their hands and giving them "so speedy a victory over so proud and insulting an enimie." A month later an English force including a company of militia from Plymouth massacred another group of Pequots near Fairfield, Connecticut. John Robinson, the Pilgrims' well-loved pastor and spiritual leader in Leiden, had died in 1625. One can imagine how shocked and saddened he would have been over the slaughter of the Pequots.

Following the Pequot massacre, the leaders in the New England colonies recognized the need to coordinate their contacts with the Indian tribes and cooperate and assist each other. After deliberating in Boston, the colony representatives formed the United Colonies of New England in September 1643, which joined the four colonies of Massachusetts, Plymouth, New Haven, and Connecticut in an association of mutual assistance and defense. The colonies would continue to maintain their own jurisdictions; they would contribute funds for the common good, mainly military expenses, based on their respective populations. Two commissioners from each colony would manage the affairs of the confederation and meet annually in each of the colonies on a rotating basis. The main focus of the new union was to cooperate in a common defense against Indian aggression and to settle boundary disputes. The outbreak of war in Europe between England and the Netherlands in 1652 also raised the possibility of conflicts with the Dutch in New Amsterdam and the Connecticut River Valley. Governor Bradford wrote that after the Pequot war "the Indeans were drawne into a general conspiracie against the English in all parts." Forming the United Colonies of New England was the first step in America toward a federal government in which citizens looked more broadly beyond their local concerns to join in a formal confederation with other colonies for their mutual benefit.

In the 1640s the total population of colonists in the United Colonies amounted to around twenty-four thousand, of which fifteen thousand were members of the Massachusetts Bay Colony. Based on the 1643 census in Plymouth Colony of men between the ages of sixteen and sixty, the colony's population was probably about two thousand. The period of the Great Migration to Massachusetts was over, but in the twenty years following the arrival of the *Mayflower* the Pilgrims and Puritans established the foundation that would shape the way of life in New England for generations. Because of its much larger population and excellent port at Boston, the Bay Colony exerted greater authority in New England affairs than the other colonies. The shallow depth of Plymouth Harbor precluded its use as a major port. Ships could not unload their cargoes at wharfs on shore. Goods were transported to the town by lighters from the ships anchored at some distance from Plymouth. While Plymouth gained in its security and economic activity from its association with the Bay Colony, its importance as an independent colony was diminished as it fell under the influence of its more powerful, cosmopolitan, and prosperous Massachusetts neighbor.

The two colonies shared the same views on key military and social issues. They recognized the importance of providing a sound education to their young people and started public schools, including the first one in America, Boston Latin. There were probably over a hundred Oxford and Cambridge graduates among the Puritans, many of whom would have supported the cause of providing higher education in the colony. When John Harvard, a church elder in Charlestown, died, he left half of his estate and his library to a small divinity school that had been founded in Cambridge in 1636. The Bay Colony assembly provided a grant of four hundred pounds, and other donations were received to establish Harvard College, the first college in

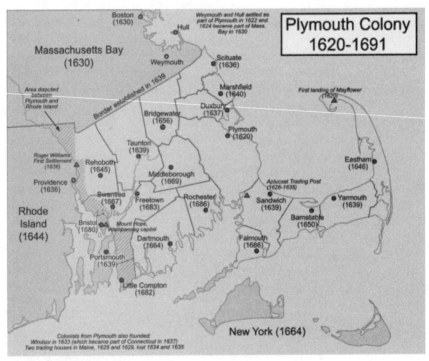

Map of Plymouth Colony, circa 1650.
Hoodinski. Creative Commons Attribution-Share Alike 3.0 Unported.

America. The literary and academic works produced near Harvard by the first printing press in America would also stimulate the pursuit of knowledge. The first book published in the English colonies, *The Whole Booke of Psalms*, was printed in 1640 on the press, which had been imported from England.

The Plymouth church, like the Massachusetts Bay Puritans, did not welcome religious dissenters such as the Quakers. Not all the Plymouth leaders were Separatists, and Miles Standish led a group that presented a petition to the Plymouth General Court recommending that the church accept all "well-behaved men." Governor Bradford, Edward Winslow, and others opposed the petition, and it was narrowly defeated. Bradford's successor, Governor Thomas Prence, led the enactment of tough laws banning the Quakers. The Plymouth church, however, was nowhere near as strict and harsh in enforcing its religious authority as the Puritans in Boston. In Plymouth Quakers were jailed, sometimes whipped, and driven away. In the Bay Colony four Quakers were hung between 1659 and 1661. The Pilgrims' treatment of Quakers was strangely inconsistent for men who had fled from religious intolerance themselves some years before. Still, there would be a growing number of voices in both colonies protesting the lack of religious freedom, and many of the citizens of Plymouth Colony came to accept Quakers in their midst later on.

In 1625 the death of John Robinson and Robert Cushman, the Pilgrims' chief advocates in Europe, spiritual and commercial, signaled the end of support by the Merchant Adventurers to finance the migration to Plymouth of the remaining Leiden Separatists. The younger generation in Leiden would increasingly be absorbed into the Dutch population. By midcentury the leadership of Plymouth began to change as the old guard, the leading Pilgrim Fathers, died off. Edward Winslow was sent on a diplomatic mission to London in 1646 and never returned to Plymouth. William Brewster, the long-standing church elder and its guiding light; Winslow; Miles Standish; Stephen Hopkins; and others all passed away, leaving their old leader, Governor Bradford, saddened and increasingly discouraged about the fate of his beloved Plymouth.

William Bradford died in 1657 at the age of sixty-nine. His successor as governor was Thomas Prence, who had arrived in Plymouth on the *Fortune* in 1621. Bradford's firm and dedicated leadership had been critical in ensuring the survival and progress of the Plymouth colony.

George Langford wrote, "He believed in the vigorous exercise of leadership and, in consultation with the men whom he trusted, he made the decisions at Plymouth. But Bradford did not forget that, in the absence of police power, he needed the confidence of the men who settled the plantation. Had he forgotten this, Plymouth could well have destroyed itself, and the landing of the Pilgrim Fathers have been only one more in a series of dreary failures to establish settlement in America."

Following the defeat of the Spanish Armada, England's dominant sea power played an effective role in expanding and protecting the nation's overseas colonies. King Charles II had appointed his brother, the Duke of York, to the post of lord high admiral of the navy, and they both viewed the New Netherlands colony at New Amsterdam as an unlawful encroachment on England's long-standing claim to the region. In 1664 England added a thriving new colony without firing a shot. Following a naval blockade by a fleet of four English gunships with hundreds of troops, the English commander demanded the town's surrender. New Amsterdam's autocratic and ill-tempered governor, Peter Stuyvesant, who had lost a leg fighting the French in the West Indies, was unable to persuade the townspeople to resist and reluctantly gave up the town to the overwhelming English force. The English acquired the entire New Netherlands colony—the region between the Delaware and Hudson rivers, which became New Jersey, New Amsterdam, and nearby parts of Long Island and Connecticut, and up the Hudson River. The area contained around six thousand people. The military undertaking had been ordered by the Duke of York, who had received a royal grant for the territory from his brother, the king. New Amsterdam became New York, and Fort Orange became Albany. There were many more Dutch inhabitants than English in New York, and Dutch traditions continued under English rule. The colony welcomed newcomers of all nationalities, creeds, and ethnic groups in sharp contrast to the intolerance of the Puritans in New England. In the Articles of Transfer that Stuyvesant and his council negotiated with the English commander, the Dutch inhabitants were assured that that they would "keep and enjoy the liberty of their consciences in religion." New York became a bustling hub of commerce and foreign trade.

In other parts of the Eastern seaboard, new English colonies—New Jersey, Maryland, and the Carolinas—were growing with the arrival of new settlers. The first colonists to settle in Maryland, Virginia's next-door neighbor, landed near the mouth of the Potomac in 1634. Led by Leonard Calvert, the brother of the second Baron Baltimore, who held the colony's charter granted by Charles I, they built the first settlement, St. Mary's City, on the northeastern shore of the Potomac. Like Virginia, the colony developed an agricultural economy producing tobacco for export. Maryland was named after Henrietta Maria, King Charles's Catholic queen. While the Calverts were Catholics, they backed a policy of religious toleration, and along with troubled English Catholics, a large number of Protestants and even Quakers settled in Maryland.

King Philip's War

$\mathcal{D}$uring the last half of 1675 and the first eight months of 1676, a fiercely fought and bloody conflict between the English colonists and Indian tribes devastated many of New England's settled areas. King Philip's War was the first large-scale confrontation with the Indians since the Pequot massacre in 1637. Two leading protagonists were Philip, who was the son of Massasoit and had assumed an English name, and Josiah Winslow, the Harvard-educated son of Edward Winslow. Edward Winslow, Plymouth's former ambassador to the Indians, had been instrumental in preserving harmony with Massasoit and the Pokanokets, based on the peace treaty that both sides had honored for over fifty years. Massasoit had died in 1660, and Philip was now "king," or the supreme sachem, of the Pokanokets. Josiah Winslow was governor of the Plymouth Colony. There had been bad blood between the two leaders stemming from several confrontations during the years leading up to the war as the colony grew in numbers and strength. The Plymouth leaders no longer treated their Indian neighbors with the respect that the Pilgrim Fathers had shown to Massasoit and his Pokanoket followers, summoning Philip and others to appear at their court on short notice with little courtesy or regard for the sachem's dignity and stature among his people.

The acquisition of new lands by the expanding population of the Plymouth Colony had put increasing pressure on the nearby Pokanokets, and their traditional tribal area was steadily shrinking. From the English viewpoint the purchase of land from the Pokanokets was perfectly legal, although sometimes they employed less scrupulous means in forcing the natives to cede their territory, such as demanding that they give up land in payment of fines for alleged misdemeanors. The Indians, however, did not accept the English concept of land ownership. In their view, selling land did not mean that they had to move away. It meant, rather, that the Indians and colonists should share the use of the land. In Virginia, many years earlier, the Powhatans, deeply resenting the English settlers' increasing occupation of their lands, had launched devastating attacks against them. For the same reason the Pokanokets in Plymouth Colony, especially the young warriors, concluded that their situation had become intolerable, as they viewed the dim prospects for their families' well-being in the future. They were largely hemmed in around their village of Mount Hope on a peninsula in Narragansett Bay. The Narragansetts were to the west, and the Plymouth settlers' homes were so close that sometimes their straying livestock damaged the Indians' cultivated fields. For their part the colonists feared that the Indians were planning an uprising against them, perhaps joined by the French. Many colonists harbored an attitude of racial superiority toward the natives, viewing them as dirty, uneducated savages. For some, hypocrisy, cruelty, and self-righteousness went hand in hand with their pious worship in the Puritan and Plymouth churches.

In meetings at Plymouth with Philip, the colonists, with the backing of the Bay Colony Puritans, were confident that they had the upper hand. They imposed harsh and humiliating conditions on Philip and his tribe: they must turn over their arms, which they had purchased from Plymouth traders and others, become subjects and abide by the laws of the English king and the Plymouth Colony, and pay an annual tribute to the colony.

Philip decided that he must free his people from the severe and unjust rule of the English. He had a plan—continue to sell off tribal lands using the proceeds to secretly buy guns from traders, English and French, engaged in that profitable business. New England Indians no longer relied solely on the bow and arrow to hunt and fight their enemies. Many were armed with muskets and flintlocks, and they were good shots. Philip also began conspiring with other tribes, urging them to join the Pokanokets in a campaign to end the English occupation of their lands. A conflict became inevitable, largely brought on by the English hunger for land and the disputes that arose when the Indians were forced to leave the lands that they had sold to the colonists.

On June 8, 1675, the Plymouth court tried and executed three Pokanokets who were implicated in the murder of another Indian who had accused King Philip of plotting against the English. Philip's angry young warriors were determined to strike back, and on June 20 they burned and looted houses a few miles north of Mount Hope belonging to Plymouth settlers who had fled earlier. Governor Winslow ordered his colony's towns to muster their militia at Taunton, and the Bay Colony agreed to send troops to join Plymouth in fighting the Pokanokets. The fighting quickly escalated in the Plymouth Colony when the Indians killed and mutilated the bodies of ten settlers and murdered and scalped a woman at Swansea north of Mount

Hope. Many years before, Powhatan's tribes had tried to drive the English settlers from Virginia. Now King Philip's warriors were starting a new war to end the spreading English occupation of New England.

The English troops soon forced King Philip's band to flee out of the confined area of Narragansett Bay, and the conflict with the Pokanokets that had begun in the Plymouth Colony spread quickly to the inland parts of New England. Joined by the Nipmucks and other tribes, King Philip's band of warriors and their new allies, about several hundred strong, conducted sudden raids on English communities throughout central and western Massachusetts and the Connecticut River Valley. They killed soldiers and settlers and murdered their women and children, or sometimes took them captive. They destroyed their crops, killed their livestock, and set fire to their homes and barns. In Plymouth Colony, Swansea, Dartmouth, and Middleborough were abandoned by their inhabitants. Deerfield was attacked three times, and only one-sixth of the houses in Springfield remained standing after the Indians' assault and arson. In September 1675 the United Colonies of New England declared war on King Philip and set a quota of soldiers for each colony to provide to the common military force. The initial quota set for the colony of Plymouth was apportioned between Plymouth and ten other towns in the colony. Later on, responding to the need for more soldiers, it was raised to three hundred men. The English militias pursued Philip's marauding band and their allies in a military campaign to protect the threatened settlements. The stealthy Indian warriors were usually one step ahead of them, however, as they burned and laid waste to New England farms and towns.

Governor Winslow and the confederation leaders were fearful that the other peaceful tribes in the region, including the Praying Indians who had converted to Christianity, would decide to join the conspiracy to attack them. The Bay Colony exiled the friendly Praying Indians to the inhospitable Deer Island in Massachusetts Bay. When over a hundred Indians, after receiving a promise of amnesty, surrendered at Plymouth, following a kangaroo court trial, Governor Winslow shipped most of them off to the Spanish slave market in Cadiz. However, it was the Narragansetts in Rhode Island, the largest tribe in New England, that posed the most imminent threat in the view of the colonies' War Council.

In December governor Josiah Winslow of Plymouth was put in command of the combined forces of about a thousand men from Plymouth, Massachusetts Bay Colony, and Connecticut that would attack the Narragansetts. (The New Haven colony had been absorbed by the Connecticut colony.) Plymouth sent 158 soldiers, and one of the two Plymouth militia companies was led by young William Bradford, the son of the former governor. After an arduous march through heavy snows and frigid temperatures, they found the Narragansett stronghold, a large palisaded and fortified village with hundreds of wigwams housing some three thousand Indian men, women, and children. It was located on an island in a dense swamp not far from today's Kingston, Rhode Island. The Narragansetts fought fiercely in defense of their homes and families, killing or wounding about two hundred English soldiers. Finally, the militias stormed into the fort and set the wigwams on fire. While many of the Narragansetts escaped into the swamp and woods, probably about four hundred men, women, and children died in the flames or were shot to death in what became known as "The Great Swamp Fight." The Pequots had suffered the same fate years before at the hands of the Puritan soldiers.

In King Philip's War the diminished Pequots, along with the Mohegans and Niantics, joined the English in fighting Philip's army, having decided that it was in their best interest to side with the English in putting down King Philip's uprising. In 1676 the Massachusetts Bay Colony released the Praying Indians from Deer Island to return to their homes. Growing numbers of them began fighting with the English troops. In March a Plymouth company of about sixty-five men and some friendly Indians was ambushed by an overwhelming force of Narragansetts near the Pawtucket River. Very few escaped. It was a stunning blow for the colony, but then the tide began to turn.

In the spring of 1676 King Philip's warriors were defeated decisively at Deerfield, Hadley, and Marlboro, and some began to surrender. After the Nipmucks had withdrawn from the war, Philip's force of Pokanokets and some Narragansetts, perhaps a thousand persons including their women and children, headed south. Hungry, exhausted, and on the run, they returned to their home territory in the Plymouth Colony where they had hidden supplies of seed corn underground for the spring planting season. They were not through fighting and attacked Clark's garrison, only a few miles from Plymouth, burned it down, and killed eleven people, including women and children.

Benjamin Church, a Plymouth officer who had fought bravely in "The Great Swamp Fight," had successfully persuaded the Sakonnets from Narragansett Bay, today's Little Compton, to join the colony's fight against Philip. During the summer of 1676 with a company of only about forty men, Sakonnets and Plymouth volunteers, he tracked Philip's band through the dense swamps and woods in the area. Several times they came close to catching Philip but failed. Church's force killed a number of Philip's men and delivered scores of captives to Plymouth, most of whom were then shipped to Caribbean islands as slaves to work in the sugar cane fields.

By August King Philip's War was over. Chased from place to place as they were hunted down by the English soldiers, Philip's warriors and people were starving and worn out. They had suffered heavy losses in battle and from starvation and disease and no longer had the will to fight. In August an Indian, whose brother had been killed by King Philip, reported that he had fled to Mount Hope, his former base. Church immediately led a company of Plymouth soldiers and friendly Indians to find him and kill him. At the sound of their attack at Mount Hope, Philip fled into the nearby swamp, but this time he did not get away. One of Church's Indians shot him to death. Benjamin Church, when viewing King Philip's corpse, described him as "a doleful great naked dirty beast" and had him drawn and quartered. Church brought back King Philip's head to Plymouth. It was impaled on the palisades for public display, and at a special church service the Plymouth congregation gave thanks to God for the victory over their hated enemy.

King Philip's War ended where it had started—in the Plymouth Colony—but the results throughout all of New England had been devastating for both sides. Many hundreds of English soldiers, Indian warriors, and innocents on both sides had been killed in raids and counterattacks. At least a hundred Plymouth men and a few women and children were killed. The war had been catastrophic for the Indians. An estimated 25 percent of their population died in battle or from illness and starvation. Some natives fled from southern New England, heading west or into Maine, where the Abenakis were attacking English coastal settlements. Probably one thousand Indians, half from the Plymouth Colony, were shipped out to become slaves in the West Indies, including King Philip's wife and son. Some of the children of Indians who had surrendered were assigned to be servants in Plymouth families until they reached the age of twenty-four. Pastor John Robinson, the former spiritual leader of the Pilgrim Fathers, would surely have been appalled by the merciless behavior of the second generation.

Over the course of about a year the Indian uprising had completely destroyed twelve English towns and villages, and overall some forty were attacked with much destruction and killing. Burned buildings and abandoned farms marked the length of the New England frontier. Around 8 percent of the colonies' men of military age were killed. So were a number of women and children. The financial burden on the colonies was heavy and took years of high taxes to pay off. The cost of the war for Plymouth, the poorest of the colonies, was £11,800. The colony's soldiers were rewarded with parcels of land, and the Mount Hope peninsula, later named Bristol, was added to Plymouth Colony. The English colonists had ended the threat of Indian attack in the populated areas, although as the colonies grew and expanded inland their new frontier settlements remained exposed to Indians' resistance to the colonists' occupation of their lands. The fierce fighting between the Indians and the New England colonists was just beginning.

Virginia and Massachusetts

$\mathscr{A}$fter the Indian massacre at Jamestown, Captain John Smith had proposed to the Virginia Company that it provide him with one hundred soldiers, together with the necessary ships and crew, and he would completely rid the Virginia tidewater region from the threat of Indian attack. His expedition would also pursue the exploration needed to join Virginia, New England, and all the territory in between on one up-to-date map. Probably he envisioned the future union of those regions under English rule. The captain was still eager to rejoin his country's efforts to build colonies in America, his visionary goal for years. Again the Virginia Company rejected his proposal; the company had a more serious Jamestown problem commanding its attention.

When the news of the massacre of about three hundred and fifty Virginia colonists in 1622 reached London, it dealt a heavy blow to the reputation of the Virginia Company. Furthermore, large numbers of settlers continued to become sick and die from famine and disease. The "bloody flux" (dysentery) and infectious diseases that spread rapidly on the crowded ships were brought ashore by the disembarking immigrants. In 1622 many more died from these natural causes than were killed in the Indian massacre. An account by Nathaniel Butler, who was visiting Virginia after his tour as governor of Bermuda, painted a frightful picture of conditions in the colony. Many colonists were "in a most sickly and desperate state." Unless the deplorable conditions were quickly addressed, "instead of a plantation, it would quickly get the name of a slaughter house." Conditions on the ground were far different than the Virginia Company's rosy propaganda in London to raise capital and recruit colonists. According to the census of 1624, although some three thousand immigrants had arrived over the preceding four years, the population of the colony was just 1,277 persons. Jamestown, the social and political capital of the colony, had about 200 residents—yeomen, merchants, farmers, hog raisers, shopkeepers, and colonial officials, including the governor. There was a church, a guardhouse, thirty-three houses, and several shops and storehouses. A "company store" was stocked with clothing and household goods supplied by the Virginia Company. Colonists normally paid for their purchases in tobacco, often used as the "coin of the realm." The bulk of the colony's population lived in the scattered outlying plantation settlements along the James and inland.

The colonists had abandoned the settlement at Henrico, where the Indians had burned down the houses and destroyed the livestock. The ambitious plans for Jamestown by the Virginia Company, including a glass factory, an ironworks, and a school for Indian children, were forgotten. The Virginia economy was unsoundly based on just one crop, tobacco. Jamestown had been a financial disaster for the company's stockholders.

In 1623 King James announced that he had resolved to close down the Virginia Company and convert Virginia from a proprietary colony to a crown colony. He had dispatched agents to investigate the state of affairs in Virginia, and he was persuaded by their reports that only royal intervention could save the colony from collapse. The colony's governor, Sir Francis Wyatt, and other company officials challenged the critical reports in vain. King James was convinced that the distressed condition of the colony was due to the poor management of the Virginia Company in directing the policies and operations in Virginia, and he did not trust its liberal-minded chief executive Sir Edwin Sandys and his successor, the Earl of Southampton. The king would appoint the governor and council in the future; the colonists would continue to elect their own representatives to the House of Burgesses to pass legislation on local matters. Naturally, the company executives and stockholders objected vehemently and presented a petition to Parliament seeking its assistance in blocking the king's plan. The Parliament, obeying King James's wishes, rejected the petition, and in 1624, following a royally directed judicial process, the Virginia Company was dissolved and all of the rights and benefits under its charter were vested in the king. By 1625, some forty years after Sir Walter Raleigh's failed attempt at Roanoke to start an English settlement, Virginia was firmly established as a crown colony with its capital at Jamestown, the first successful English settlement in America.

Although King James disdained his subjects' fondness for smoking, he had granted Virginia planters the exclusive right to sell tobacco in England, which generated significant revenues for the government. King Charles I, who ascended to the throne after James died in 1625, shared his father's abhorrence of tobacco and smoking. In a letter to Virginia governor Yeardley, whom he had reappointed to the post, he expressed his concern that the colony had been unable to raise any other staple than tobacco. "Well might it be said," he wrote, "that the plantation was wholly built on smoke, which would easily turn into air" if tobacco continued to dominate Virginia's agriculture. After delivering this Shakespearean play on words, Charles instructed the colony to produce various new products to diversify its economy—silk, pitch, flax, hemp, and potash.

By 1629 the quality of Virginia tobacco had deteriorated, probably suffering from soil depletion resulting from the huge volume produced to meet the steadily growing demand. London merchants, and even the king, admonished the colony officials about the inferior product being shipped to England, and the Virginia House of Burgesses passed an act limiting the culture of tobacco to so many plants per head. The plantation owners were also instructed to allot at least two acres for producing corn, the basic food in the colony. Often ships arrived without enough provisions to even feed the immigrants that they had brought to Virginia. The availability of enough food to feed the growing number of colonists remained a serious problem. So was their tense and sometimes violent relationship with the Powhatan Indians.

The Powhatans conducted small-scale assaults on English farms and plantations from time to time, sometimes seizing and holding English children for ransom. In view of the ongoing threat of an Indian attack, a government proclamation commanded the colonists to be extremely careful in the use of gunpowder, which was in short supply and heedlessly wasted in celebrating weddings and other festive events. The new rule had one serious drawback. When the Indians outside the forts noted the colonists' reluctance to fire their muskets, they became increasingly bold in stealing corn from the colony's cornfields.

The steady encroachment of the growing numbers of English settlers into their lands infuriated the Powhatans, and in 1644 Opechancanough's warriors launched another devastating attack on the outlying plantations and settlements. They massacred some three hundred and fifty settlers and their families and torched their homes and farms. Again the colonial militia, summoned by Governor William Berkeley, retaliated fiercely and took control of all the lands between the James and York rivers south of James Falls. They captured Opechancanough, and a soldier, disobeying orders, shot the frail and proud old chief in the back and killed him. The death of the Powhatans' formidable leader marked the dissolution of the great confederation, which had been formed by the genius of Powhatan. While some Indian families chose to leave their old homes and head north and west beyond the English settlements, many elected to stay in the same area on lands allotted to them by the general assembly. They paid an annual tribute of twenty beaver skins to the colonial government and lived peacefully under their sachems. From time to time the assembly approved the purchase of additional lands from the Indians. However, sporadic Indian attacks on the frontier continued as the growing number of colonists pushed further inland to plant new farms and plantations.

In 1642 King Charles had appointed Sir William Berkeley, a military veteran and member of his court, to be the new governor of Virginia; he held office for ten years before retiring. Unlike some of his predecessors, in his first years as governor Berkeley was respectful of the rights and opinions of the colonists and their elected representatives to the House of Burgesses in Jamestown. In 1653, when the colony's population was about twenty thousand, thirty-four burgesses were elected from fourteen counties to attend the general assembly meetings in Jamestown; four came from Jamestown. The seats on Virginia's Royal Council were all held by gentlemen from the elite families of Virginia, usually related by blood or marriage, and they were often passed down within families from generation to generation. In the beginning often they were younger sons of prominent English families who, with no hope of inheriting the family estate in England, had come to Virginia to seek their fortunes.

For years sometimes as many as ten ships a year had been arriving in the Chesapeake Bay from England to disembark their passengers, and they continued to come. The new arrivals were by no means all sturdy yeomen or skilled workers. Several hundred vagrant children, mainly teenagers taken from detention centers and street urchins, were rounded up and shipped to Virginia. There were also Irish military prisoners, homeless beggars, and criminals that the authorities forced the colony to accept. The colony officials became increasingly disturbed over the continuing inflow of these undesirable types, and finally the House of Burgesses voted to prohibit the further import of criminals. More hands were needed in homes and fields to tend to the steadily expanding production of tobacco and to replace the many workers felled by hunger and disease. The mortality rate in Virginia was much higher than in New England. To meet this demand for more labor, increasing numbers of slaves were brought to Virginia, mainly from the West Indies. In 1660 there were about nine hundred slaves in the colony, and ten years later at least half the plantations and farms owned slaves. In 1681 the governor estimated that there were about three thousand "black slaves" in Virginia. The combination of tobacco and slavery was significantly shaping the economic and social structure of the colony.

Over time the quality of immigrants steadily improved; they had little hope for their future in England, prompting their desire to move on. The availability of land for immigrants attracted growing numbers of ambitious young men to Virginia, where they could acquire landed estates for themselves and their children. A few were sons from elite English families, perhaps royalist sympathizers fleeing from the civil war in England; some were yeomen farmers with a modest stake, but most were indentured servants who went to work on the large tobacco plantations. After fulfilling a four- or five-year work contract they received tools and land to farm. Life was not easy for the plantation workers, both whites and blacks. Their masters worked them very hard and punished them severely for any misconduct with beatings or extending the servants' years of servitude. Some plantation owners exercised a "droit de seigneur" over their slave and servant girls.

Not everyone coming to Virginia was welcomed. Quakers were initially treated as they were in Plymouth Colony: they were denied the rights of citizens, harassed, and persecuted, but never executed or punished physically. Yet gradually they and other dissenters from the Anglican Church would come to be accepted by their fellow Virginians as they were in neighboring Maryland.

After the early years of hardship and near collapse, Virginia, with its capital at Jamestown, grew in numbers and steadily expanded. Many plantations now had their own wharfs, houses, and gardens a few miles apart on the James River, a pattern of settlement that dispersed the growing population. Incoming ships delivered goods that the plantation owners had ordered directly to them and departed with cargoes of tobacco. There was less need for a central market and port town for shipping tobacco exports abroad. The House of Burgesses had persuaded Sir William Berkeley to reassume the office of governor, and, based on his report, Virginia had a population of about thirty thousand people in 1660, still with many more men than women.

In the 1660s saturation of the English market for tobacco, causing rock-bottom prices for exports, and a destructive hurricane brought about an economic decline, but not for long. The European craving for smoking tobacco was insatiable. Jamestown merchants opposed England's enforcement of the Navigation Acts, which required that all of the colony's foreign trade be transacted with England, with imports and exports carried on English or colonial ships. Disobeying the law carried heavy penalties; obeying the law would handicap the colony's foreign commerce. Some of the colony's merchants accepted the risk of illegal trading with the Dutch, with whom Virginia had earlier enjoyed a thriving trade.

In 1676 an outbreak of attacks on frontier plantations by the Susquehanna Indians from the upper Chesapeake Bay led to a rebellion against the colonial government and its elderly governor, Sir William Berkeley. The leader of the rebels was Nathaniel Bacon, a young, hot-headed plantation owner in Henrico, whose overseer had been killed in an attack on his plantation. Bacon raised a small army, and, against Governor Berkeley's orders, tracked down the Indian raiders and routed them; for good measure they also killed some Indians from a local tribe. The governor, who didn't want to get into another Indian war, declared that Bacon was a traitor.

Governor Berkeley's second term in office was marked by his increasingly autocratic style of governing, submitting to the king's orders without question and ignoring the rights and role of the House of Burgesses. Nathaniel Bacon had won over a large number of followers, mainly backcountry farmers, who were no longer willing to accept Governor Berkeley's dictatorial rule. Many members of the newly elected House of Burgesses, including Bacon, were now opposed to Berkeley. There were several angry confrontations between the Bacon and Berkeley factions in Jamestown, with Bacon's forces holding the upper hand. Finally, Bacon occupied Jamestown with his soldiers, burned it down, including the church and statehouse, and forced Governor Berkeley to flee to the eastern shore briefly. Then Bacon suddenly died. Without its leader the rebellion collapsed, and Berkeley and his supporters regained control of Jamestown and the colony.

Governor Berkeley exacted a cruel revenge on those who had opposed him earlier. Some were imprisoned, twenty-three were executed, and Governor Berkeley confiscated estates or levied heavy fines on others. The colonists and royal commissioners roundly condemned him for his vengeful and cruel punishments. He was summoned by the king, who had pardoned Bacon's supporters and demanded Berkeley's resignation, to return to England to answer for his conduct. King Charles II muttered that "the old fool has hung more men in that naked country, than I have done for the murder of my father." (Charles I had been executed in 1649 by Oliver Cromwell's Roundheads in the English Civil War.) The king would not see Berkeley. Suffering from various ailments at the age of seventy-two, Sir William Berkeley, Virginia's longest-serving governor and now a bitter old man, died in England soon after his arrival.

Relations between the House of Burgesses and some of the royally appointed governors, both before and after Berkeley, were often tense. The Navigation Acts' harmful effects on commerce and the governors' imposition of taxes and fees without the approval of the House of Burgesses were subjects of bitter dispute. Sometimes governors arbitrarily dissolved the assemblies of the House of Burgesses and refused to permit new meetings to take place for long periods. The colonists' protests against taxation without representation would be heard for years to come. Some colonists were imprisoned for allegedly speaking out seditiously against the governor or king. They may have bitterly observed that the government's decisions were based on what actions would enhance the king's revenues rather than what was beneficial for Virginia. Virginians had complained for some time that the burdensome royal duty on tobacco imports from Virginia was hurting their market.

In 1698 the rebuilt Jamestown, with some fine new houses including a brick statehouse and church, was heavily damaged by an accidental fire, which again destroyed the statehouse and other buildings and houses. The following year the seat of government was moved from Jamestown to the Middle Plantation, soon to be named Williamsburg after King William III. The Middle Plantation, a fortified community built in 1632, was about eight miles north of Jamestown. In arguing to make the change permanent, some noted that it would be wise to move the government to higher ground away from Jamestown's unhealthy, low, and swampy land that bred mosquitoes and the threat of disease. Williamsburg was also the home of the newly founded College of William and Mary, the second college to be established in the English colonies, and the colony's House of Burgesses met initially in its handsome new brick building. From its precarious beginnings at Jamestown, colonial Virginia was on its way to becoming a cultivated society with a prosperous future.

Losing its role as the colony's capital after ninety-two years sounded the death knell for Jamestown, as its population dwindled rapidly until the town was finally abandoned. Today its ruins remain as an informative archeological site and tourist attraction, not far from the impressively reconstructed town of colonial Williamsburg. A Virginian view of the importance of Jamestown's role in American history was summed up in a 1907 Virginia guidebook: "The first and foremost being Jamestown, the sire of Virginia, and Virginia, the mother of this great Republic."

The defiant insistence of the Massachusetts Bay Colony on retaining its self-governing independence from the Crown had increasingly become a thorn in the side of the English government. When Governor Winthrop sent Edward Winslow to London as his ambassador, his final instructions declared, "Our charter gives us an absolute power of government." Like their fellow colonists in Jamestown, the Boston merchants and ship captains sometimes ignored the English Navigation Acts. The Massachusetts General Court declared, "The subjects of his majesty here being not represented in Parliament, so we have not looked at ourselves to be impeded in our trade by them." The Puritans had been trading directly with the Dutch for years.

Plymouth, followed by other colonies, accepted their government's decree that people of all religious faiths were welcome in the English colonies. The Bay Colony Puritans, however, continued to defy this official policy by denying their Massachusetts citizens the freedom to worship as they chose. In 1684 King Charles II decided that he would not tolerate the colony's acts of disobedience to the rulings of the Crown any longer, and he revoked the Massachusetts Bay charter. The rights of citizens who were not members of the church to vote in elections and to worship in their chosen faith were now affirmed by law. It marked the end of the Massachusetts theocracy.

Two years later following the death of Charles, King James II decided to consolidate and tighten his government's control over the American colonies. James II was not unfamiliar in dealing with colonial affairs in America. Before succeeding to the throne in 1685, as the Duke of York he had ordered the seizure of New Amsterdam from the Dutch in 1664 and had overseen the development of New York, New Jersey, and other colonies. Starting in 1686 he created a new royal province in several steps, the Dominion of New England.

The Dominion of New England eventually incorporated the Massachusetts Bay Colony, Maine, New Hampshire, Plymouth, Connecticut, Rhode Island, New York, and the Jersies. The king appointed the Dominion's new governor, Sir Edmund Andros, and the local councils. The colonial legislatures were dissolved, and the individual colonies lost their local political rights. Authority resided with the ironhanded Governor Andros and ultimately the Crown. The new governor imposed taxes by fiat, ignoring the views of the people. The local self-governing independence of the Plymouth colonists for the last sixty-six years, prescribed by the Mayflower Compact, was over.

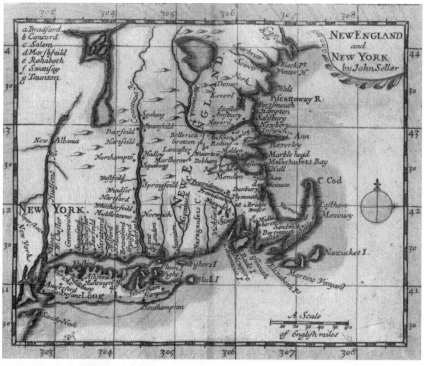

Map of New England in the late 1600s.
Map Image Courtesy of the Sidney R. Knafel Collection at Phillips Academy, Andover, MA.

The looming threat of war between England and France had been a significant factor calling for a change in the governance and steps to protect the New England colonies. King William's War, as it was called in the English colonies, lasted from 1688 to 1697, and wars between the English and the French and their Indian allies would continue on and off well into the eighteenth century. In 1690 a force of French and Indians burned the frontier hamlet of Schenectady, killing and capturing dozens of residents. They later launched fierce attacks on English settlements in Maine, New Hampshire, and Massachusetts. The colony of Plymouth sent 153 men to join an army raised by the Massachusetts Bay Colony for an expedition by sea to capture Quebec. When the fleet reached Quebec, their attack on the town was a disastrous failure, and twenty-two Plymouth Colony soldiers died. It was an especially sad outcome for the people of Scituate. Of all the Plymouth towns, the largest number killed, about a third, came from that town.

At the time there were seventeen towns in the Plymouth Colony, which was divided into three counties, Plymouth, Barnstable, and Bristol. Plymouth County contained the towns of Plymouth, Scituate, and four smaller towns. Scituate was now the biggest and richest town in the colony and the one most closely associated with Boston and the Bay Colony. An estimate based on military levis in 1690 put the population of the whole colony at about ten thousand, roughly a third of that of its neighbor, the Massachusetts Bay Colony. In 1689, following the overthrow of the autocratic and unpopular James II, Parliament proclaimed William of Orange and Mary, daughter of James II, to be the new king and queen of England. Under a new royal charter issued in 1691, the Plymouth Colony became part of Massachusetts, along with Maine. A royal governor appointed by the king and a governor's council elected by the general assembly would govern the colony. The right of citizens to vote for their representatives to the assembly was based on property ownership.

The story of the Pilgrim Fathers, who crossed a dangerous ocean to a forbidding new land to worship in their own way, has always inspired Americans, and thousands flock each year to visit Plymouth and the rebuilt Plymouth Plantation. Their memory has been honored in other ways. At the royal coronation of Edward VII in 1902, a group of distinguished gentlemen from America and Great Britain founded The Pilgrims, an organization with hundreds of members in separate branches in New York and London. Its purpose is to promote brotherhood between Americans, the British, and other English-speaking peoples.

William Bradford was justifiably proud of the Pilgrim community that he had led, which became the sturdy foundation of an expanding colony, and of the religious and moral way of life of the Pilgrims. "Thus out of small beginnings," he wrote near the end of his life, "greater things have been produced by His hand that made all things of nothing, and gives being to all things that are; and as one small candle may light a thousand, so the light here kindled hath shone unto many, yea in some sort to our whole nation." William Bradford knew how close the flickering candle had come to going out when the Pilgrims faced the terrible hardships that they encountered in their new home. So did John Smith from his experience in leading Jamestown.

William Bradford and John Smith are two of the most renowned pioneers and trailblazers in American history. Their very different personalities were reflected in their writings and the observations of their colleagues. James Truslow Adams wrote about John Smith, "It must be frankly admitted that no one will ever think as highly of the Captain as he thought of himself." Smith was boastful and brash; Bradford was modest and circumspect. Both were fair, brave, and effective leaders who faced different conditions and challenges, notably in the character of the colonists that they led and in their relations with the neighboring native tribes. The New England coastal Indians had been decimated by the plague a few years before the Pilgrims arrived, and when the Pilgrims landed, the badly weakened local tribe was unable to resist the English occupation of their lands. Negotiating the long-lasting treaty with the loyal Massasoit and the Pokanokets was critical in maintaining peaceful relations with the Indians and advantageous for both sides. At the same time Captain Miles Standish was vigilant and forceful when necessary in protecting Plymouth.

In the beginning, cultivating good relations with the natives was essential for both Plymouth and Jamestown to obtain desperately needed food supplies. Both colonies also faced the challenge of feeding the unexpected boatloads of new settlers who usually arrived poorly equipped and provisioned. In the early years of both colonies the settlers were hired hands working for the absentee investors in England. After failing to produce enough food when the colonists were working on a communal basis, both colonies adopted plans for their settlers to own and farm their own lands, a move that significantly increased agricultural output with important collateral benefits for the colonies. New Englanders enjoyed one special advantage over their fellow colonists in Virginia: the mortality rate was much lower in New England than Virginia, where so many colonists died from malnutrition and disease. After the first year the New England settlers apparently found the challenging climate healthy and invigorating.

Later on agriculture in the two colonies developed in different directions. The thin soil, stony fields, and long, harsh winters in New England made the region unsuitable for the kind of large plantations based on a single cash crop that were started in Virginia. Fishing, shipbuilding, and foreign trade became major activities in New England. The scattered and isolated Virginian plantations, farms, and homes produced a very different pattern of living than in New England with its many small towns beyond Boston. In later years the initial importance of both Jamestown and Plymouth was diminished by the surging influx of immigrants developing new regions and towns, and their role as the seat of colonial government was transferred elsewhere.

Most importantly, the highly motivated Pilgrims had the will and courage to overcome the challenges and hardships in the new life that they had chosen in America, where they could worship God in their own way. They were English men and women who found that living in Holland had become increasingly difficult for them. Many had been small farmers in England. In Holland they had had to labor long hours at low-wage common crafts to provide for their families. Facing the challenge of building their settlement at Plymouth in midwinter did not daunt them—they were accustomed to hard work. Most of them had brought their families to their new home, and they were determined to remain and build a successful community.

Conditions were quite different in Jamestown, a settlement in its early years that was more similar to a military garrison than a community. There the first groups of settlers, all men, were mainly undisciplined and uninspired adventurers and hired hands. They needed a strong leader to direct them and maintain order, one who also possessed the diplomatic and military skills to obtain food from the Indians and protect the little colony from Powhatan's hostile warriors. Until the marriage of his daughter, Pocahontas, to an English colonist, the formidable chieftain, who may have slaughtered the Roanoke settlers, was almost relentless in his scheming against the colony and launched frequent attacks on the colonists, especially after John Smith's departure. After Powhatan's death his successor, Opechancanough, resumed the assaults on the colony, whose soldiers retaliated brutally.

William Bradford and John Smith both believed that every settlement needed a strong fort and a well-trained band of soldiers. After Smith had left Jamestown, colonist Richard Potts wrote

> thus we lost him, that in all his proceedings made Justice his first guide and experience his second, ever hating baseness, sloth, pride and indignity more than any danger, that never allowed more for himself than for his soldiers with him; that upon no danger would send them where he would not lead them himself . . . that loved action more than words and hated falshood and cozenage worse than death; whose adventures were our lives and whose losse our deathes.

William Bradford and John Smith both shared the same vision of building a free society in America. Bradford Smith, the author of the excellent biography, *Captain John Smith*, said about Smith, "He was in love with America, and America for him meant a place where a man could prosper according to his merits, not according to his place in a rigid hierarchy. America meant a place where a man could have free land and an opportunity to make the most of it."

In 1622 the second edition of *New Englands Trials* by Smith was published, which reported on the founding of the new Pilgrim colony at Plymouth. Referring to Jamestown and Plymouth, Smith wrote, "By that acquaintance I have with them, I may call them my children, for they have bin my wife, my hawks, my hounds, my cards, my dice, and in total my best content, as indifferent to my heart as my left hand to my right." He described the latest English "discoveries" in New England as "pigs of my own sowe."

The prolific author continued to produce travel books promoting English colonization in America—*The Generall Historie of Virginia, New England, and the Summer Isles* in 1624 and *Advertisements for the Unexperienced Planters of New England, or Anywhere* in 1631, the year Smith died. In *Advertisements* he described the emigration of growing numbers of Puritans to Massachusetts Bay and the building of the new settlements at Salem, Charlestown, and Boston, under John Winthrop's able leadership. He cited again the many attributes of the region that would enable the new colony to prosper and gave advice to the new colonists, based on his own experience, to help them succeed in their new home. Smith's perseverance in promoting the establishment of colonies in New England, backed by his exploration, books, and maps, certainly encouraged the Pilgrims and the Puritans in their plans to emigrate. He had every right to call the new colonies in the region his "children," along with Jamestown and its Virginia offshoots. Captain John Smith's accomplishments and the legacy that he left for America were extraordinary.

After a number of explorations and a few failed attempts, the English finally succeeded in planting their first two colonies in America, a seminal event in American history. The original purpose that motivated the pioneering settlers of Jamestown and their investment backers was commercial. They expected their ships to return filled with valuable cargoes, including gold and silver. They hoped to find a short northwest passage to the riches of the Orient. The London investors were also incited by the profit motive in the Plymouth enterprise. However, the Pilgrim settlers had another goal: they were seeking to start a new life in a place where they could worship and live freely. In the new colonies, John Smith's vision of a new society where advancement and status were derived from merit and accomplishment, not birth, grew steadily over time. While for generations citizens of English colonies would continue to be proud of their English heritage and were loyal subjects of the king, at the same time the concept of an independent and democratic American nation was growing from its roots in the first two colonies. The new Americans, who faced a challenging environment and hostile natives, steadily became more separated from the old ways of life in England. The waves of English immigrants to the colonies left home to seek a better life and greater freedom than what lay in store for them in England. Several thousand of miles of ocean now divided them from England's rule of kings and rigid hierarchical boundaries.

By 1675, after overcoming a brief insurrection by the Dutch in New York, the English had succeeded in occupying and governing the coastal regions of the Atlantic seaboard stretching from Maine to the Carolinas. The colonists would continue to be ruled by England for the next one hundred years leading up to the American Revolution, as their numbers grew and expanded, pushing the frontiers steadily westward. Two centuries later President Ronald Reagan declared in a Thanksgiving Day proclamation that "a divine plan placed this great continent here between the oceans to be found by people from every corner of the earth who had a special love of faith and freedom."

It all began with the first English settlements at Jamestown and Plymouth. Just forty years after Sir Walter Raleigh's failed Roanoke project, these two new settlements were secure and expanding after their early desperate struggle to survive. Their founding led the way for the flow of immigrants from the British Isles that populated Virginia and Massachusetts, the two largest colonies in the 1600s, and the other English colonies, whose political and cultural legacy informed our nation's history. These two colonies, and later states, produced most of the leaders that inspired America's successful struggle for independence and the formation and workings of our constitutional government. It can truly be said that the founding of Jamestown and Plymouth gave birth to America.

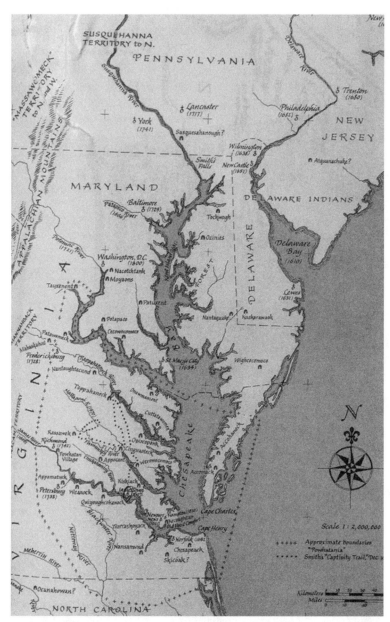

Map of the Chesapeake Bay. From The Complete Works of Captain John Smith, 1580–1631, edited by Philip L. Barbour, with a foreward by Thad W. Tate. Published for the Omohundro Institute of Early American History and Culture. Copyright 1986 by the University of North Carolina Press.
Used by permission of the publisher. www.uncpress.unc.edu.

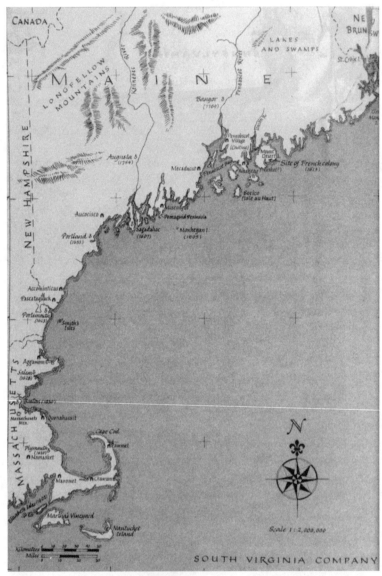

Map of the New England coast. From *The Complete Works of Captain John Smith, 1580–631*, edited by Philip L. Barbour, with a foreword by Thad W. Tate. Published for the Omohundro Institute of Early American History and Culture. Copyright 1986 by the University of North Carolina Press.
Used by permission of the publisher. www.uncpress.unc.edu.

Acknowledgments

$\mathcal{I}$ first acknowledge and salute Captain John Smith, 1580–1631, whose life story gave me the inspiration to write this book. Some years ago I came across a framed reproduction of John Smith's 1614 map of the New England coast. I generally remembered John Smith's connection to Jamestown and how the Indian maiden, Pocahontas, had saved him from execution by appealing to her father, Powhatan, the great chieftain in the Virginia tidewater region. But what the heck was Smith doing exploring the New England coast? That was news to me, and I decided to look into it.

I had spent many summer vacations on the island of North Haven off the coast of Maine and cruised the coastal waters from Long Island Sound to Maine's Penobscot Bay a number of times, covering the same territory visited by Smith, Champlain, and other early explorers. And like many thousands of tourists, we visited Plymouth, the home of the Pilgrims. When we had lived in Washington, DC, we often visited Jamestown, Williamsburg, and the tidewater region where my wife's parents had settled in their retirement years. So I was quite familiar with the territory.

I am very grateful to a handful of friends for their assistance and encouragement. William and Susan Sheeline read my manuscript and made sound suggestions. Susan also introduced me to Sara Gronin, professor of history at Long Island University–Post, who read my manuscript and provided helpful comments. So did historian Evan Thomas and Phyliss Lee Levin. Ross and Pamela Meurer helped by preparing the pictures that I selected to use in the book. Cindy Connett reviewed my manuscript and undertook the onerous task of obtaining permissions from various sources to use the pictures and maps. Cindy was especially helpful in searching and finding appropriate pictures of some of the subjects that I had selected, including the handsome book jacket. She has my wholehearted thanks for a job well done.

I am still a computer amateur and welcomed the expert and prompt assistance of Carol Solinger. My dear wife, Buz, was also always ready to come to my rescue when things went amiss. Finally, I am very grateful to my grandfather, Edward G. Miner, who was a voracious reader and an avid book collector. When he died he left me several rare old books about the early history of Virginia and the Pilgrims that provided useful information enriching the story.

I deeply appreciate the enthusiastic support I received from these friends and others, which enabled us to cross the finish line with a book that tells the remarkable story about the birth of our nation.

Notes

CHAPTER 1: TREASURE, COD, AND THE NORTHWEST PASSAGE

The sources for this chapter are Samuel Eliot Morison, *The European Discovery of America, The Northern Voyages A.D. 500–1600*, New York: Oxford University Press, 1971; Louis B. Wright, *The American Heritage History of the Thirteen Colonies*, New York: American Heritage Publishing Company, Inc., 1967; *America's Historylands, Landmarks of Liberty*, Washington, DC, National Geographic Book Service, National Geographic Society, 1967; John Bakeless, *America as Seen by Its First Explorers: The Eyes of Discovery*, New York: Dover Publications, 1961; James Truslow Adams, *The Founding of New England*, Boston: The Atlantic Monthly Press, 1921.

Quotation by Giovanni da Verrazzano is from his letter to French king François I describing his discoveries after completing his voyage in 1524, contained in Morison, *The European Discovery of America*.

The New Encyclopedia Britanica, Chicago: University of Chicago, 1989; Wikipedia, the Free Encyclopedia, and *The Almanac of American History*, Arthur M. Schlesinger Jr., ed., New York: G. P. Putnam's Sons, 1983, were useful reference sources throughout the book. The source of many quotations is identified in the text.

CHAPTER 2: THE ELIZABETHAN YEARS

The sources for this chapter are Lacy Baldwin Smith, *The Horizon Book of the Elizabethan World*, New York: American Heritage Publishing Company, 1967; Winston S. Churchill, *A History of the English-Speaking Peoples, Vol. II, The New World*, London: Cassel and Company Ltd., 1956; James Horn, ed., *Captain John Smith: Writings with Other Narratives of Roanoke, Jamestown and the First English Settlement in America*, New York: Library Classics of America, 2007; David Platt, ed., *One Land/Two Worlds*,

Rockland, Maine: Island Institute, 2005; Raleigh Trevelyan, *Sir Walter Raleigh*, New York: Henry Holt and Company, 2002; Samuel Eliot Morison, *The European Discovery of America, The Northern Voyages A.D. 500–1600*; Louis B. Wright, *The American Heritage History of the Thirteen Colonies*; *America's Historylands, Landmarks of Liberty*.

The following sources are contained in *Captain John Smith: Writings with Other Narratives*: Arthur Barlowe's quotation about Roanoke from his account in *Discourse of the First Voyage: The First English Voyage to Virginia: 1584*; Sir Richard Grenville, *The Journal of the* Tiger: *The Second Voyage to Virginia: 1585*; Ralph Lane, *Discourse on the First Colony, Roanoke 1585–86*; John White, *Narrative of His Voyage: The Fourth Virginia Voyage: 1587*; Thomas Harriot, *A Brief and True Report; A Description of Virginia: 1588*; John White, *Narrative of the 1590 Voyage, The Fifth Virginia Voyage: 1590*.

Captain Edward Hayes's account of Sir Humphrey Gilbert's last words and actions (contained in all editions of Richard Hakluyt's *The Principal Navigations, Voyages, and Discoveries of the English Nation*) is from Morison, *The European Discovery of America*. Quotation by Prince Henry about Sir Walter Raleigh's imprisonment is from the chapter by Neil Rolde in *One Land/Two Worlds*. Quotations by Raleigh are from *America's Historylands, The Horizon Book of the Elizabethan World*, and Trevelyan, *Sir Walter Raleigh*.

CHAPTER 3: PROBING THE FORBIDDING SHORES

The sources for this chapter are Louis B. Wright, *The American Heritage History of the Thirteen Colonies*; James Truslow Adams, *The Founding of New England*; John Bakeless, *America as Seen by Its First Explorers: The Eyes of Discovery*; James Rosier, annotated by David C. Morey, *The Voyage of Archangell: James Rosier's Account of the Waymouth Voyage of 1605: A True Relation*, Gardiner, Maine: Tilbury House, 2005; David Hackett Fischer, *Champlain's Dream*, New York: Simon & Schuster Paperbacks, 2008; Nathaniel Philbrick, *Mayflower*, New York: Viking, 2006; Louise Dickinson Rich, *The Coast of Maine*, New York: Thomas Y. Crowell Company, 1956; Dana Huntley, *Bartholomew Gosnold: The Man Who Was Responsible for England's Settling in the New World*, historynet.com; Karle Schlieff, ed., "Gosnold: 1602," ancientlights.org, contains complete *Briefe and True Relation of the Discoverie of the North Part of Virginia in 1602* by John Brereton, published by George Bishop of London.

James Horn, ed., *Captain John Smith: Writings with Other Narratives* contains quotations by John Brereton of the Gosnold expedition and Martin Pring (or possibly Robert Salterne) of the Pring expedition. Quotations about Cape Cod and Indians from *Briefe and True Relation* by John Brereton are from *The American Heritage History of the Thirteen Colonies*. Quotation about Indians in "a Biscay shallop" in Gabriel Archer's account, *The Relation of Captaine Gosnolds Voyage to the North part of Virginia*, is from John Bakeless, *America as Seen by Its First Explorers*. (The Archer journal was published by Samuel Purchas, in *Hakluytus Posthumus or Purchas His Pilgrimes IV*, in 1625.) Quotations by Martin Pring from his account, *A voyage set out from the citie of Bristol . . . for the discoverie of the North part of Virginia*, also published by Purchas in 1625, are taken from *The American Heritage History of the Thirteen Colonies*.

CHAPTER 4: THE ENGLISH ARE COMING

The main source for Captain Waymouth's expedition is James Rosier, annotated by David C. Morey, *The Voyage of Archangell: James Rosier's Account of the Waymouth Voyage of 1605: A True Relation*. Rosier's title of his account was *A True Relation of the most prosperous voyage made this present yeere 1605 by Captain George Waymouth in the discovery of the land of Virginia: where he discovered 60 miles up a most excellent River together with a most fertile land. Written by James Rosier, a gentleman employed in the voyage*, published by George Bishop of London, 1605. All the quotations describing the expedition are from Rosier's account. Other sources: Bill Caldwell, *Islands of Maine: Where America Really Began*, Portland, Maine: Guy Gannet Publishing Co., 1981; Colin Woodward, *The Lobster Coast: Rebels, Rusticators, and the Struggle for a Forgotten Frontier*, New York: Viking Penguin, 2004; Louis B. Wright, *The American Heritage History of the Thirteen Colonies*; William H. Tabor, "Maine's Popham Colony," athenapub.com/popham.htm.

Quotation describing Chief Justice John Popham is from a chapter by Matt Simmons in David Platt, ed., *One Land/Two Worlds*; quotation of Captain Thomas Hanham and those describing George Popham and Raleigh Gilbert are from Sir Ferdinando Gorges, *Briefe Relation*, contained in James Truslow Adams, *The Founding of New England*. Quotation from Popham letter to King James is from Bill Caldwell, *Islands of Maine*. Quotation about the failure of the Popham colony is from Sir Ferdinand Gorges, *A Briefe Relation*, contained in Colin Woodward, *The Lobster Coast*. Quotation of Popham's last words is from John Abbot, *History of Maine*, 1875, contained in Ellen Barry, "Colony Lost and Found," *Boston Phoenix*, October 27, 1997.

CHAPTER 5: SOLDIER OF FORTUNE

John Smith's own books, written at different times, provided the main source of detailed information about his career; they are contained in James Horn, ed., *Captain John Smith: Writings with Other Narratives of Roanoke, Jamestown and the First English Settlement in America*.

In chronological order according to date of publication are Smith's books dealing with his early life and the founding of Jamestown: *A True Relation of such occurrences and accidents of note, as hath hapned in Virginia, since the first planting of that collony, which is now resident in the south part thereof, till the last retourne*, by John Smith (1608); and *The Proceedings of the English Colonie in Virginia, since their first beginning from England in the yeare of our lord 1606 till this present 1612* (1612). For this book Smith assembled the accounts of nine Jamestown colonists. (See text for further explanation.) The colonists' accounts contained verbatim statements by Smith to Powhatan, Opechancanough, the settlers, the London Company, and others, as well as statements by Powhatan and other Indians to him. They were undoubtedly written by Smith and provided by him to the authors. Smith also wrote a section describing Virginia and its Indian inhabitants: *The Generall Historie of Virginia, New England,*

and the Summer Isles with the names of the Adventurers, Planters, and Governours from their first beginning 1584–1624 (1624). This book incorporated the 1612 *Proceedings* together with some changes and significant additions. Also, *The True Travels, Adventures, and Observations of Captaine John Smith in Europe, Asia, and America, A.D. 1593 to 1629* (1630).

The main source for this chapter about Smith's early life, military campaigns, and travels before Jamestown is Smith's own book, *The True Travels*. Bradford Smith, *Captain John Smith: His Life and Legend*, New York: J. B. Lippincott Co., 1953, provides a well-researched account of Smith's military campaigns in Hungary. Other sources: Dorothy and Thomas Hoobler, *Captain John Smith: Jamestown and the Birth of the American Dream*, Hoboken, New Jersey: John Wiley & Sons, Inc., 2006; *The New Yorker*, April 2, 2007. All the quotations are from Smith's *The True Travels*.

CHAPTER 6: THE FIRST ENGLISH COLONY

The sources for this chapter are the three books by Smith in 1609, 1612, and 1624, listed above. Of the three, the more comprehensive 1624 version was generally relied on as the main source. George Percy, *Discourse: The Founding of Jamestown: 1606–1607*; Gabriel Archer, *A Relatyon of the Discovery of our River: Exploration Inland: 1607*; Edward Maria Wingfield, *A Discourse of Virginia: Famine and Disease at Jamestown: 1607–1608*. All quotations are taken from the books by Smith and other authors and are identified in the text. All of the above accounts are contained in James Horn, ed., *Captain John Smith: Writings with Other Narratives of Roanoke, Jamestown and the First English Settlement in America*.

Other sources: Lyon Gardiner Tyler, ed., *Narratives of Early Virginia*, New York: Charles Scribner's Sons, 1907; Bernard Bailyn, *The Barbarous Years: The Peopling of North America, The Conflict of Civilizations, 1600–1675*, New York: Alfred A. Knopf, 2012; Edward Wright Haile, *Jamestown Narratives: Eyewitness Accounts of the Virginia Colony*, Champlain, Virginia: Roundhouse, 1998; Louis B. Wright, *The American Heritage History of the Thirteen Colonies*; John Bakeless, *America as Seen by Its First Explorers: The Eyes of Discover*; Dorothy and Thomas Hoobler, *Captain John Smith: Jamestown and the Birth of the American Dream*; Bradford Smith, *Captain John Smith: His Life and Legend*; *America's Historylands, Landmarks of Liberty*. Quotation from Captain Newport's letter to the Earl of Salisbury is from Accounts of 1607 in Edward Wright Haile, *Jamestown Narratives*. Quotation by Edward Wingfield about Kendall's execution is from *A Discourse of Virginia* in Edward Wright Haile, *Jamestown Narratives*.

CHAPTER 7: THE KING AND HIS PRINCESS

The main sources for this chapter are Smith's three books listed above, especially the 1624 book, the only one to include Smith's account of how Pocahontas saved his life. (See text for further explanation.) These books are contained in James Horn, ed., *Captain John Smith: Writings with Other Narratives*. All quotations are from the books by Smith and his selected authors and are identified in the text. Other sources: Bradford Smith, *Captain John Smith: His Life and Legend*; Dorothy and Thomas Hoobler, *Captain John Smith: Jamestown and the Birth of the American Dream*; Louis B. Wright, *The American Heritage History of the Thirteen Colonies*; Lyon Gardiner Tyler, ed., *Narratives of Early Virginia*

CHAPTER 8: EXPLORING THE CHESAPEAKE

The main sources for this chapter are Smith's books of 1612 and 1624, especially the 1624 version, contained in James Horn, ed., *Captain John Smith: Writings with Other Narratives*. All quotations are from the books by Smith and his selected authors and are identified in the text. Other sources: Bradford Smith, *Captain John Smith: His Life and Legend*; Dorothy and Thomas Hoobler, *Captain John Smith: Jamestown and the Birth of the American Dream;America's Historylands, Landmarks of Liberty*; Lyon Gardiner Tyler, ed., *Narratives of Early Virginia*.

CHAPTER 9: CAPTAIN NEWPORT RETURNS

The main sources for this chapter are Smith's books of 1612 and 1624, especially the 1624 version, contained in James Horn, ed., *Captain John Smith: Writings with Other Narratives*. All quotations are from the books by Smith and his selected authors and are identified in the text. Other sources: Bradford Smith, *Captain John Smith: His Life and Legend*; Dorothy and Thomas Hoobler, *Captain John Smith: Jamestown and the Birth of the American Dream*; Louis B. Wright, *The American Heritage History of the Thirteen Colonies*; Lyon Gardiner Tyler, ed., *Narratives of Early Virginia* .

CHAPTER 10: TROUBLES FOR THE PRESIDENT

The main sources for this chapter are Smith's books of 1612 and 1624, especially the 1624 version, contained in James Horn, ed., *Captain John Smith: Writings with Other Narratives*. All quotations are from the books by Smith and his selected authors and are identified in the text. Quotation of the London Company's instructions to Sir Thomas Gates and the company's broadside about Jamestown are from Bradford Smith, *Captain John Smith: His Life and Legend*. Other sources: Dorothy and Thomas Hoobler, *Captain John Smith: Jamestown and the Birth of the American Dream*; Louis B. Wright, *The American Heritage History of the Thirteen Colonies*; *America's Historylands, Landmarks of Liberty*; Lyon Gardiner Tyler, ed., *Narratives of Early Virginia*.

CHAPTER 11: UNDER NEW MANAGEMENT

The main sources for this chapter are Smith's books of 1612 and 1624, especially the 1624 version; Henry Spelman, *Relation of Virginia: An English Boy among the Indians: 1609–1611*; William Strachey, *A True Reportory: Shipwreck and Rescue: 1609–1610*; William Strachey, from *The Historie of Travell into Virginia Britania: The Indians of Virginia: 1612*; George Percy, *A Trewe Relacyon: Dissention in Virginia: 1609–1612*; Ralph Hamor, *A True Discourse on the Present State of Virginia: Expanding the Colony: 1609–1614*; Lord De La Warre, *A Short Relation: Securing the Colony: 1610–1611*. All of the above are contained in James Horn, ed., *Captain John Smith: Writings with Other Narratives of Roanoke, Jamestown and the First English Settlement in America*.

Other sources: John Burk, *The History of Virginia from Its First Settlement to the Present Day*, Petersburg, Virginia: Dickson & Pescod, 1804; Samuel Eliot Morison, *The Oxford History of the American People*, New York: Oxford University Press, 1965; Page Smith, *A New Age Now Begins*, New York: McGraw-Hill Book Company, 1976; Edward Wright Haile, *Jamestown Narratives*; Bradford Smith, *Captain John Smith: His Life and Legend*; Dorothy and Thomas Hoobler, *Captain John Smith: Jamestown and the Birth of the American Dream*; Louis B. Wright, *The American Heritage History of the Thirteen Colonies*; Lyon Gardiner Tyler, ed., *Narratives of Early Virginia*; Bernard Bailyn, *The Barbarous Years*.

The report that the Powhatans had killed the Roanoke settlers is from William Strachey, *The Historie of Travell into Virginia Britania*, and Smith's chronology in Horn, *Captain John Smith: Writings with Other Narratives*. The Council of Virginia instructions, 1609, name a place "where you shall find four of the English alive left by Sir Walter Raweley which escaped from the slaughter of Powhaton of Roanocke upon the first arrival of our colony" are from Haile, *Jamestown Narratives*. No survivors were found.

Quotations taken from the books by John Smith and his selected authors are identified in the text. Quotation of the London Company appointing Smith to be military commander is from Bradford Smith, *Captain John Smith*. The Sir Thomas Gates decree regarding rape and fornication is from *The Laws Divine and Moral* in Edward Wright Haile, *Jamestown Narratives*. The Gates decree regarding hygiene discipline and morality is from John Burk, *The History of Virginia*. Quotations of Gates from his report to the Virginia Company are from the company's *A True Declaration of Virginia* contained in Strachey's *A True Reportory* in Haile, *Jamestown Narratives*. Quotation of Gates regarding "famine and pestilence" is from *America's Historylands*. Quotation from the 1610 Council of Virginia's *A True and Sincere Declaration* is from Haile, *Jamestown Narratives*. Certain population figures and information pertaining to the Virginia Company stock issue and the regimes of governors De La Warr, Gates, and Dale are from Barnard Bailyn, *The Barbarous Years*. Quotation regarding censorship from the summary of 1609 Virginia Company instructions to Sir Thomas Gates, quotations from the 1612 charter issued to the Virginia Company, and Governor Dale's letter to the Earl of Salisbury are from Haile, *Jamestown Narratives*.

Quotation of Strachey in *A True Reportory* regarding poor condition of the colonists is from Haile, *Jamestown Narratives.* Quotation of Dale regarding workers is from Bailyn, *The Barbarous Years.* Quotation about implementation of censorship is from *The Ancient Planters of Virginia, A Brief Declaration,* in Haile, *Jamestown Narratives.* Quotations from the Dale letter to the Virginia Company and by George Percy in *A True Relation* about treatment of Indian captives are in Haile, *Jamestown Narratives.* Quotation by Alexander Whitaker in the letter to Sir Thomas Smythe is from Haile, *Jamestown Narratives.* Quotation of William Crashaw supporting Jamestown is from Page Smith, *A New Age Now Begins.* Quotation by Crashaw admiring John Smith's book is from Haile, *Jamestown Narratives.*

The Oxfordian school of historians believes that Shakespeare's plays and sonnets were written by Edward de Vere, the Earl of Oxford, who died in 1604. According to this theory, *The Tempest* could not have been based on Strachey's account.

CHAPTER 12: NORTHERN VIRGINIA BECOMES NEW ENGLAND

The sources for this chapter are Dorothy Simpson, *The Maine Islands in Story and Legend,* Nobleboro, Maine: Blackberry Books, 1987; Carl Carmer, *The Hudson,* New York: Farrar & Rinehart, 1939; Peter C. Mancall, "Strangers in a New Land: Henry Hudson's First American Adventure," *American Heritage* 59, no. 1 (2009); "Mount Desert Island" and "Castine, Maine" from Wikipedia, the Free Encyclopedia; George J. Varney, *History of Mount Desert, Maine,* Boston: B. B. Russell, 1886; Colin Woodward, *The Lobster Coast*; Bradford Smith, *Captain John Smith: His Life and Legend*; James Truslow Adams, *The Founding of New England* ; Dorothy and Thomas Hoobler, *Captain John Smith: Jamestown and the Birth of the American Dream*; Louis B. Wright, *The American Heritage History of the Thirteen Colonies*; David Hackett Fischer, *Champlain's Dream.*

James Horn, ed., *Captain John Smith: Writings with Other Narratives* contains Smith's *A Description of New England* published in 1616, Smith's *New England Trials,* published in 1622, and Smith's *The Generall Historie of Virginia, New England, and the Summer Isles* published in 1624. *A Description of New England* contains the deposition by Daniel Baker regarding Smith's failed third expedition to New England. All quotations by Smith are from *A Description of New England. The Generall Historie* contains Captain Edward Harlow's account of his New England expeditions.

CHAPTER 13: INDIAN PARTNERS

The sources for this chapter are Samuel Eliot Morison, *Oxford History of the American People*; James Horn, ed., *Captain John Smith: Writings with Other Narratives;* Bradford Smith, *Captain John Smith: His Life and Legend*; Dorothy and Thomas Hoobler,

Captain John Smith: Jamestown and the Birth of the American Dream; Lyon Gardiner Tyler, ed., *Narratives of Early Virginia*; James Truslow Adams, *The Founding of New England*; Louis B. Wright, *The American Heritage History of the Thirteen Colonies*; Edward Wright Haile, *Jamestown Narratives*.

Quotation by Alexander Whitaker about Pocahontas's conversion to Christianity is from Haile, *Jamestown Narratives*. The following are contained in *Captain John Smith: Writings with Other Narratives*: quotations about Pocahontas by Ralph Hamor and Hamor's meeting with Powhatan from *A True Discourse of the Present Estate of Virginia: Expanding the Colony: 1609–1614* by Hamor; quotations from Smith's letter to Queen Anne introducing Pocahontas, Smith's meeting with Pocahontas, and his idea to give free land to colonists are from *Smith's Generall Historie of Virginia, New England, and the Summer Isles*. Quotations from John Rolfe's letter to Sir Thomas Dale about his pending marriage are from Tyler, *Narratives of Early Virginia*. Quotations about Pocahontas in London by Samuel Purchas are from *Purchas His Pilgrimes, 1625*, contained in Wikipedia, the Free Encyclopedia. Quotation describing young women sent to Jamestown is from Morison, *The Oxford History of the American People*. Quotation about the Yeardley regime and tense Indian relations is from *The Ancient Planters of Virginia* in Haile, *Jamestown Narratives*. Quotation about Thomas Hunt by Sir Ferdinando Gorges is from Gorges, *Briefe Relation* contained in Bradford Smith, *Captain John Smith, His Life and Legend*. Quotation from the letter of Thomas Dermer to Gorges is from Gorges, *Briefe Relation*, contained in Adams, *The Founding of New England*. Quotations regarding the first Yeardley administration and tense Indian relations by *Ancient Planters of Virginia* are from Haile, *Jamestown Narratives*.

CHAPTER 14: THE LEIDEN SEPARATISTS

The sources for this chapter are William Bradford, *Of Plymouth Plantation 1620–1647*, edited by Samuel Eliot Morison, New York, Random House, 1981; John Brown, *The Pilgrim Fathers of New England and Their Puritan Successors*, New York: Fleming H. Revell Company, 1897; Nathaniel Philbrick, *Mayflower*, New York: Viking, 2006; John Alden, *Story of a Pilgrim Family*, Boston: James H. Earle, 1889; George B. Cheever, *The Journal of the Pilgrims at Plymouth in New England, in 1620*, New York: John Wiley, 1848. This book contains the account that has come to be known as *Mourt's Relation*, largely written by Edward Winslow with the early parts by William Bradford and published in 1622 by George Morton, Bradford's son-in-law; *Mourt's Relation* covers the first year the Pilgrims spent at Plymouth.

Other sources: James Horn, ed., *Captain John Smith: Writings with Other Narratives*; James Truslow Adams, *The Founding of New England*; Samuel Eliot Morison, *The Oxford History of the American People*; Louis B. Wright, *The American Heritage History of the Thirteen Colonies*; Page Smith, *A New Age Now Begins*; *America's Historylands, Landmarks of Liberty*.

The quotation of King James regarding treatment of the Separatists is from William Bradford, *Of Plymouth Plantation*. The quotation of Edward Winslow regarding the Dutch and the Sabbath is from Adams, *The Founding of New England*. The quotation of John Smith about the Pilgrim's use of his map is from his book, *The True Travels, Adventures, and Observations of Captaine John Smith*, published in 1630, contained in *Captain John Smith: Writings with Other Narratives*. The quotation by Thomas Weston in Southampton is from Adams, *The Founding of New England*. The demographic breakdown of the Pilgrims by gender, age, and other factors is from Brown, *The Pilgrim Fathers of New England*. The numerical division between the two groups signing the Mayflower Compact is from Adams, *The Founding of New England*. The following quotations and all those by William Bradford are from Bradford, *Of Plymouth Plantation*: quotation from the Leiden Pilgrims' letter of August 3, 1620, to Merchant Adventurers; quotation from John Robinson's letter of July 1620 to the Leiden Pilgrims; quotation from the Mayflower Compact.

CHAPTER 15: THE PLYMOUTH PLANTATION

The sources for this chapter are Henry Martyn Dexter, William Bradford, Edward Winslow, *Mourt's Relation or Journal of the Plantation at Plymouth*, Boston: John Kimball Wiggin, 1865; William Bradford, *Bradford's History of Plymouth Plantation 1606–1646*, New York: Charles Scribner's Sons, 1908; William Bradford, *Of Plymouth Plantation: 1620–1647*; John Brown, *The Pilgrim Fathers of New England and Their Puritan Successors*; George B. Cheever, *The Journal of the Pilgrims at Plymouth in New England, in 1620*, New York: John Wiley, 1848; Nathaniel Philbrick, *Mayflower*; James Truslow Adams, *The Founding of New England*; John Alden, *Story of a Pilgrim Family*, Boston: James H. Earle, 1889; Samuel Eliot Morison, *The Oxford History of the American People*, New York: The Oxford University Press, 1965; Louis B. Wright, *The American Heritage History of the Thirteen Colonies*.

The following quotations and scenes are from *Mourt's Relation or Journal of the Plymouth Plantation*: women going ashore to bathe; the first attack by the Indians on Cape Cod; Samoset welcoming the English; Edward Winslow's speech to Massasoit; text of treaty between the Pilgrims and Massasoit. Historians believe that this section of *Mourt's Relation* was written by William Bradford. Other quotations by Bradford, as indicated in the text, are from Bradford, *Of Plymouth Plantation*. Regarding the question as to whether the Pilgrims had a copy of John Smith's map, Reverend John Alden states in *Story of a Pilgrim Family* that the Pilgrims consulted Captain John Smith's map when they anchored their shallop in Plymouth Harbor, which "they found to be named Plymouth." Nathaniel Philbrick in the notes for *Mayflower* states that James Baker, the Plymouth historian and author, reported that William Brewster had Smith's map and book in his library. John Smith also stated in *The True Travel, Adventures, and Observations of Captaine John Smith* that the Pilgrims had his map.

CHAPTER 16: INDIAN SUMMER

The sources for this chapter are Eugene Aubrey Stratton, *Plymouth Colony: Its History and People 1620-1691*. Provo, Utah: Ancestry Publishing, 1986; Henry Martyn Dexter, William Bradford, Edward Winslow, *Mourt's Relation or Journal of the Plantation at Plymouth*; William Bradford, *Bradford's History of Plymouth Plantation 1606–1646*; William Bradford, *Of Plymouth Plantation: 1620–1647*; John Brown, *The Pilgrim Fathers of New England and Their Puritan Successors*; George B. Cheever, *The Journal of the Pilgrims at Plymouth, in New England, in 1620*; Nathaniel Philbrick, *Mayflower*; James Truslow Adams, *The Founding of New England*; John Alden, *Story of a Pilgrim Family*; Samuel Eliot Morison, *The Oxford History of the American People*; Louis B. Wright, *The American Heritage History of the Thirteen Colonies*.

The accounts of Winslow's visit to Massasoit, the rescue of the Billington boy, the missions of Standish to find Squanto and meet with the Massachusetts Indians are contained in *Mourt's Relation or Journal of the Plantation at Plymouth*, as are the quotations cited in these episodes. The quotations of Bradford are from *Of Plymouth Plantation*, as are the letters from Weston and Bradford's reply. Quotations from the letter of Edward Winslow are contained in *Mourt's Relation or Journal of the Plantation at Plymouth*.

CHAPTER 17: EMERGING CONFLICTS

The sources for this chapter about Jamestown are Edward Winslow, *Good Newse from New England. A True Relation of Things Very Remarkable at the Plantation of Plimoth in New England*. Printed for William Bladen and John Bellamie, 1624; John Burk, *The History of Virginia: From Its First Settlement to the Present Day*; James Horn, ed., *Captain John Smith: Writings with Other Narratives*; Bradford Smith, *Captain John Smith: His Life and Legend*; Lyon Gardiner Tyler, ed., *Narratives of Early Virginia*; Bernard Bailyn, *The Barbarous Years*; Louis B. Wright, *The American Heritage History of the Thirteen Colonies* The quotations from Governor Wyatt's instructions for governing the colony are from *The History of Virginia: From Its First Settlement to the Present Day*, the description of the Indian massacre and colonist casualties is largely from the same source and Bernard Bailyn, *The Barbarous Years*. The quotation by the Virginia Company after the massacre is also from *The Barbarous Years*. Martin's Hundred and Smith's Hundred, named after Sir Thomas Smythe of the Virginia Company, were both established in 1617. The name was derived from the practice of awarding one hundred acres to a group of colonists or that one hundred colonists would be sent to settle on a particular plantation. By 1619 six additional "hundreds" had been settled and more would follow.

The main sources for the chapter about Plymouth are Eugene Aubrey Stratton, *Plymouth Colony: Its History & People, 1620–1691*; Bernard Bailyn, *The Barbarous Years*; Edward Winslow, *Good Newes from New England, A True Relation of Things Very Remarkable at the Plantation of Plimoth in New England*; Samuel Eliot Morison, *The Oxford History of the American People*; William Bradford, *Bradford's History of Plymouth Plantation, 1606–1646*. Quotations from these sources are indicated in the text.

Quotations from letters by Thomas Weston, Robert Cushman, and John Pierce are from *Bradford's History of Plymouth Plantation*. Quotations concerning Massasoit's illness and his warning to the English regarding the plot of the Massachusetts; Bradford's letter to John Sanders about stealing Indian corn; the instructions to kill Wituwamat; Phineas Pratt's report; statements by Standish, Peksuot, and Hobbamock; Bradford's message to Obtakiest; and John Robinson's letter to Bradford are from Edward Winslow, *Good Newse from New England*. Robert Cushman's letter to Bradford about recruiting settlers is from *Bradford's History of Plymouth Plantation*. Bradford's quotation regarding the good year of 1625 is from Morison, *The Oxford History of the American People*. Information about the arrival of the Leiden Pilgrims in 1629 to 1630 is from Bernard Bailyn, *The Barbarous Years*. Information about the Pilgrims' repayment of debt to the Merchant Adventurers and the visit of Issac de Rasieres to Plymouth is from Eugene Aubrey Stratton, *Plymouth Colony*.

CHAPTER 18: JOHN WINTHROP AND THE PURITANS

The sources for this chapter about Plymouth are Wesley Frank Craven, *The Colonies in Transition*, New York: Harper Torchbooks, 1968; William Bradford, *Bradford's History of Plymouth Plantation 1606–1646*; William Bradford, *Of Plymouth Plantation*; John Brown, *The Pilgrim Fathers of New England and Their Puritan Successors*; George B. Cheever, *The Journal of the Pilgrims at Plymouth, in New England, in 1620*; Nathaniel Philbrick, *Mayflower*; John Alden, *Story of a Pilgrim Family*; Samuel Eliot Morison, *Oxford History of the American People*; Edward Winslow, *Good Newes from New England, A True Relation of Things Very Remarkable at the Plantation of Plimoth in New England*; Bernard Bailyn, *The Barbarous Years: The Peopling of North America*; Louis B. Wright, *The American Heritage History of the Thirteen Colonies*; Eugene Aubrey Stratton, *Plymouth Colony: Its History & People, 1620–1691*.

Information about crime in Plymouth, the treatment of Quakers, the changing political status of Plymouth, and the quotation about Bradford by George Langford are from Eugene Aubrey Stratton, *Plymouth Colony*. Quotations from the Massachusetts Bay Colony charter and the Reverend Francis Higginson are from *The American Heritage History of the Thirteen Colonies*. Quotation from the Winthrop letter about conditions in England is from Morison, *The Oxford History of the American People*. Quotations from John Winthrop's letter to his wife and John Endicott's letter to William Bradford are from John Brown, *The Pilgrim Fathers of New England*. Quotations of Bradford are from *Of Plymouth Plantation*. The quotation from Edward Winslow's advice to potential investors in the colonies is from *Good Newes from New England*. The 1630 New England population figures are from James Truslow Adams, *The Founding of New England*. The 1643 population estimate of Plymouth Colony is from Eugene Aubrey Stratton, *Plymouth Colony*. The quotation from the Articles of Transfer regarding religious freedom in New York is from World Digital Library, Atlantic World Collection, National Library of the Netherlands, The Hague.

CHAPTER 19: KING PHILIP'S WAR

The sources for this chapter are Benjamin Church, *The History of King Philip's War*. Boston: Howe & Norton, 1825; Wesley Frank Craven, *The Colonies in Transition*; Nathaniel Philbrick, *Mayflower*; Eugene Aubrey Stratton, *Plymouth Colony: Its History & People, 1620–1691*; Louis B. Wright, *The American Heritage History of the Thirteen Colonies*; Arthur M. Schlesinger Jr., ed., *The Almanac of American History*; James Truslow Adams, *The Founding of New England*; the quotation by Benjamin Church about King Philip is from *The History of King Philip's War*.

CHAPTER 20: VIRGINIA AND MASSACHUSETTS

The sources for this chapter about Jamestown are Wesley Frank Craven, *The Colonies in Transition*; Marcus Lee Hansen, *The Atlantic Migration 1607–1860*, New York: Harper & Row, 1961; David Hackett Fischer, *Albion's Seed*, New York: Oxford University Press, 1981; Warren M. Billings, *Virtual Jamestown: Sir William Berkeley*, National Park Service, *Historic Handbook: The Story of Jamestown*; John Burk, *The History of Virginia: From Its First Settlement to the Present Day*; James Horn, ed., *Captain John Smith: Writings with Other Narratives of Roanoke, Jamestown and the First English Settlement in America*; Bradford Smith, *Captain John Smith: His Life and Legend*; Lyon Gardiner Tyler, ed., *Narratives of Early Virginia*; Samuel Eliot Morison, *Oxford History of the American People*; Bernard Bailyn, *The Barbarous Years: The Peopling of North America, The Conflict of Civilizations, 1600–1675*; Eugene Aubrey Stratton, *Plymouth Colony: Its History & People, 1620–1691*; Louis B. Wright, *The American Heritage History of the Thirteen Colonies*.

The account of events leading up to Jamestown's conversion to a royal colony and the quotation from Nathaniel Butler's report on Virginia is based largely on John Burk, *The History of Virginia* and *The American History Heritage of the Thirteen Colonies*. Developments in the Virginia tobacco industry and King Charles's quotation about its economic dominance are from John Burk, *The History of Virginia*. The story of Nathaniel Bacon's rebellion is based on Warren M. Billings, *Virtual Jamestown* and Samuel Eliot Morison, *The Oxford History of the American People*. Statistics about the importation of slaves are from Bernard Bailyn, *The Barbarous Years*. Information about the composition of the Virginia House of Burgesses and Royal Council is from David Hackett Fischer, *Albion's Seed*. Quotation of King Charles II about Governor Berkeley is from *American History Heritage of the Thirteen Colonies*. Quotation from the Richard Potts's tribute to John Smith is from *Captain John Smith: Writings with Other Narratives*. The 1660 Virginia population figures and the 1690 Plymouth and Massachusetts population figures are from Wesley Frank Craven, *The Colonies in Transition 1607–1860*. Quotations of Winthrop's instruction to Edward Winslow regarding Massachusetts and the General Court's comment on the Navigation Acts are from Samuel Eliot Morison, *The Oxford History of the American People*. The account of the formation of the Dominion of New England and the grant of a new charter of Massachusetts incorporating Plymouth was taken from Stratton, *Plymouth Colony*. Quotation by President Ronald Reagan is from *The Almanac of American History*.

References

BOOKS AND ARTICLES

Adams, James Truslow. *The Founding of New England*. Boston: The Atlantic Monthly Press, 1921.

Alden, John. *Story of a Pilgrim Family*. Boston: James H. Earle, 1889.

Bailyn, Bernard. *The Barbarous Years: The Peopling of British North America: The Conflict of Civilizations, 1600–1675*. New York: Alfred A. Knopf, 2012.

Bakeless, John. *America as Seen by Its First Explorers: The Eyes of Discovery*. New York: Dover Publications Inc., 1961.

Barry, Ellen. "Colony Lost and Found." *Boston Phoenix*, October 27, 1997.

Beard, Charles A., and Mary R. Beard. *The Rise of American Civilization*. New York: Macmillan, 1927.

Blow, Michael, ed., and Louis B. Wright, author. *The American Heritage History of the Thirteen Colonies*. New York: The American Heritage Publishing Company Inc., 1967.

Bradford, William. *Bradford's History of Plymouth Plantation, 1606–1646*. New York: Charles Scribner's Sons, 1908.

———. *Of Plymouth Plantation, 1620–1647*. New York: Alfred A. Knopf, 1952.

Bragdon, Henry W., and Samuel P. McCutchen. *History of a Free People*. New York: Mcmillan, 1964.

Brown, John. *The Pilgrim Fathers of New England and Their Puritan Successors*. New York: Fleming H. Revell Co., 1897.

Burk, John. *The History of Virginia*. Virginia: Dickson & Pescud, 1804.

Butler, Nathaniel, author, and C. F. E. Hollis Hallett, trans. and ed. *Butler's History of the Bermudas*. Bermuda: Bermuda Maritime Museum Press, 2007.

Caldwell, Bill. *Islands of Maine: Where America Really Began*. Maine: Guy Gannett Publishing Co., 1981.

Carmer, Carl. *The Hudson*. New York: Farrar & Rinehart Inc., 1939.

Castine, Maine. Wikipedia, The Free Encylopedia. wikipedia.org., http://en.wikipedia .org/wiki/Castine,_Maine.

Cheever, George B. *The Journal of the Pilgrims at Plymouth, in New England, in 1620.* New York: John Wiley, 1848.

Church, Benjamin. *The History of King Philip's War.* Boston: Howe and Norton, 1825.

Churchill, Winston S. *A History of the English-Speaking Peoples, Vol. II, The New World.* London: Cassell & Co. Ltd., 1956.

Craven, Wesley Frank. *The Colonies in Transition.* New York: Harper & Row, 1968.

Deans, Bob. "Captain John Smith." *Time*, April 26, 2007.

Fischer, David Hackett. *Albion's Seed.* New York: Oxford University Press, 1981.

———. *Champlain's Dream.* New York: Simon & Schuster Paperbacks, 2008.

"Gilbert, Humphrey." Answers.com, http://www.answers.com/topic/humphrey-gilbert.

Gratwick, Harry. "Main's First Ship Will Sail Again." *The Working Waterfront*, published by The Island Institute, August 3, 2011.

Haile, Edward Wright. *Jamestown Narratives: Eyewitness Accounts of the Virginia Colony, The First Decade, 1607–1617.* Champlain, VA: RoundHouse, 1998.

Hansen, Marcus Lee. *The Atlantic Migration, 1607–1860.* New York: Harper & Row, 1961.

Hoobler, Dorothy, and Thomas Hoobler. *Captain John Smith: Jamestown and the Birth of the American Dream.* New Jersey: John Wiley & Sons, Inc., 2006.

Horn, James, ed. *Captain John Smith: Writings with Other Narratives of Roanoke, Jamestown and the First English Settlement in America.* New York: Library of America, 2007.

Hoxie, Frederick E., ed. "Squanto (Tisquantum)." *Encyclopedia of North American Indians.* New York: Houghton Mifflin Harcourt, 1996.

Huntley, Dana. *Bartholomew Gosnold: The Man Who Was Responsible for England's Settling in the New World.* historynet.com, http://www.historynet.com/bartholomew-gosnold-the-man-who-was-responsible-for-englands-settling-the-new-world.htm.

Jameson, J. Franklin, ed. *Narratives of Early Virginia 1606–1625: Original Narratives of Early American History.* New York: Charles Scribner's Sons, 1907.

Mancall, Peter C. "Strangers in a New Land: Henry Hudson's First American Adventure." *American Heritage* 59, no. 1 (Spring 2009).

Mann, Charles C. "America Found & Lost." *National Geographic*, May 2007.

Morey, David C., anno. *The Voyage of Archangell: James Rosier's Account of the Waymouth Voyage of 1605: A True Relation.* Gandiner, Maine: Tilbury House, 2005.

Morison, Samuel Eliot. *The Oxford History of the American People.* New York: Oxford University Press, 1965.

———. *The European Discovery of America: The Northern Voyages A.D. 500–1600.* New York: Oxford University Press, 1971.

Morton, Thomas. *The New English Canaan.* Boston: Prince Society, 1883. Reprinted digitally by the University of Michigan Libraries.

"Mount Desert Island." Wikipedia, The Free Encyclopedia. wikipedia.org, http:// en.wikipedia.org/wiki/Mount_Desert_Island.

The *New Encyclopaedia Britannica*. Chicago: Encyclopaedia Britannica Inc., 1989.

Philbrick, Nathaniel. *Mayflower*. New York: Viking, 2006.

Platt, David, ed. *One Land/Two Worlds: A Symposium to Celebrate the 400th Anniversary of George Waymouth's Voyage to New England*. Rockland, Maine: Island Institute, 2005.

"Pocahontas." Wikipedia, The Free Encylopedia. wikipedia.org, http://en.wikipedia. org/wiki/Pocahontas.

"Pring, Martin." Wikipedia, The Free Encylopedia. wikipedia.org, http://en.wikipedia .org/wiki/Martin_Pring.

Quinn, David B., and Alison M. Quinn, eds. *The English New England Voyages, 1602–1608*. London: The Hakluyt Society, 1983.

———. *The Hakluyt Handbook Vol. I*. London: The Hakluyt Society, 1974.

Randall, Willard Sterne. "First Encounters." *American Heritage* 59, no. 1 (Spring 2009).

Rich, Louise Dickinson. *The Coast of Maine*. New York: Thomas Y. Crowell Company, 1956.

"Samuel de Champlain." Wikipedia, The Free Encyclopedia. wikipedia.org, http:// en.wikipedia.org/wiki/Samuel_de_Champlain.

Schlesinger, Arthur M. Jr., ed. *The Almanac of American History*. New York: G. P. Putnam's Sons, 1983.

Schlieff, Karle, ed. "Gosnold: 1602." ancientlights.org, http://ancientlights.org/gosnold.html.

Severy, Merle, ed. *America's Historylands: Touring Our Landmarks of Liberty*. Washington, DC: National Geographic Society, 1967.

Simpson, Dorothy. *The Maine Islands in Story and Legend*. Nobleberry, Maine: Blackberry Books, 1987.

"Sir Ferdinando Gorges." EncyclopediaBritannica.com, http://www.britannica.com/ EBchecked/topic/239240/Sir-Ferdinando-Gorges.

Smith, Bradford. *Captain John Smith: His Life and Legend*. New York: J. B. Lippincott Co., 1953.

Smith, Lacey Baldwin. *The Horizon Book of the Elizabethan World*. New York: American Heritage Publishing Co., Inc., 1967.

Smith, Page. *A New Age Now Begins, Vol. I*. New York: McGraw-Hill Book Co., 1976.

Stratton, Eugene Aubrey. *Plymouth Colony: Its History & People, 1620–1691*. Provo, Utah: Ancestry Publishing, 1986.

Tabor, William H. "Maine's Popham Colony." athenapub.com/popham.htm.

"Tisquantum" ("Squanto"). MayflowerHistory.com, http://mayflowerhistory.com/ tisquantum/.

Tooley, R. V. *Maps and Map-Makers*. London: B. T. Batsford Ltd., 1949.

Trevelyan, Raleigh. *Sir Walter Raleigh*. New York: Henry Holt and Co., 2002.

Tyler, Lyon Gardiner, ed. *Narratives of Early Virginia, 1606–1625*. New York: Charles Scribner's Sons, 1907.

Van de Gohm, Richard. *Antique Maps for the Collector*. New York: Macmillan, 1973.

Varney, George J. *History of Mount Desert, Maine*. Boston: B. B. Russell, 1886.

Winslow, Edward. *Good Newes from New England.* London: Printed by I. D. for William Bladen and John Bellamie, 1624.

Winslow, Edward, William Bradford, and Henry M. Dexter, ed. *Mourt's Relation or Journal of the Plantation at Plymouth.* Boston: J. K. Wiggin, 1865.

Woodard, Colin. *The Lobster Coast: Rebels, Rusticators, and the Struggle for a Forgotten Frontier.* New York: Viking Penguin, 2004.

PRIMARY SOURCES

Archer, Gabriel. *A Relatyon of the Discovery of Our River.* Exploration Inland: 1607.

———. "Letter from Jamestown," 31 August 1609.

Argall, Samuel. "Letter to Hawes," June 1613.

Barlowe, Arthur. *Discourse of the First Voyage. The First English Voyage to Virginia: 1584.*

Bradford, William, and Edward Winslow. *Mourt's Relation: A Journal of the Pilgrims at Plymouth.* London, 1622.

———. *The 1630 Bradford Patent. Plymouth's third patent granted to William Bradford and his associates by the Council of New England.*

———. *Of Plymouth Plantation. Written 1630–1654.* Boston: Massachusetts Historical Society, 1856.

Brereton, M. John. *A Brief and True Relation of the Discovery of the North Part of Virginia; being a most pleasant, fruitful and commodious soil: Made this present year 1602 by Captain Bartholomew Gosnold, Captain Bartholomew Gilbert, and diverse other gentlemen and their associates, by the permission of the honourable knight, Sir Walter Raleigh, & c. Imperis Geor. Bishop.* Londini, 1602.

Biard, Pierre. "Letter of Father Pierre Biard, 1614: To the Very Reverend Father Claude Acquaviva, General of the Society of Jesus, at Rome, May 26, 1614."

Cartier, Jacques. *A Shorte and Briefe Narration (Cartier's Second Voyage), 1535–36.*

Church, Benjamin. *The History of King Philip's War.* Boston: Howe & Norton, 1825.

Dale, Thomas. "Letter to Salisbury," 17 August 1611.

———. "Letter to Smythe," June 1613.

———. "Letter from Henrico," 10 June 1613.

———. "Letter to D.M.," 18 June 1614.

———. "Letter to Winwood," 3 June 1616.

De La Warr, Lord. West, Thomas. "Letter to Salisbury," rec'd September 1610.

———. *A Short Relation, Securing the Colony: 1610–11.*

Gorges, Sir Ferdinando. *A Brief Relation of the Discovery and Plantation of New England.* London, 1622.

Grenville, Sir Richard. The Journal of the Tiger: The Second Voyage to Virginia: 1585.

———. *The Voyage made by Sir Richard Greenvile, for Sir Walter Raleigh, to Virginia in the yeere, 1585.*

Hamor, Ralph. *A True Discourse of the Present Estate of Virginia. Expanding the Colony: 1609–14.*

Harriot, Thomas. *A Briefe and True Report, A Description of Virginia: 1588.*

Lane, Ralph. *Discourse on the First Colony, Roanoke: 1585–86.*

Le Challeux, Nicolas. *Narrative of Captain Jean Ribaut's last voyage in 1565.*

Letters: To the Council of Virginia in England from the Council in Jamestown, Virginia, 22 June 1607.

The Council of Virginia: A True and Sincere Declaration. *Lord De La Warr and the Jamestown council declared it to be "our own approved discourse."*

The Council of Virginia: *A True Declaration of the estate of the colony in Virginia, 1610.*

A Brief Declaration, The Ancient Planters of Virginia.

The General Assembly. *The Answer of the General Assembly 1624.*

Newport, Christopher. "Letter to Salisbury," 29 July 1607.

Percy, George. *Observations Gathered out of a Discourse of the plantation of the Southern colony in Virginia by the English, 1606.*

———. *Discourse, The Founding of Jamestown: 1606–7.*

———. *A Trewe Relacyon, Dissension in Jamestown: 1609–12.*

Perkins, Francis. "Letter from Jamestown to a Friend," 28 March 1608.

Pory, John. "Letter of John Pory, 1619: Secretary of Virginia," To Sir Dudley Carelton.

Pring, Martin. *A Voyage set out from the Citie of Bristoll,* 1603.

Purchase, Samuel. *An Interview in London: Uttamatomakkin.*

Ratcliffe, John. "Letter to Salisbury," 4 October 1609.

Rich, Richard. *News from Virginia, 1610.*

Rolfe, John. "Letter of John Rolfe, 1614: The coppie of the Gentle–mans letter to Sir Thomas Dale, that after married Powhatans daughter, containing the reasons moving him thereunto."

———. *A True Relation of the State of Virginia, The Colony Prospers: 1616.*

———. "Letter of John Rolfe to Sir Edwin Sandys," January 1620.

Rosier, James. *A True Relation of the Most Prosperous Voyage Made this Present Year 1605 by Captain George Weymouth.* London, 1605.

Saltonstall, Nathaniel. *The Present State of New England, 1675.*

Settle, Master Dionise. *The Second Voyage of Master Martin Forbisher, 1577.*

Smith, Captain John. *The True Travels, Adventures, and Observations of Captaine John Smith in Europe, Asia, and America, A.D. 1593 to 1629.*

———. *A True Relation of such occurrences and accidents of note, as hath hapned in Virginia, since the first planting of that Collony, which is now resident in the South part thereof, till the last returne. May 1608.*

———. *The Proceedings of the English Colonie in Virginia. 1612.*

———. *A Description of New-England.* London, 1616.

———. *The Generall Historie of Virginia, New England and the Summer Isles.* London, 1624.

———. *New England Trials, and Present Estate.* London, 1624.

———. *Advertisements: For the unexperienced Planters of New-England, or anywhere, or The Path-way to Experience to erect a Plantation, 1631.*

Somers, George. "Letter to Salisbury," 15 June 1610.

Spelman, Henry. *Relation of Virginia, An English Boy among the Indians: 1609–11.*

Strachey, William. *A True Reportory, Shipwreck & Rescue: 1609–10.*

———. *The Historie of Travell into Virginia Britania, The Indians of Virginia: 1612.*

Virginia Statutes, 1661.

Whitaker, Alexander. *Good News from Virginia: 1612.*

White, John. *Narrative of His Voyage, The Fourth Virginia Voyage: 1587*.

———. *Narrative of the 1590 Voyage, The Fifth Virginia Voyage: 1590*.

Wingfield, Edward Maria. *A Discourse of Virginia, Famine and Disease in Jamestown: 1607–8*.

Winslow, Edward. *Journal of the Pilgrims at Plymouth. Letter of Winslow, December 11, 1621. A letter sent from New England to a friend in these partes sailing forth a briefe and true Declaration of the Worth of that Plantation*.

———. *Good Newes from New England, 1624*.

Index

About the Author

Edward M. Lamont was a banker for twenty-three years with the World Bank and JP Morgan & Co. He also worked for the Marshall Plan and NATO in Paris and the U.S. Department of Housing and Urban Development in Washington, DC. He is a chairman emeritus of The Children's Aid Society in New York City. Lamont is the author of *The Ambassador From Wall Street: The Story of Thomas W. Lamont, J. P. Morgan's Chief Executive* and *Ned Miner and His Pioneering Forebears*. He and his wife Camille live in Laurel Hollow, Long Island, New York. They have three children and five grandchildren.